Student's Gluten-Free Cookbook

FOR DUMMIES®

A Wiley Brand

by Nancy McEachern

Founder of the Gluten Freeville blog

P9-DED-215

Student's Gluten-Free Cookbook For Dummies®

Published by
John Wiley & Sons, Inc.
111 River St.
Hoboken, NJ 07030-5774
www.wiley.com

Copyright © 2013 by John Wiley & Sons, Inc., Hoboken, New Jersey

Published simultaneously in Canada

For general information on our other products and services, please contact our Customer Care Department within the U.S. at 877-762-2974, outside the U.S. at 317-572-3993, or fax 317-572-4002.

For technical support, please visit www.wiley.com/techsupport.

Wiley publishes in a variety of print and electronic formats and by print-on-demand. Some material included with standard print versions of this book may not be included in e-books or in print-on-demand. If this book refers to media such as a CD or DVD that is not included in the version you purchased, you may download this material at http://booksupport.wiley.com. For more information about Wiley products, visit www.wiley.com.

Library of Congress Control Number: 2013931131

ISBN 978-1-118-48584-2 (pbk); ISBN 978-1-118-50238-9 (ebk); ISBN 978-1-118-50239-6 (ebk); ISBN 978-1-118-50242-6 (ebk)

Manufactured in the United States of America

10 9 8 7 6 5 4 3 2 1

About the Author

Nancy McEachern lives in northern California with her husband. She is a business owner, consultant, author, speaker, champion of gluten-free issues, and mom to a college student who had to go gluten-free when he was in high school, which started her research of everything she could find out about living gluten-free and enjoying it. Nancy set out to help others who need or want to eliminate gluten from their diets.

As the founder of Gluten Freeville (`http://glutenfreeville.com`), Nancy runs a popular website and writes about all aspects of gluten-free living, including new products, restaurants offering gluten-free menus, gluten-free medical news, travel options for families, practical tips for moms and students, and how to make great-tasting food. The website empowers tens of thousands of people to live a healthy and happy gluten-free life.

Nancy also runs the companion health and wellness Facebook fan page Gluten Freeville. With more than 50,000 members from throughout the world, this large and active online community discusses the everyday struggles and victories of living gluten-free and shares information and advice. Thousands also follow Gluten Freeville on Twitter and Pinterest as a way to connect with the gluten-free community and stay up-to-date on gluten-free news, food, and advice.

Dedication

To my son, Michael, who handles his diet with grace and embraces his options, not his limitations. And to my daughter, Leah, who encouraged me to take on this book and graciously accepted our home's gluten-free fare without complaining long before she officially went gluten-free.

Author's Acknowledgments

I owe a mountain of thanks to my husband Rick for his kindness while embracing my experimental meals and for being my awesome tech support guy for Gluten Freeville. Gratitude, too, to Dee and Walt, Beth and Mc: Thanks for sharing family recipes and allowing me to doctor them so everyone can enjoy them and for changing your cooking habits to accommodate us so lovingly.

Thanks to my thousands of gluten-free friends on GlutenFreeville. com. You all make this gluten-free journey more fun and more worthwhile.

Special appreciation to the Wiley editorial team. Thanks to Mike Lewis, acquisitions editor, for asking me to write this book and guiding me through the process. It's been an adventure that I never expected. Sincerest thanks to Jenny Larner Brown, project editor; you've been such a pleasure to work with and have put as much heart into this project as I have. Thanks to Danielle Voirol, copy editor; Emily Nolan, recipe tester; and Patty Santelli, nutritional analyst, for your time and input in this project. Your expertise and attention to detail are appreciated!

Special thanks to my respected friend and colleague in this gluten-free universe, Jules Shepard, for agreeing to be the technical editor of this project. Your activism on behalf of the gluten-free community is appreciated, and your flour and gluten-free mixes rock! I wouldn't even bother baking without them.

Thanks to my personal product and recipe testers: Rick, Leah, Michael, Amanda, Dee, Walt, Glenda, Lauren, Shelley, and Jadon. And to all my family and friends, thanks so much for your support and encouragement throughout this project. I'm excited to look up from my computer and rejoin the festivities with you all.

Publisher's Acknowledgments

We're proud of this book; please send us your comments at http://dummies.custhelp.com. For other comments, please contact our Customer Care Department within the U.S. at 877-762-2974, outside the U.S. at 317-572-3993, or fax 317-572-4002.

Some of the people who helped bring this book to market include the following:

Acquisitions, Editorial, and Vertical Websites

Project Editor: Jenny Larner Brown

Acquisitions Editor: Michael Lewis

Senior Copy Editor: Danielle Voirol

Assistant Editor: David Lutton

Editorial Program Coordinator: Joe Niesen

Technical Editor: Jules Shepard

Recipe Tester: Emily Nolan

Nutritional Analyst: Patty Santelli

Editorial Manager: Christine Meloy Beck

Editorial Assistant: Alexa Koschier

Art Coordinator: Alicia B. South

Cover Photos: © Lauri Patterson/ iStockphoto.com

Composition Services

Project Coordinator: Sheree Montgomery

Layout and Graphics: Carrie A. Cesavice, Jennifer Creasey, Joyce Haughey, Christin Swinford

Proofreaders: Melissa Cossell, Penny L. Stuart

Indexer: Sharon Shock

Illustrator: Elizabeth Kurtzman

Publishing and Editorial for Consumer Dummies

    Kathleen Nebenhaus, Vice President and Executive Publisher

    David Palmer, Associate Publisher

    Kristin Ferguson-Wagstaffe, Product Development Director

Publishing for Technology Dummies

    Andy Cummings, Vice President and Publisher

Composition Services

    Debbie Stailey, Director of Composition Services

Contents at a Glance

Recipes at a Glance

Dinners

Snacks

Soups, Salads, and Sides

Desserts

Table of Contents

Part IV: The Part of Tens *295*

Chapter 17: Ten Tips for Going to College Gluten-Free 297

Chapter 18: Ten Simple Ways to Make a Recipe Gluten-Free. 303

Introduction

· ·

College likely marks your first time having to buy groceries and make meals for yourself on a regular basis. You need to decide what to eat, when to eat, and how to eat. You probably prepare single servings most of the time, scrounge for food when you don't have time to go to the store, and eat at odd hours. So how do you manage all that and avoid consuming gluten, too? This book addresses all that and more!

Whether you're gluten-free to relieve symptoms of a medical condition or simply to feel better in general, you're in good company these days. Athletes are trying the gluten-free diet to improve their energy and physical performance. Celebrities are in the news for going gluten-free in hopes of looking better. And people with all sorts of aches, pains, and discomfort are becoming increasingly aware that eliminating gluten from their diets can help.

This a great time to start exploring new ingredients and find out how to prepare delicious gluten-free foods. Flour blends, pastas, and ingredients that used to be off-limits for people on a gluten-free diet are now readily available in gluten-free form for use in the kitchen. Gluten-free cooking has come a very long way.

In addition, many restaurants provide gluten-free menus, and kitchen crews now tend to have at least a little education on how to make a great meal for you. Companies are producing some great-tasting glutenless substitutes for gluten-filled favorites, which means most grocery stores offer sizable and growing gluten-free sections. Even universities are beginning to understand how to better serve gluten-free students.

About This Book

Student's Gluten-Free Cookbook For Dummies includes more than 150 easy-to-prepare recipes and lots of information on how to begin and maintain a gluten-free lifestyle — even in the cramped and often-shared quarters of the typical college environment.

This book is easy to read and hopefully kind of fun, too. There's no test at the end, but familiarizing yourself with the basics makes it a lot easier to stick with gluten-free cooking and eating. You may need to refer back to some sections now and then at first, but I provide cross-references throughout the book to direct you to need-to-know information. Everything you need is here to help you go gluten-free in no time.

Conventions Used in This Book

Here are a few things to know before you read this book or make any of the recipes:

- People follow a gluten-free diet for many reasons, some of which involve serious illnesses. These folks need to be extremely diligent about avoiding any little bit of gluten. If you read something about cross-contamination, I'm referring to when gluten gets into gluten-free food.

- The term *glutened* is my made-up word for how you may feel when you unknowingly eat something with gluten in it.

- You can use nondairy substitutions for any dairy-containing recipe in this book. I provide specific ideas within the recipe chapters, but if you see milk in a recipe, for example, you can replace it with a nondairy substitute such as rice, almond, soy, or coconut milk.

- All the ingredients I list for recipes and recommend in the text are the gluten-free versions. Be sure to check all your food labels for gluten-free status.

- I use large (not extra large) eggs in these recipes.

- To measure flour, I scoop it out of the bag with a measuring cup and then level it off with a straight edge.

- All oven temperatures are in degrees Fahrenheit.

Here are a few other standard conventions to help you navigate this book:

- **Bold** text highlights action items in numbered lists and keywords in bulleted lists.

- *Italics* draw your attention to new terms and add emphasis.

- All web addresses appear in `monofont`.

- URLs that need to break across two lines have no extra characters added. If you type exactly what you see, you should land at the right website.

What You're Not to Read

I realize that you're in college and have plenty of other reading to do, so you don't have to read this book from cover to cover (although I think it's a fantastic idea). Each chapter includes helpful, sometimes witty supplemental information that you can skip if you're pressed for time. Here's what you can skip:

- ✔ **Technical Stuff:** Following this icon, you find extra information on a given subject. If you're not looking for details, move on.

- ✔ **Sidebars:** I provide interesting information in the shaded boxes throughout the book. You may miss something downright fascinating or really helpful if you skip them, but you won't miss anything crucial.

- ✔ **Vary It!** Following this phrase in a recipe, you see some ways to change a recipe to make it lower in fat, dairy-free, different in texture and flavor, and so on. Check out this information if you're interested.

Foolish Assumptions

You're a unique individual with one-of-a-kind talents and charisma, but I had to make some assumptions about my readers in order to decide what kinds of information to include. I'm guessing that one or more of the following statements apply to you:

- ✔ You're heading to college or are already there, and you're probably a bit short on extra cash and time.

- ✔ You need to learn to cook gluten-free on your own, but you don't have tons of experience in the kitchen.

- ✔ A doctor told you to steer clear of gluten. Or you have a coach, a friend, or maybe a family member who suggested that you try a gluten-free diet. You're wondering whether a gluten-free diet will help you feel better.

- ✔ You're a supportive friend or relative who's looking for information to understand or to pass along to someone on a gluten-free diet.

- ✔ You're curious about all the fuss related to gluten.

- ✔ This book was on the sale table and that bright yellow and black cover caught your eye.

If any of these apply, you have the right book! I don't spend a lot of page space on dreary details of gluten or bore you with tons of medical information. I try to quickly answer your questions about the gluten-free lifestyle and help you save money and time while living and cooking delicious gluten-free food.

Here are some things you can assume about me:

✔ I know what I'm talking about. My household went gluten-free years ago, and I've put two kids through high school and college on a gluten-free diet. We searched for colleges; dealt with dorm food and cafeteria directors; figured out social situations and dating on a special diet; and learned to travel, eat out, cook simply with limited space and time, live with roommates who aren't gluten-free, and more. If a piece of info is in here, it's because we've lived it, and I have personal experience and tips to share with you.

✔ I write a popular blog and run a busy Facebook site where I answer questions about this stuff every day, and I've done tons of research over the years, but I have no medical training, and nothing you read here is to be taken as medical advice. Don't pick up a book or read any website without seeing a medical professional if you have medical questions.

✔ I don't write about picking berries on the old farm and then making Grandma's pie crust from scratch in an all-day pie-making extravaganza. I'm busy. I want a 30-minute pie (with shortcuts if possible), or forget it. The recipes you find here are quick and no-nonsense — not gourmet but great. They taste good and don't require tons of time or skill to prepare. So invite your friends over to eat; they'll never guess they're eating gluten-free. *That's* the mark of a great recipe!

How This Book Is Organized

This book's content is a blend of lifestyle information and gluten-free recipes. It's organized in the following parts.

Part 1: Getting Started with Gluten-Free Cooking

Find the basics of the gluten-free diet here. I start by telling you what gluten is, where to find it, and why people go gluten-free. The chapters in this part cover nutrition basics and how to handle social situations, stock your kitchen, shop on a dime, and safely share your space with gluten-eating people.

Part II: Preparing Gluten-Free Goodies

Here's where you get cooking. This part offers super-fast-prep breakfasts, lunches, and dinners along with recipes for meals that take a bit longer. None of these recipes take more than 30 minutes, and all are easy to prepare, call for common ingredients, and taste great.

Part III: Going Beyond Three Squares

This part showcases recipes that go beyond breakfast, lunch, and dinner. It includes sensational soups, salads, and sides as well as study snacks and dazzling desserts. You also find some great ideas on turning leftovers into the star of another meal, getting the most for your money, and preparing ingredients ahead of time to make meal-time prep even quicker.

Part IV: The Part of Tens

All *For Dummies* books have cool lists at the end to help you even further. In this book, Chapter 17 gives you crucial tips for going to college gluten-free, Chapter 18 points out how to make recipes gluten-free, and Chapter 19 highlights product recommendations so you don't waste a lot of time and money on gluten-free brands that you probably won't enjoy.

Appendixes

Appendix A directs you to some great gluten-free books, magazines, websites, and apps, and Appendix B has useful information on metric conversions and oven temperatures.

Icons Used in This Book

This book uses a few icons to help you quickly find the info you need.

This icon points out ideas to pay special attention to — in other words, remember them!

Tip icons mark great ideas that help you cook with a little more ease or save some time or money.

The Warning icon is followed by information that helps you avoid some common mistake or danger associated with your gluten-free diet.

These lists, facts, or statistics aren't necessary to your understanding of the material, but they may interest you if you're a factophile.

Where to Go from Here

The great thing about any *For Dummies* book is that you can pick it up and turn to any section and get something out of it. If you're totally new to the idea of a gluten-free lifestyle, turn to Part I and get the basics. If you're a little more familiar with the foundational concepts of gluten, you may find the info on social situations, shopping, and stocking the kitchen in Chapters 4 to 6 really interesting. And the well-versed and experienced gluten-free readers may want to head straight for Parts II and III and start cooking!

No matter how much you know about going gluten-free, you can find practical tips, ideas, lists, and tons of great recipes in this book.

Part I

getting started with gluten-free cooking

Visit www.dummies.com for valuable Dummies content online.

In this part . . .

✔ Find out what you need to know and buy before you begin cooking without gluten.

✔ Explore ways to approach a gluten-free diet based on your health goals and check out nutritional do's and don'ts.

✔ Consider the symptoms of celiac disease and gluten sensitivity.

✔ Discover all the places that gluten hides.

✔ Stay social while avoiding gluten.

Chapter 1

Gluten-Free 101

● ●

● ●

*G*luten. This is probably the hundredth time you've seen that word in print in the past couple of months. It's everywhere — magazines, television commercials, websites, celebrity Tweets, Facebook feeds, restaurant menus, and even entire grocery aisles. Gluten-free has become a hip way to eat. Some people are embracing the trend by choice; others are forced into it for a range of medical reasons.

If you still wonder what this whole gluten thing is all about, you're not alone. In this chapter, I point out what gluten is, tell you where it lives, and introduce you to the basics of gluten-free living and cooking. Knowing the basics can help you better support a gluten-free friend or loved one or make the transition to gluten-free yourself — due to choice or necessity — and start enjoying the benefits of going gluten-free.

Getting Familiar with Gluten

Gluten, which is a natural element of wheat, is a food protein — technically a mixture of two types of protein, *gliadin* and *glutenin.* The gliadin is what causes problems for people with celiac disease (see Chapter 3). Rye and barley contain proteins similar to gliadin, so for simplicity, people use the term *gluten* to refer to the troublemaking proteins in wheat, rye, barley, and related grains.

Questioning an increasingly sensitive world

Gluten sensitivity, celiac disease, obesity, and a myriad of other diet-related chronic illnesses seem to be on the rise. Why is the world suddenly so darn sensitive? At the heart of the story is the evolution of wheat. This is not your grandparents' wheat.

Wheat has been scientifically manipulated to be a more efficient size, hardier, and higher yielding. Over the past 50 years, wheat has experienced three major hybridization changes that benefit the food industry but not necessarily human bodies. According to Dr. Mark Hyman, a practicing physician, founder of The UltraWellness Center, and a five-time *New York Times* bestselling author, today's wheat is a super starch (and thus super fattening), a super gluten (that is, super inflammatory), and a super drug (as in super addictive).

The starch in today's wheat is a rapidly digested carbohydrate, making it a fast train to stored body fat. Dr. William Davis, in the bestseller *Wheat Belly*, claims that two slices of commercial wheat bread raise blood sugar levels more than 6 teaspoons of straight sugar does. This modified form of gluten in modern-day wheat causes a significant amount of inflammation in the body, which leads to a host of chronic diseases, including celiac disease, heart disease, diabetes, and other autoimmune diseases.

The super addictive nature of wheat acts as an appetite stimulant and actually alters brain chemistry. Wondering why you get the urge to binge on cookies but don't feel hungry enough to scarf down a plate of veggies? The concentrated gluten in wheat turns into chemicals that can trigger cravings, affect behavior and mood, and even contribute to autism, depression, and schizophrenia, according to many experts.

Source: Hyman, MD, Mark. "Three Hidden Ways Wheat Makes You Fat." February 13, 2012. http://drhyman.com/blog/2012/02/13/three-hidden-ways-wheat-makes-you-fat/

For some people, the gliadin in wheat and the similar proteins in barley and rye cause the immune system to produce antibodies, leading to a host of health issues.

Finding Gluten's Hideouts

Not only is gluten present in foods that contain wheat, rye, or barley, but it also resides in some not-so-expected places, including soy sauce and natural flavorings and spices as well as beer, vitamins, and even lotions. In this section, I point out foods, beverages, and other products that contain gluten.

Food stuff: Discovering gluten's natural habitat

Gluten shows up in most baked goods and processed foods because it helps dough rise and stick together. Gluten gives baked goods that fluffy, bready texture or a crispy, crackery crunch. Without it, foods are denser and flatter, and they crumble more easily.

Gluten is in wheat, rye, and barley. Of all the grains that contain gluten, wheat is the most prevalent. It has a variety of names and related varieties, which makes gluten-free eating confusing at first. I recommend familiarizing yourself with these gluteny aliases so you aren't caught off-guard when shopping, dining, cooking, and eating gluten-free:

- ✔ Bulgur
- ✔ Bran
- ✔ Couscous
- ✔ Durum
- ✔ Einkorn
- ✔ Graham
- ✔ Matzo, matzah
- ✔ Seitan
- ✔ Semolina
- ✔ Spelt

Spelt is definitely not gluten-free, but it's marketed as a wheat alternative for people with wheat allergies. Be careful, because spelt breads and tortillas are often erroneously grouped with gluten-free products on the grocery store shelf.

Similarly, barley often masquerades as *barley malt, malt vinegar,* or just *malt* and is used as a flavoring and a sweetener. Malt can also come from corn, but if the label just says "malt," assume that it comes from barley and isn't gluten-free.

A good way to start your gluten-free journey is to avoid common foods with flour in them. Wheat flour is a popular base ingredient for most traditional baked goods, including bread, bagels, buns, cookies, cake, pie crust, muffins, donuts, and brownies as well as crackers, pasta, and pizza crust.

But don't worry! You don't have to live without your favorite foods, because great gluten-free versions of almost everything that contains gluten are available. You just need to know how to make the swap. Check out Chapter 5 to find out how to decode food labels and avoid hidden gluten in salad dressings, baking ingredients, spices, soups, and other groceries. Find more than 150 already gluten-free recipes in Parts II and III of this cookbook.

You may find glutinous rice in an Asian recipe, but that rice doesn't contain gluten. *Glutinous* (with an *i*) simply means "sticky." However, *glutenous* with an *e* does mean "related to gluten."

Choosing booze you can use

Some alcoholic beverages are unsafe for people on a gluten-free diet. These popular products are among the beverages to avoid:

- ✔ Beers made from barley (unless they're deglutenized)
- ✔ Malt beverages (like wine coolers)
- ✔ Beverages with barley-based flavorings (such as some teas)

However, the list of alcohol you can drink on a gluten-free diet is actually pretty long, and it includes a growing list of gluten-free beers. Here are some of the most popular gluten-free alcoholic beverages:

- ✔ **Gluten-free beer:** Most beers are made from barley and therefore contain gluten, but a growing list of gluten-free beer comes from sorghum, rice, corn, buckwheat, or other gluten-free grains.

  Some new beers on the market are made from barley, but through a process similar to distillation, the gluten is removed. These beers are called *deglutenized beers*. Whether you feel comfortable trying these beers or prefer to stick to beers made from gluten-free grains is a personal choice that probably depends on the severity of your body's response to gluten.

- ✔ **Hard cider:** Ciders that don't contain barley as a flavoring are gluten-free.

- ✔ **Rum:** Most rums are made from sugar cane, which is gluten-free.

- ✔ **Tequila:** Tequila is made with the gluten-free blue agave plant.

- ✔ **Wine and champagnes:** Nearly all wines and champagnes (sparkling wines) are gluten-free because they're made from grapes.

Gluten is included in some flavorings, which contaminates otherwise gluten-free beverages, so always read labels and check specific brand websites to verify gluten-free status — even on products that are known to be predominately gluten-free. Contact the manufacturer if you're unsure of the gluten content in your favorite beverage.

In addition to the naturally gluten-free adult beverages, some liquor that's made from gluten-containing grains can be gluten-free due to the distillation process, which removes the gluten. So as long as these liquors are distilled and the gluten-containing mash isn't added back into the spirits, these beverages are also on the gluten-free party list:

- **Vodka:** Most vodka is made from potato or corn. Some vodkas are made from glutenous grains, but vodkas are distilled, which removes the gluten. Yet some celiac specialists recommend sticking with the potato and corn-based versions to ensure safety.

- **Whiskey:** Most whiskey is made from glutenous grains, but it's still considered gluten-free because whiskey is distilled. However, if the gluten-containing mash is added back into the whiskey (which is uncommon), then this beverage is definitely not gluten-free. Contact the distiller if you have questions about its products.

Making sure medications are gluten-free

Gluten may be in medicine, vitamins, and herbal supplements, too! Finding out the source of each ingredient in medications is much more difficult than reading food labels because different regulations apply to different products and because the source of some ingredients is unclear.

Some companies are beginning to label over-the-counter liquids and pills as gluten-free because more consumers are now looking for that information. And some companies list the gluten-free status of supplements, over-the-counter drugs, and prescription medicines on their websites.

Many, if not most, medications do not contain gluten, but if you become sick from a little gluten, it's important to confirm that pills you may be taking daily aren't going to trigger your gluten-related symptoms. Look out specifically for starch, wheat, flour, or malt listed as an ingredient, especially in herbal and vitamin supplements that may use gluten as a binder and filler. In addition, Vitamin E can be derived from wheat.

Here are some credible resources for finding out whether a medication is gluten-free:

- A shopping guidebook such as *Cecelia's Marketplace Gluten-Free Shopping Guide* by Matison and Matison

- Gluten-free apps, including ScanAvert

- A prescription website such as www.glutenfreedrugs.com

- FDA package inserts (which are often online as well)

- Drug company websites

- Pharmacists

Be sure to ask your pharmacist to make a note in your file that you're gluten-free.

Avoiding gluten in cosmetics and hair and skincare products

If you're just trying out a gluten-free diet, you probably don't need to worry about topical gluten; but if you're gluten-free due to a medical condition, then what you put *on* your body may be important.

Some experts say that gluten molecules are too large to enter the skin and that they're fine unless you ingest them, but a few doctors disagree, claiming that topical skincare products enter the bloodstream after being absorbed through the skin.

Swearing that they feel "off" or "glutened" when they use gluten-containing products, some people prefer to avoid gluten even for nonfood products. Others get contact rashes and other skin problems from gluten-containing skin products. But no matter what you decide in terms of lotion and makeup in general, lipstick needs to be gluten-free (and lots of it isn't) if you — or someone you're kissing — is gluten-free due to a medical condition.

Cosmetics companies aren't required to list wheat as an ingredient on the label, and they aren't obligated to declare the presence of gluten. As with food, check manufacturer websites, shopping guides, and smartphone apps to find the gluten-free status of cosmetics, lotions, shampoos, and other nonfood products.

Here are some ingredients that may contain gluten in your cosmetics:

- **Glutens:** Hydrolyzed wheat gluten, *Triticum vulgare* (wheat) gluten

- **Flours:** *Avena sativa* (oat) kernel flour, hydrolyzed oat flour, *Secale cereale* (rye) seed flour

✔ **Extracts and oils:** Barley extract, fermented grain extract, hydrolyzed malt extract, phytosphingosine extract, *Triticum vulgare* (wheat) germ extract, *Triticum vulgare* (wheat) germ oil, yeast extract

✔ **Proteins:** Hydrolyzed vegetable protein, hydrolyzed wheat protein, hydrolyzed wheat protein/PVP crosspolymer

✔ **Starches:** Hydrolyzed wheat starch, *Triticum vulgare* (wheat) starch

✔ **Dextrins:** Dextrin and maltodextrin (usually gluten-free because it's derived from corn in the U.S., but not always), dextrin palmitate, and cyclodextrin

✔ **Vitamins:** Vitamin E (may have wheat germ as the source)

✔ **Other:** Samino peptide complex, sodium C8-16 isoalkylsuccinyl

Choosing Naturally Gluten-Free Foods

The good news is that the list of foods you can eat on a gluten-free diet is much longer than the list of things you can't. For starters, finding gluten-free replacements for almost all the gluten-containing foods you love is getting easier. But you can also decide to just eat more naturally gluten-free foods, especially if you're newly gluten-free or you want to eat healthier in general.

Here are some food options that naturally contain no gluten:

✔ Fresh vegetables, fresh fruits, fruit juice

✔ Unseasoned beef, pork, chicken, turkey, fish, seafood

✔ Fresh eggs

✔ Milk, butter, margarine, cream, yogurt, cheese

✔ Beans, lentils, corn, rice, potatoes

✔ Unseasoned nuts and seeds

✔ Oils

✔ Sugar, honey, molasses

✔ Pure spices and herbs

Eating naturally gluten-free is a call to cooking! The key is to combine ingredients — soften the garlic and onions in the butter or oil, brown the meat, add vegetables and herbs, and learn to use new sauces and spices. Choosing naturally gluten-free foods isn't about subtracting things from your diet; it's about adding to your cooking!

Many people who are just beginning to explore the gluten-free diet are surprised to find out that many satisfying grains and seeds are also gluten-free, including these:

- Amaranth

- Arrowroot

- Buckwheat

- Chia

- Corn (*Note:* All forms of corn are gluten-free, including maize, polenta, hominy, grits, cornmeal, and cornstarch.)

- Flax

- Flours made from nuts, beans, seeds, coconut, or rice

- Millet

- Oats (*Note:* Oats are naturally gluten-free but are often contaminated with wheat in growing, processing, or storing, so buy oats that are marked gluten-free.)

- Quinoa

- Rice

- Sorghum

- Soy (but not soy sauce unless it's marked gluten-free)

- Tapioca (cassava)

- Teff

Staying Nourished on a Gluten-Free Diet

The gluten-free diet isn't so much a diet as it is a lifestyle. If you have celiac disease, then permanently and exclusively eating gluten-free foods is the only treatment. Staying gluten-free is also important if you're treating other medical conditions, such as a gluten sensitivity or wheat allergy, autoimmune disorders, and more. (Find information on reasons to go gluten-free in Chapter 2, and find details on celiac disease, gluten sensitivity, and nutrition in Chapter 3.)

Cutting out nearly an entire food group means you need to be careful that you get enough of the nutrients your body requires for optimal operation from other foods. After all, a food labeled "gluten-free" isn't necessarily good for you — it just doesn't contain gluten.

When cutting gluten from your diet, you may inadvertently cut something else: fiber. Fiber improves digestive function, lowers blood cholesterol, helps control diabetes and weight, plays a role in the prevention of colon cancer, and supports friendly gut bacteria. People are often told that whole-wheat bread is the best way to get fiber in their diets. Wrong! There are plenty of healthy, gluten-free ways to make sure you add this important element to your diet.

Steer clear of low-fiber processed foods and eat plenty of these high-fiber, naturally gluten-free foods:

- ✔ Gluten-free whole grains

- ✔ Fresh fruits and vegetables

- ✔ Nuts and seeds

- ✔ Beans

- ✔ Almond flour

- ✔ Popcorn

- ✔ Gluten-free oatmeal

 If you're worried you may be lacking key vitamins and minerals when you go gluten-free, consult a dietitian or nutritionist during a visit home or on campus.

Socializing in a Gluten-Loving World

Socializing can be a little tricky when you're gluten-free. Fortunately, it's getting easier each day, as more and more people understand the ins and outs of gluten-free eating. There are still many challenges, though, in mingling socially with gluten-consuming family, friends, and schoolmates.

 Don't let your dietary requirements or choices keep you away from all the fun! Try these simple tips to raise your confidence in dealing with those around you:

- ✔ Tell your friends and relatives about your decision or need to begin eating gluten-free and ask for their support in meeting your goals, but don't turn the focus of a gathering on your dietary restrictions. (See Chapter 4 for more advice on dealing with social situations.)

✔ Be specific with roommates about your expectations for sharing kitchen space and keeping your food gluten-free. (Find guidance on setting up and maintaining a gluten-free cooking space in Chapter 6.)

✔ When planning to eat out — or order in — check the menu online and pick out some options ahead of time. (Check out Chapter 4 for more tips on gluten-free dining.)

✔ Keep a few gluten-free snacks with you when visiting friends, traveling, and attending parties. (Find recipes for great take-along snacks in Chapter 14.)

Preparing Gluten-Free Meals

There are lots of details to manage when living gluten-free, but when you get down to it, it's all about the food: shopping, cooking, and eating! Knowing what to buy and how to cook it is the key to a happy gluten-free experience. Not only will you improve your health by cooking your own food, but you'll likely enjoy a wide range of additional perks, including finding new foods to love, developing cooking skills, and being able to serve friends and dates delicious homemade food.

Shopping smart

Smart gluten-free shopping is a bit of an art. Here are some things to keep in mind when shopping:

✔ Keep your pantry and fridge stocked with gluten-free staples to make mealtime quick and to avoid emergency trips to the grocery store (see Chapter 6).

✔ Check labels and ingredients for obvious and not-so-obvious gluten (see Chapter 5).

✔ Buy at a discount. Chapter 5 helps you find ways to save some (ahem) dough on gluten-free groceries.

Naturally gluten-free foods are most often found along the edges of the grocery store. Start in the produce section to gather fruits and veggies. Enjoy all you want of these items. Even starches such as potatoes and corn are safe on a gluten-free diet.

 The back or side wall of many grocery stores contains seafood, meat, and poultry. In their natural forms, these foods are gluten-free, but you need to watch out for these potentially gluten-containing additives:

> ✔ Flavorings
>
> ✔ Spice mixes
>
> ✔ Breading, coating
>
> ✔ Marinades
>
> ✔ Injected broth

Continuing around the store, you find dairy and eggs. Milk, yogurt, sour cream, butter, and eggs are all gluten-free. Just watch for gluten on the labels of flavored yogurts and flavored coffee creamers. Most are fine, but a few brands contain gluten.

The bakery and deli areas are also on the perimeter of most grocery stores. Run, don't walk past the bakery. All those breads and desserts likely contain gluten, unless your store has a little gluten-free section. In the deli, almost all cheese is fine, but sometimes wheat is used as an anti-caking agent in shredded, packaged cheese. Blue cheese sometimes contains gluten as well.

If your gluten-free deli meat is sliced on the same cutter as the gluten-containing stuff, then it's no longer safe for you. It's often safest to go with prepackaged deli meat that's marked gluten-free to avoid cross-contamination.

Setting up your kitchen

Student living is filled with more time and space challenges than almost any other time of life. Living with gluten-loving roommates who share your kitchen is another challenge — and that's if you even have the luxury of a kitchen. Turn to Chapter 6 for info on setting up your kitchen and working with your roommates to avoid cross-contamination. If you live in a dorm, find help in Chapter 17.

Get cooking!

After you stock up on gluten-free ingredients and have your kitchen in some semblance of order, you're ready to get cooking! Here are some general cooking tips:

> ✔ **Start simple.** If you're cooking a main dish, keep the sides simple — a lettuce salad, veggie sticks, fresh fruit, or a microwaved potato is perfect.
>
> ✔ **Do some planning.** Think about what you'd like to make before you head to the store, and think about what you want to eat before you're hungry. Thaw meat overnight in

the fridge, and get the butter and eggs out a couple of hours before you bake so they can warm to room temp.

✔ **Get organized.** Read through the entire recipe of the dish you hope to prepare — before you start cooking. Make sure that you have enough of each ingredient, that you have the right tools (or a way to improvise), and that you understand the directions. Chop and measure ingredients so they're ready to go. Keep your space clean.

✔ **Use your senses, not just the clock, to tell when food is ready.** Cooking equipment varies, and stoves, ovens, and pans don't always heat the same way. Pay attention to the food's appearance, texture, flavor, and so on when deciding whether to adjust the heat and when to move to the next recipe step.

✔ **Measure carefully when baking.** For some dishes, you can eyeball the measurements and adjust ingredients to taste. If you're baking, however, measurements should be precise. You can experiment with add-ins like chocolate chips, nuts, and flavorings, but in general, keep the recipe's ratios of dry ingredients, wet ingredients, and fats intact.

✔ **Be patient.** Give ovens and skillets time to heat up, and let water come to a full boil. Skillet temperature can mean the difference between steaming meat and giving it a tasty brown crust. Don't try to rush things by turning up the heat — you may burn the food instead of making it cook faster.

✔ **Relax, have fun, and expect mistakes.** Having recipes not turn out is a sign that you've tried cooking, not a sign that you're a bad cook. You gain skills with experience. Enjoy the process, learn from your mistakes, and regale your friends with your best kitchen disaster stories.

The recipe chapters of this book, Chapters 7 through 15, offer more than 150 great but easy gluten-free dishes that you can enjoy and share with your gluten-consuming friends and family.

Finding Support and Reliable Information

As the gluten-free diet continues to become more popular — and, dare I say, mainstream — more and more resources and people are emerging to help gluten-free newbies and vets alike live and dine more comfortably. Still, connecting with others who share your perspective and accessing other kinds of information and support is pretty helpful. Find a list of valuable resources in Appendix A.

Chapter 2

Why Go Gluten-Free?

Millions of people are eliminating gluten from their diets and seeing great improvements in their health. People are making the shift to a gluten-free diet for a wide range of reasons that include managing disease, fulfilling curiosity about different ways of eating, supporting gluten-free friends, and even tapping into the coolness of gluten-free living.

Seriously, gluten-free eating is hip! Top athletes such as the Garmin-Transitions pro cycling team, tennis great Novak Djokovich, and gold medalist swimmer Dana Vollmer have stopped consuming gluten and attribute improved performances in part to their change in diet. Even pop stars like Lady Gaga and Miley Cyrus are gluten-free and looking great. These high-profile examples of gluten-free living motivate many people to try the diet to find out if it can benefit them, too.

In this chapter, I point out the main reasons people embrace the gluten-free lifestyle and offer some examples of the kinds of benefits that different groups of people enjoy as a result of avoiding gluten.

Addressing Medical Concerns

Going gluten-free may not seem so exciting and adventurous if a medical condition forces you into it and eating gluten-free suddenly becomes a long-term necessity.

The most common medical reasons that people have to be gluten-free are celiac disease, gluten sensitivity, and an allergy to a gluten-containing grain. But many people choose to go gluten-free to help manage a host of other conditions, too, such as autoimmune disorders, autism, migraines, and more (see Chapter 3 for details).

If you're eliminating gluten due to celiac disease or another medical condition, here are guidelines for your gluten-free diet:

- ✔ Don't cheat! It's not worth the damage or discomfort you'll cause. Be especially strict if you have celiac disease.

- ✔ Be vigilant about making sure your food isn't cross-contaminated with any gluten-containing foods. Flip to Chapter 6 for guidelines on avoiding cross-contamination.

- ✔ When in doubt, leave it out.

- ✔ Work with a doctor or nutritionist to make sure you're getting all your vitamins and other nutrients (find info on nutrition in Chapter 3).

Treating celiac disease

Celiac disease is an autoimmune disorder in which the immune system attacks healthy cells in the presence of gluten. Experts believe as many as 1 in 100 Americans have celiac disease.

Most people who have celiac disease don't know it. They often think something else is causing their health symptoms; perhaps they've been told they're imagining their symptoms, or maybe they just live with uncomfortable symptoms without seeking help. Recent studies claim it takes an average of 11 years of misdiagnoses before someone is correctly diagnosed with celiac disease.

The lining of the intestines contains *villi,* little fingerlike projections that help absorb nutrients. When people with celiac disease eat foods that contain gluten, their immune system reacts by damaging these villi. Malnutrition occurs because the body can't absorb nutrients. There's no cure for celiac disease, but a totally gluten-free diet allows the intestines to heal, and the symptoms can disappear.

The exact cause of celiac disease is unknown, but if you have a relative who has it, you're more likely to have it as well. And if you already have another autoimmune disorder, you may be more likely to develop celiac disease.

Handling gluten sensitivity or an allergy

New research confirms what many people have known for years: Gluten sensitivity is a real condition that's separate from celiac disease. Recent studies show that many more people have this condition than celiac disease — as many as 1 in every 15 to 20 people — but very little information is available on how prevalent gluten sensitivity really is. Some people just can't tolerate gluten and must stay away from it to feel well. Gluten sensitivity symptoms can take many forms and may be different for each person.

If you're experiencing any of the 300 possible symptoms of gluten sensitivity (check out the short list in Chapter 3), then slashing gluten may be just the solution you're looking for. By the time many people decide to try a gluten-free diet to improve specific health issues, they've already been to several doctors with no luck, and they've suffered at least a little for quite a long while.

Some people who have an allergy to wheat, barley, or rye are eating gluten-free as well. In fact, wheat is one of the most common food allergens. Gluten-free foods are wheat-free as well, but if you see "wheat-free" on a label, gluten may still be in the product in the form of barley or rye.

There isn't a condition called a "gluten allergy," but sometimes it's easier to describe gluten sensitivity that way. People understand what a food allergy is; they know you can't eat a certain food. A sensitivity somehow sounds optional, and well-meaning friends and family may try to influence these folks to "just have a little."

Managing an autoimmune disorder

A healthy immune system is your friend, but with an autoimmune disorder, the body can't tell the difference between an invader and itself. It becomes your *frenemy*. Many health experts believe that cutting out gluten may help ease the immune system's confusion and reduce the body's inflammatory response, improving some symptoms of autoimmune conditions. I hear from people all the time who claim remarkable results for various autoimmune disorders when they change their diets.

Here are just a few autoimmune conditions that may diminish with a gluten-free diet:

- ✔ Hashimoto's thyroiditis
- ✔ Systemic lupus erythematosus
- ✔ Type 1 diabetes
- ✔ Rheumatoid arthritis
- ✔ Sjögren's syndrome
- ✔ Multiple sclerosis
- ✔ Chronic inflammatory bowel disease

Improving other medical conditions

People may choose a gluten-free diet to manage many medical conditions aside from celiac disease and gluten sensitivity, including the following:

- ✔ Migraines
- ✔ Fibromyalgia
- ✔ Autism
- ✔ Attention deficit disorder
- ✔ Anemia
- ✔ Inflammation
- ✔ Irritable bowel syndrome, colitis, diarrhea, constipation, gas, cramps, bloating
- ✔ Behavioral issues, psychiatric issues, seizures, memory issues
- ✔ Brain fog, depression, fatigue
- ✔ Ataxia (a muscle coordination disorder)
- ✔ Skin conditions like eczema, psoriasis, acne, and rashes

Maximizing Athletic Performance

All kinds of great athletes are going gluten-free. When athletes with celiac disease and gluten sensitivity take gluten out of their diets, they typically see improvements in their performance because they no longer suffer from the uncomfortable or painful symptoms that gluten can cause them. But why are nonceliac athletes dropping the gluten, too?

People in all walks of life, especially athletes who depend on feeling in top shape, are finding that they feel healthier and perform better without a gut full of gluten. There doesn't seem to be much scientific evidence that cutting gluten improves your game unless you're gluten-free for medical reasons, but people have lots of reasons for cutting gluten, and many athletes swear by it.

You may see some of these physical advantages of eliminating gluten from your diet even if you don't have celiac disease or gluten sensitivity:

- ✔ Stabilized blood glucose levels
- ✔ Reduced inflammation and joint pain

✔ Increased energy and endurance

✔ Improved digestion and reduced bloating and gas

✔ More efficient muscle recovery due to an improved immune system and better absorption of nutrients

If you want to cut the gluten and see whether you experience the benefits that many athletes claim, discuss your plan and your athletic goals with your coach. And if you need to cut gluten for health reasons, you can eat gluten-free and feel great while playing. Even if you're on a high-carb diet, you can easily replace gluten-containing grains with gluten-free grains (see Chapter 18).

Improving General Health

Entire grocery aisles are dedicated to foods designated *gluten-free,* so eliminating gluten from your diet must be a smart move, right? Otherwise, why would anyone give up the "normal" version of so many favorite foods — and fork over a bunch more money on the alternative version in most cases — if something really magical weren't packed in those gluten-free foods?

Going gluten-free can help you make better food choices, and it can be part of a plan to lose weight, but cutting out gluten isn't an automatic ticket to good health. In this section, I explain how going gluten-free can work with your general health goals.

Making better food choices

Maybe you've been paying attention to the buzz about gluten-free foods and have decided to cut the gluten in an attempt to live a healthier lifestyle. Recent surveys show that most people believe that if a product is marked gluten-free, it's healthier than its gluten-filled counterpart. But this isn't necessarily true.

Some gluten-free foods are full of empty calories or contain a higher fat or sugar content in order to make up for unusual flavors or textures. There are good and bad gluten-free foods, just like regular food; however, you can certainly make your diet healthier while eating strictly gluten-free.

Think about all the processed foods you eat in just one day as a student away from Mom and Dad's home cooking. You may have cereal or toast for breakfast and enjoy some cookies for snacks. Maybe you have two slices of bread on your sandwich with sliced deli meat, or perhaps you have a couple of slices of pizza. Dinner may be a frozen meal or restaurant takeout, and then you have chips or crackers for a late-night snack. Even if you eat only a couple of those things and add in salads, fruit, and vegetables, you've still consumed tons of processed food and empty calories in a day.

Now just imagine that you go through that list and cross off every processed food. Most of it contains gluten, anyway. If you fill your menu with the naturally gluten-free foods — such as fresh lean proteins, high-fiber whole grains, and fruits and veggies — you'll most certainly be eating better. And if you combine the non-gluten, minimally processed way of eating with the exercise and portion control that's part of all health and fitness guidelines, you've got yourself a very healthy way of living.

Including easy fitness

If your goal is to improve your general health, making good food choices is only half the picture. Look for some easy ways to meet your fitness goals and have some fun. Try some of these simple ideas to get started:

- ✔ **Walk or bike to class:** If you skip the bus or car, you'll get some exercise, save some money, and likely run into some friends on the way across campus. Just make sure you leave enough time for the trip.

- ✔ **Take the stairs:** Take the stairs instead of the elevator to your class or dorm room. If you're fast, you may beat the elevator-riders to the top.

- ✔ **Join an intramural sport:** Get a little exercise in as you make new friends and tap into your competitive spirit.

- ✔ **Go for a walk with friends:** Instead of taking a shortcut across campus, take a friend and the scenic route. Pack a gluten-free snack if you'll be out for a while.

- ✔ **Register for a course:** Most degree programs require at least a few activity classes. Add fitness into your routine and earn credit at the same time.

- ✔ **Use your college resources:** Tennis and racquetball courts, discounted gym memberships, climbing walls, and swimming pools are just a few of the fitness resources you find at most universities.

So grab some friends and hit the gym, or go for a walk, or start a basketball game, or have a large-scale snowball fight, or make up inspired new versions of tag. You could probably use a break from school work, anyway!

Simply cutting out gluten-filled junk food and replacing it with gluten-free junk food will not improve your health. Your gluten-free food choices must be deliberate.

Losing weight

When you hear the word *diet,* you probably automatically think weight loss, and maybe that's why you're looking into going gluten-free. But going gluten-free doesn't necessarily mean that you're trying to lose weight or that you *will* lose weight. In fact, the gluten-free diet isn't designed to help people lose weight.

Still, going gluten-free can be part of a weight-loss plan. And programs that allow you to choose your own food, such as Weight Watchers and the South Beach Diet, can work along with eating gluten-free.

Here are some specific ways to meet your health goals on a gluten-free diet:

- ✔ Choose mostly naturally gluten-free foods.
- ✔ Choose high-fiber, minimally processed foods.
- ✔ Choose lower-calorie foods and smaller portions.
- ✔ Choose lower-glycemic foods (Check out "The Essentials of Choosing Low-Glycemic Foods" at www.dummies.com/ how-to/content/the-essentials-of-choosing- lowglycemic-foods.html).
- ✔ Exercise more. See the sidebar "Including easy fitness" for ideas.

An online search can yield some good weight-loss websites that are specifically designed to work with gluten-free diets.

Choosing grain-free diets

Saying goodbye to all grains goes against the . . . uh, grain, but some people still don't feel totally well even after going gluten-free and checking for other intolerances and allergies, so they drop all grains from their diets. Some claim the only "true" gluten-free diet is a grain-free diet. You can certainly choose to go grain-free; just don't say it's the *only* way to go gluten-free, or you'll be wrong.

On a grain-free diet, you can eat foods made with these grain-free flours:

✔ Coconut flour

✔ Bean flours, such as soy, fava, and garbanzo/chickpea

✔ Nut flours, such as almond and cashew

✔ Buckwheat, quinoa, and amaranth flour

✔ Starch flours, such as tapioca, potato, and arrowroot

The Paleo diet, or primal diet, is grain-free and therefore is gluten-free, but it's a bit more specific than a general grain-free diet. Very simplified, the idea is to eat only what could have been hunted or gathered in the Paleolithic period. Today's hunting and gathering can be at the grocery store! Just keep it clean and unprocessed.

Here's a sample of approved foods on a Paleo diet:

✔ Lean meats

✔ Wild seafood

✔ Fats — tallow, lard, coconut oil, olive oil (uncooked or lightly cooked)

✔ Eggs

✔ Vegetables and fruits

✔ Nuts and seeds

For details on the Paleo diet, check out *Living Paleo For Dummies* by Melissa Joulwan and Dr. Kellyann Petrucci.

Chapter 3

Jumping Over Health Hurdles

● ●

● ●

*R*emember all those stories your parents told you about
the wise and mature decisions they made during their
college years? Me, neither. Look around. Your friends are probably
not making the wisest and healthiest choices right now. But that
doesn't mean you shouldn't be making good decisions about your
health. But I bet you already know this. After all, you're reading
this book!

Good nutrition is important in the high-stress college years,
especially if you're gluten-free for medical reasons. Highly
processed convenience foods and extra-salty and high-fat snacks
are fairly common mainstays of a college diet — as are late-night
eating binges. Don't let your daily time crunch leave you unprepared
to take care of yourself and eat nourishing foods.

In this chapter, you can read up on nutrition, consider health
symptoms you may be experiencing, and find out about other food
intolerances. Even if you know you have no medical issues and are
trying a gluten-free diet for other reasons, reading the first few
sections on fiber and vitamins can help you find out what you need
to eat to stay healthy and strong.

This information isn't intended to replace professional medical
advice or care; it's general information that applies to basic health
and nutrition.

Knowing (and Getting) Proper Nutrition

Whether you're investigating the gluten-free lifestyle to speed up your race time, to improve a medical condition, or for some other reason, consuming a balanced diet makes a world of difference.

Just because a food is labeled "gluten-free" doesn't necessarily mean it's good for you. Gluten-free processed foods can be just as nutritionally deficient as any other kind of junk food. When making food choices, seek low-sugar, lowfat, whole-grain, and minimally processed options. While gluten-free, you need to be particularly vigilant about getting enough fiber, vitamins, and other nutrients.

In this section, I describe the basics of good nutrition without wheat, including info on fiber, vitamins, and minerals. (And check out the nearby "Noshing nutritiously" sidebar for some tips on organizing a day's worth of foods that include protein, fats, dairy or dairy substitutes, grains, fruits, and vegetables.)

Getting enough fiber

Fiber includes the part of plants that your body doesn't absorb. A sufficient amount of fiber is necessary to help with digestion, blood sugar levels, and healthy cholesterol. Because of its role in digestion, fiber is especially important for people who've gone on a gluten-free diet due to trouble in the gut. The recommended daily dose of fiber is about 25 grams for women and 35 to 40 grams for men.

Fiber, which may be insoluble or soluble, passes relatively easily through your system and serves a couple of important purposes:

- ✔ **Insoluble fiber:** Insoluble fiber aids in digestion. Whole grains, nuts, seeds, fruits, and legumes can be good sources of insoluble fiber.

- ✔ **Soluble fiber:** Soluble fiber helps regulate your cholesterol and glucose levels. You can find it in foods such as apples, beans, citrus fruits, carrots, oats, and peas.

You've probably heard that whole-wheat bread is the best way to get fiber in your diet. Whole grains are definitely important, but you can skip the wheat, barley, and rye to get a good amount of fiber without the gluten. You just need to increase your intake of other high-fiber foods such as nuts, seeds, legumes, fruit and vegetables, and gluten-free grains.

Noshing nutritiously

Nutrition is complex, but the need-to-know info is really pretty simple. Choose food for what it gives you (nutrients), not only for what it doesn't have, such as less fat, no sugar, reduced calories, and no gluten. That is, raise your standards so you eat food that's nourishing, not just not-bad-for-you. Eat food that looks like it came from a plant or animal — such as fruit, vegetables, meat, dairy, and gluten-free whole-grains — rather than stuff born in a box. That usually means cooking!

Use these simple guidelines to organize a healthy diet:

- **Fruits and vegetables:** To provide vitamins and minerals for healthy skin, hair, nails, and immune system, try having at least five servings of fruits and vegetables — like apples, broccoli, tomatoes, carrots, or salad — each day.

- **Proteins:** To help maintain muscle, try to include beans, eggs, fish, nut butter, chicken, or lean beef in two meals each day.

  If you're a noodle lover, you'll be glad to know that gluten-free pasta packs in two to four times the amount of protein in the gluten-filled variety. That is, pasta made from brown rice, white rice, corn, and quinoa all offer about 4 grams of protein per serving, compared to the 1 to 2 grams provided by wheat pasta.

- **Fats:** To keep you feeling full and maintain good cholesterol levels, include some healthy fats from foods such as olive oil, guacamole, nuts, or seeds at every meal.

- **Dairy and dairy substitutes:** To build strong bones, try having three servings each day of lowfat dairy such as milk, cheese, or yogurt.

- **Grains:** To provide energy for your muscles and brain, include gluten-free grains, rice, pasta, or bread at every meal. Choose whole-grain gluten-free options as often as possible.

Supplementing vitamins and minerals

Along with gluten, grains tend to dish out a generous amount of certain vitamins and minerals. Fortified wheat bread contains a lot of vitamins and minerals, including B vitamins, calcium, iron, potassium, manganese, and selenium. Therefore, people who follow a gluten-free diet need to seek out alternative sources for these nutrients.

Along with healthy food choices, a daily multivitamin can ensure that you get the nutrients your body needs to function properly. Just make sure your vitamin is gluten-free.

If you're a long-term gluten-freer or plan to become one, you may want to ask a dietitian or doctor to review your diet to make sure you're getting enough of the following vitamins, minerals, and healthy fats:

- ✔ **B vitamins:** The B vitamins include thiamin, riboflavin, niacin, and folate/folic acid. Some good sources are meat, poultry, fish, asparagus, broccoli, spinach, bananas, potatoes, dried apricots, dates and figs, milk, eggs, cheese, yogurt, nuts and seeds, and brown rice.

- ✔ **Vitamin D:** Salmon, tuna, sole, milk, eggs, mushrooms, and ricotta cheese are good sources of vitamin D. Your body can also make vitamin D with exposure to sunshine.

  Vitamin D is a common deficiency in people with celiac disease because the intestines have trouble absorbing and metabolizing this vitamin. Your doctor can check your level of vitamin D with a simple blood test if you think you need one.

- ✔ **Iron:** Some good sources of iron are clams, oysters, lean beef, gluten-free whole grains, soybeans, white beans, lentils, pumpkin seeds, and spinach.

- ✔ **Calcium:** Calcium sources include yogurt, cheese, milk (including rice and almond milk), broccoli, kale, black beans, peanuts, peas, and oranges.

- ✔ **Omega-3 fatty acids:** Some good sources are salmon, flax seeds, walnuts, soybeans, shrimp, and tuna.

Exploring the Symptoms of Gluten Intolerance

Celiac disease and gluten sensitivity (see Chapter 2) motivate many people to seek gluten-free diets. People with these medical conditions have one thing in common: Eating gluten causes trouble in their bodies. The kind of trouble varies from person to person.

Gluten can trigger a wide range of symptoms in people with gluten intolerance. In fact, more than 300 symptoms are associated with celiac disease and gluten sensitivity.

You may experience just one or two symptoms as a reaction to consuming gluten, or you may experience many of them at one time or another. Some of the most common symptoms are gastro-intestinal; other symptoms may not seem related to food at all.

Removing gluten from your diet may help alleviate these symptoms or cause them to go away completely if you do in fact have a sensitivity or intolerance to gluten.

Here are just a few of the many gastrointestinal symptoms that gluten sensitivity can trigger:

- Diarrhea
- Constipation
- Gas
- Acid reflux
- Cramping
- Stomach pain
- Bloating
- Irritable bowel

And here are some common symptoms of gluten intolerance that you may not associate with food:

- Headaches, migraines
- Brain fog
- Itchy skin, rashes
- Mouth sores
- Joint and muscle pain
- Inflammation throughout the body
- Dental enamel problems
- Stunted growth
- Infertility and miscarriages
- Chronic fatigue and weakness
- Depression, anxiety, and other psychiatric and behavioral problems
- Malabsorption
- Seizures

Identifying Food Intolerances

When people talk about a *food intolerance* or *food sensitivity,* they're referring to a condition in which the body can't completely process a food. A *food allergy,* on the other hand, is the body's response to a perceived threat.

If you suspect that your health issues may be due to an adverse reaction to gluten, listen to your hunch. To figure out whether gluten may be the cause of some of your health issues, rule out a more serious disease with your doctor and then leave gluten out of your diet for a week or two and see whether your symptoms subside.

Maybe you've already eliminated gluten but suspect some other foods may also be disagreeing with your body. Having more than one food intolerance is common. Food intolerances seem to do the group thing, presenting themselves in pairs more often than as individuals.

There are lots of ways to substitute for the ingredients you have to stop consuming (see Chapter 18), but how do you find out which foods you need to avoid? An elimination diet and blood tests can both help you figure out which food sensitivities and allergies you may have.

Trying an elimination diet

An elimination diet is the most accurate way to identify which foods are making you feel bad. The goal of an elimination diet is to test all possible foods that may be triggering your symptoms. By eliminating one food at a time for at least a few weeks and then adding suspect foods back into your diet one at a time, you can find out which food or foods are making you sick.

An elimination diet isn't fun, but it's a surefire way to find out which foods you should be avoiding, including foods that contain gluten! But don't bother with this approach to solving your food-related mysteries unless you can commit to it for a while. Sort of cutting out certain foods won't help you figure out how you feel without those foods.

Before you begin an elimination diet to sort out possible food intolerances, you may want to seek the guidance of a doctor, naturopath, or dietitian. Your school probably even has someone who can advise you on how to complete an elimination diet successfully. Check with your food director, health center, or nutrition department.

You can find tons of elimination-diet plans online. Some last longer than others or focus on a few different ingredients, but most are essentially the same. Find one that looks right for you, and be sure to keep a food diary, because it's very easy to forget what you ate and how you felt before and after.

The first phase: Limiting what you eat

Pick a time when you can realistically commit to following the elimination diet — maybe not during finals or over holidays. Every website and book you refer to gives a different amount of time for the elimination phase; five to ten days seems to be a pretty common recommendation, but some suggest longer.

To begin with, you stop consuming anything processed, and you avoid sugar, gluten, dairy, eggs, alcohol, and caffeine. So what on earth can you eat? Keep it simple. Start with unprocessed and simply prepared meats, fish, poultry, and vegetables. For instance, you can eat filet mignon, mashed potatoes (without milk or butter), and vegetables for three meals a day and even snacks. Grill a week's worth of steak in advance and then fry it in a pan with some garlic at mealtime.

Some elimination diet plans recommend that you avoid potatoes, too, but definitely avoid foods you normally eat every day or every week to get a good picture of how eliminating them from your diet makes you feel.

Initially, you want to limit your diet to the following foods:

- Vegetables (but avoid corn, peas, or beans)
- Fruit (but avoid citrus and any fruit that you currently eat two or more times a week)
- Meat (but avoid highly processed meats such as bacon and hot dogs)
- Rice and gluten-free grains such as amaranth, quinoa, and buckwheat
- Bottled or distilled water
- Herbal teas

Avoid consuming all foods that are highly processed and artificial as well as foods that are likely to trigger an adverse reaction, such as these:

- Dairy products (rice milk is good alternative)
- Caffeine, soda, and alcohol

- ✔ Sugar and artificial sweeteners (stevia is okay)

- ✔ Wheat, rye, barley, oats, and anything containing gluten

- ✔ Eggs

- ✔ Highly processed meats: bacon, sausage, hot dogs, and lunch meats

- ✔ Nuts

- ✔ Peas, beans, and corn

- ✔ Citrus fruit

- ✔ All processed foods, food colors, dyes, and additives such as MSG

- ✔ Any food you currently eat more than twice a week

It's normal to crave foods that you eat frequently, and you need to expect some withdrawal from caffeine if you drink it regularly. A couple of days with a whopping headache should put you over it.

The challenge phase: Introducing new foods

After five to ten days of eliminating most foods, you start the challenge phase. Add back one new food every three to four days and eat a generous amount of that food. Keep out glutenous grains, corn, soy, and dairy products until the end, because allergies to these foods are common.

Continue to write in your food journal as you reintroduce foods, and be sure to note any symptoms that appear with a newly introduced food or reappear with an old favorite. Common symptoms of food allergy or sensitivity include fatigue, depression, anxiety, nasal congestion, dark circles under the eyes, headaches, irritability, abdominal pain, digestive issues, hives, itchy skin, hyperactivity, attention deficits, and memory issues. You may be surprised to find that foods you frequently crave are the bad guys.

After you identify triggers for unpleasant symptoms, avoid eating those foods for several months before trying them in your diet again. This period of rest may allow your immune system time to recover its tolerance to some, or all, previously reactive foods, but it may not. Be careful to avoid the foods that increase any unpleasant symptoms.

Undergoing blood tests and allergy testing

Blood tests and allergy testing are certainly easier than an elimination diet, but these tests can be inaccurate and thus not so helpful for determining which foods are making you sick. That said, these tests can offer important information about your health.

Some things you're reacting to won't show up in tests, and other things may show up as a minor allergy but cause major symptoms. Sometimes, though, you can have a big "aha!" moment from an allergy or blood test.

 To figure out which tests may help you the most, see a medical doctor who specializes in allergies or a licensed naturopathic doctor. Tests for foods, additives, environmental chemicals, molds, and more are available.

Questioning conventional wisdom

Michael ran cross-country and track and loved it. When he began to suffer severe cramps, shortness of breath, and dizziness while running — he came close to blacking out a few times — his father, a marathon runner, thought he may need more carbs and began taking bagels for the team to each meet. Michael's dad encouraged his son to eat a bagel before he ran, although Michael was always reluctant to do so. Michael's coach also complained that the young runner wasn't sticking to the carb-loaded eating program she had designed. "Eat more carbs before you run," everyone advised Michael.

During the summer following tenth grade, medical testing confirmed that Michael had a gluten intolerance and had to remove gluten from his diet. Finally! It all made sense! Instinctively, Michael had resisted the wheat-filled carbs, knowing that, despite conventional wisdom, the bagels and pasta were killing his desire and ability to run.

The lesson: Conventional wisdom is not always right! When runners with an undiagnosed gluten intolerance, wheat allergy, or celiac disease consume the standard pre-race diet of wheat-filled carbs, they harm themselves, making it unpleasant if not impossible to continue running.

Addressing Your Issues with Specific Foods

This section covers some common food intolerances that may accompany issues with gluten, including dairy, soy, and egg intolerances. These foods are also highly allergenic for many people and can sometimes work along with gluten to make you feel bad.

Nuts and fish can cause strong allergic reactions, but these reactions tend to differ significantly from symptoms related to intolerances for gluten, dairy, eggs, and soy. That's why I don't address health issues with nuts and fish in this section.

Ditching dairy

If some uncomfortable symptoms spike after you consume dairy products, you're not alone. As many as 60 percent of adults worldwide have trouble digesting lactose, the enzyme found in dairy products. And if you have celiac disease, then you're even more likely to have dairy issues than other people.

 People with celiac disease are often lactose intolerant because the gluten damages the small intestine's villi and microvilli, making the hair-like projections incapable of catching and breaking down the lactose molecule.

After being on a strict gluten-free diet for a while — I'm talking as long as a few years — you may be able to add dairy back into your diet. Take it slow, though; you need to see just how much dairy you can tolerate. A lactase enzyme supplement can help some people enjoy dairy again without feeling ill effects.

 If you need to avoid dairy, try cheeses and milks that are made from rice, almond, or coconut. Or try goat's milk and goat's milk cheeses. Goat's milk is easier to digest, especially if your issue is the casein in cow's milk rather than the lactose.

Breaking up with eggs

You'd be surprised by how many people write in to "correct" dairy-free recipes I post, telling me that eggs are dairy. Last time I looked, eggs come from birds, and dairy comes from cows! Nevertheless, eggs represent one of the top eight allergens in the U.S.

Symptoms of an egg allergy or intolerance include skin problems; asthma-like symptoms; hives; flatulence; bloating; abdominal cramping; sudden change in the frequency, texture, and color of feces; severe headaches; hot-flash sensations; and tiredness not attributable to another cause.

If you must eliminate eggs from your diet, you can still bake successfully. See Chapter 18 for specific egg substitution ideas.

Saying sayonara to soy

Food sensitivities often travel in groups, and if you have an intolerance to gluten, your body may also have a tough time with soy. Soy and gluten seem to hang out together a lot.

In a person with a soy *allergy,* the immune system recognizes the soy protein as a foreign substance and responds with symptoms like hives, rashes, and tingling of the mouth and tongue. With a soy *intolerance,* the body may have trouble breaking down soy or find it irritating to the digestive system, resulting in symptoms ranging from general moodiness and irritability to gastrointestinal discomfort to headaches.

There's no handy substitution for soy like there is with dairy and eggs; you simply have to avoid soy if your body reacts poorly to it. Soy is an ingredient in most processed foods, so if you can't eat soy, start cooking! That's the easiest way to steer clear of soy.

Overcoming Emotional Obstacles

Choosing to be gluten-free may be exciting. After all, look at how many celebrities and sports heroes are doing it. Being gluten-free right now is actually pretty cool.

But what if you *have* to go gluten-free? What if you just got a devastating diagnosis or have discovered that you function better without gluten and now you can't imagine how you're going to survive without pizza, sandwiches, and cookies?

It may be difficult to believe, but you *can* have a great social life with wonderful food that happens to contain no gluten. You can have fun family holidays, you can eat out at restaurants and friends' homes, and you can even have pizza and cookies (see Chapter 4 for hints on handling social situations). It's not the end of the world if you can't eat gluten. It's the beginning of a wonderful future, knowing you'll feel better than ever.

Type "stages of grief" — yes *grief* — into a search engine to find some ways for coping with the emotional fallout of your situation and necessary changes. Grieving over the loss of life as you've known it is okay, and it's a process.

This section addresses the emotional aspects of being forced to live without gluten.

Handling shock and denial

It's normal to feel shocked when you receive a diagnosis and suddenly face big changes in your life. You may even grapple with denial. Especially if you feel great after a while, you may start to doubt your diagnosis or the need to remain gluten-free.

Or perhaps someone else in your life is the one in denial. She may not believe that you really need to cut gluten out of your life; she may even accuse you of being unnecessarily high maintenance. Sadly, you can't change other people. If someone important to you is unable to support you during this time of change, maybe she's just uneducated, not unfeeling. Give her some to time to adjust to the idea of your drastic life change and how it may affect her.

Even if you have super supportive people around you, you can make your transition to gluten-free a little more pleasant by following this advice:

- ✔ **Don't share all the reasons you've found that gluten is harmful.** You'll be an expert in no time and may be tempted to tell people everything you know, especially if you have a friend or relative you know would benefit from a gluten-free diet. Just let it go! Make your own decisions and let others make theirs without judgment.

- ✔ **Remember that it's not all about you.** Don't monopolize dinner conversations to talk about your health. If events, meals, and outings aren't focused on you and your health issues, you may just find that those unpleasant confrontations with insensitive people begin to fade away.

- ✔ **Don't expect people to cater to you.** With a condition like celiac disease or gluten sensitivity, people don't always believe that you must be strict with your food intake. Be prepared to feed yourself for a little while. The people who really care about you will eventually see your resolve and catch on.

Accepting your situation

Acceptance doesn't mean you have to love your situation but that you reach a point of seeing the good in it. After you figure out what to order at your favorite restaurants, what to eat at parties, and what to cook for yourself that tastes great and keeps you healthy, your new gluten-free life is likely to feel better than anything that came before.

You may be tempted to turn down social invitations and not eat much of anything at first. Try to resist that urge and keep putting yourself out there. Remember that you're on the road to good health, so you're better off without gluten. Besides, exploring new cuisines and ingredients while becoming a great cook can be pretty fun!

Sticking with It

Temptation to quit or to try a bite of some gooey gluten-containing pizza or dessert rears its ugly head every so often. Just a little peer pressure can catch you off-guard if you're not careful. But if you're gluten-free to help treat a medical condition, keep in mind that even a little gluten can significantly affect your health.

Avoiding temptation can be a little easier if you're prepared with ideas like these:

- ✔ Keep a gluten-free snack in your car, purse, or backpack so you have a good food choice to go to in a pinch.

- ✔ Bring your own dessert, sandwich, beer, or meal. Be prepared with your own version of whatever everyone else is having so you aren't tempted to give in and have some of theirs.

- ✔ Volunteer to bring food for the group and show up with chips and homemade guacamole, veggies and dip, fruit, popcorn, ice cream, and so on. There are plenty of things that everyone can enjoy, gluten-free or not.

- ✔ Go online and look at restaurant menus ahead of time. Most have gluten-free items you can order, and it helps to have your order figured out before you go so you aren't tempted to cheat.

- ✔ Remember why you're doing this. You're working on getting or staying healthy. It's worth it. The consequences of consuming gluten may not be.

Supplying your own refreshments

John has celiac disease and knows that gluten is a poison that his body rejects, but he has only minor outward symptoms of the disease. He hasn't told his college buddies about his illness because he's self-conscious about talking about his health and embarrassed about being different. While hanging out with his friends, he has the pizza and beer but feels guilty because he knows he's doing inward damage to his body.

The lesson: BYOGFB! Bring your own gluten-free beer! Be prepared to be in social settings with your own gluten-free stuff for the sake of your health. (See Chapter 4 for tips on handling social situations, and see Chapter 1 for info on gluten-free alcoholic beverages.) Gluten-free frozen pizzas, homemade pizzas, and even restaurant pizzas are fairly accessible in most places, and so is gluten-free beer. Mention it once, and move on with your gluten-free living. Your friends aren't likely to be mad that you won't be raiding *their* stash!

Living gluten-free to improve your health requires positive thinking, strategy, planning, training, and endurance. So build yourself a team of supporters to help you stay on track. Over time, you'll learn to take control of your health and get better at resisting temptation.

Chapter 4

Surviving Social Situations

● ●

In This Chapter

▶ Discussing your new diet with family and friends

▶ Dining away from home

▶ Traveling on your gluten-free diet

● ●

*E*ating away from home and entertaining guests at your place
can be intimidating when you're on a restricted diet, but you
really can do it successfully! All it takes is a few supplies and an
adventurous attitude. And with some easy food-preparation
techniques, whipping up a delicious and satisfying meal — even for
people who can eat anything — is no trouble at all.

Fortunately, gluten-free eating is popular. Most people have heard
of the gluten-free diet, and many restaurants are prepared to
accommodate you. So surviving social situations on a gluten-free
diet may not be as tough as you fear.

In this chapter, you can find suggestions for talking to friends
and family about the gluten-free diet as well as info on food options
at restaurants, parties, and special events. I also address managing
travel on a restricted diet.

Informing Family and Friends

You probably know how annoying it is to hang out with people
who never do what you want to do or eat where you want to eat
and constantly try to change the plans of the group. But that
doesn't need to describe you just because you need to avoid
gluten. In this section, I offer some tips for talking about the
gluten-free diet with other people, dating while gluten-free,
keeping the peace with roomies, and creating a strategy for staying
positive and fending for yourself so you don't end up feeling left
out in social situations.

Educating without lecturing

One of the first ways for you to set the stage for social survival is to tell your family and friends about the limitations of your gluten-free diet. Be specific but brief about what you can and can't eat. If someone asks for information about gluten or your new diet, feel free to share the basics in a positive light. No need for tons of detail on personal health issues or a lecture on the evils of gluten. If no one asks, assume people aren't interested in making it a topic of discussion.

Some people may feel you're judging them when you decide not to eat something they do, so try not to dwell on things you've read that led you to trying a gluten-free diet or on the ills of wheat in the modern diet. And don't expect your friends and family to adopt your new gluten-free lifestyle or even remember what you can eat. You may be lucky enough to have people around who want to go the extra mile for you, but that has to be their choice, not your demand.

Use these tips to be an upbeat gluten-free diner:

✔ Asking if something contains gluten is very important because you can't tell by looking. Ask, "Can you tell me if this contains gluten?" If it does, just skip it. No need for a big explanation. If the person you're talking to doesn't know what gluten is, it's often easier to say you're allergic to anything with flour in it. Most people understand that.

For people especially close to you, such as parents or a sweetheart, consider making a copy of the simple diet card in this chapter's "Gluten-free dining card" sidebar to help them grasp what you're attempting to avoid.

✔ Avoid saying, "I can't eat that." Just say, "No thanks," when offered a gluten-containing item.

✔ Don't pout or complain if there's nothing you can eat at that moment. You can always eat before or after an event.

✔ Always be prepared with a protein bar or snack in your car or backpack.

✔ Avoid discussing diet or digestion issues during a meal!

✔ Don't generalize why everyone should go gluten-free.

Daring to date while gluten-free

In an ideal world, you find a special someone who's good-looking, funny, smart, caring, and also on a gluten-free diet. It can happen, but it's not too likely. In fact, people often ask me how to deal with a girlfriend or boyfriend who's hostile toward their gluten-free diet. It sounds crazy, but this situation is more common than you may think. My answer is that your significant other needs to show respect for your needs and health goals. If not, you may need to consider that this person isn't the best relationship fit for you, especially if you're committed to a gluten-free diet forever.

When dating, avoid being negative about other people's food choices, acting like a know-it-all, and discussing gastrointestinal issues. That's not hot. Instead, try one of these tactics:

- ✔ Pick places for dates that offer good gluten-free choices (most do, including many fast food places).

- ✔ Gauge your date's level of respect for you by how well she respects your food choices.

- ✔ Avoid talking about your food choices, diet needs, or the results of not following your diet during a meal.

- ✔ Cook for or with a date to show her how delicious gluten-free fare can be and how it's prepared.

Okay, on to the important stuff: Kissing. If your date eats gluten or drinks a gluten-filled beer, should you ask her to brush her teeth or at least rinse well so you can safely make out? Should you both eat gluten-free at a meal if you want the option of more-spontaneous kissing later? It depends on why you're gluten free. If you have a serious wheat allergy or a very sensitive case of celiac disease, the answer is yes. If extremely tiny amounts of gluten cause negative effects when you eat them, they may also affect you negatively when someone else eats them and then kisses you. Lipstick also needs to be gluten-free.

The good news is that you can quickly gauge who is worth more of your time by how they respond to your needs. And just think how well their dental visits will go from now on with all that brushing!

Relating to roommates

Successfully cohabitating with people who don't share your gluten-free lifestyle requires a bit of organization and communication. Here are a few simple ideas to help you keep your environment safe and your roommate relations strong:

✔ Be kind and specific about your expectations of cooking and cleaning procedures. Reassure roomies that you're not limiting what they can prepare, just asking that they keep things clean.

✔ Keep your foods and preparation items as separate from others' as possible.

✔ Clean your kitchen well daily.

✔ If you find your frustration level rising because of lack of cooperation on the part of your roommates, take on kitchen duty yourself.

If you're gluten-free because of celiac disease, gluten sensitivity, or serious allergies, avoiding cross-contamination with gluten-containing foods and kitchen gadgets is critical. Keep a chart of who's supposed to clean the kitchen each day if necessary, but make sure it actually gets done — every day. See Chapter 6 for tips on organizing and setting up a shared kitchen and details on avoiding cross-contamination.

Going Out on the Town

Venturing out of the house on a gluten-free diet doesn't need to be daunting. Gluten-free eating is much more popular and understood now than it was even a couple of years ago. A little preparation goes a long way toward triumphant gluten-free dining and travel. This section offers tips on ordering at a restaurant and finding gluten-free food when traveling.

Eating at restaurants

Every day it seems like a new chain or local eatery is announcing a gluten-free menu. But menu or not, you can find great gluten-free food choices almost anywhere.

When dining out, ask questions every time. Does the server know what gluten is? Does the restaurant have a gluten-free menu? Will the chef come out to speak with you about how to prepare your meal? If you feel uncomfortable with the answers you receive, then take your business elsewhere. Making sure your meal is gluten-free takes some effort, but you can enjoy eating at restaurants that accommodate your needs.

Another bonus: When you ask questions, you help increase awareness of gluten intolerance! And hopefully this results in more food choices for everyone in the future.

Here are some suggestions for making your restaurant experience a little easier:

- ✔ **Check out the menu ahead of time.** If you know where you're dining, check the restaurant's website. Restaurants often have menus online; if not, then call and ask before you go.

- ✔ **Narrow down your choices.** At the restaurant, find two or three dishes that look good to you and that seem "safe" (no obvious gluten) and ask the server for details. Don't expect the server to spend time going over the entire menu with you. It's easier and safer to have him check on just a few dishes than, say, all the salads offered by the place.

- ✔ **Get the server's attention.** Try to spend a few minutes talking with the server about your gluten-free diet and food ingredients before everyone else orders. A good time may be when he comes to take drink orders or to tell you about the specials.

- ✔ **Communicate.** Explain your dietary needs before you order and always ask the server to ask the chef whether something contains gluten or how it's prepared. See the nearby sidebar for a restaurant card you can share.

- ✔ **Speak to the manager.** If your server doesn't seem to get it, talk with the restaurant manager before you order. I've had many restaurant managers approach me during a meal and say, "Feel free to ask for me when you get here next time, and I'll make sure you're taken care of."

- ✔ **Substitute.** Don't be afraid to ask for modifications to your selections. For example, request rice, polenta, potatoes, or a vegetable instead of pasta. (Check out Chapter 18 for the lowdown on savvy food substitutions.)

- ✔ **Check your food.** When your food comes, check everything — twice; mistakes happen! If your salad has croutons on it or your hamburger comes with a bun, *don't* actually send it back. Keep it at the table and alert your server that you need another order. Don't let them take the contaminated plate away, as sometimes kitchen staff simply remove croutons or a bun (not good enough!) and return the contaminated dish to you.

- ✔ **Enjoy!** When you're confident that your food is safe, eat up and enjoy!

Even when you take precautions, risk of cross-contamination and mistakes exists. Everyone has a different level of tolerance, but the goal is always zero tolerance — no gluten! Over time, you'll compile a list of places you know can accommodate you safely, and your gluten-free life will become easier because you'll be ready with suggestions when your friends want to order late-night pizza, go celebrate at a restaurant, or order carryout for dinner.

When dining out with a group of friends, splitting the bill may not always be equitable if you didn't share that pitcher of beer or bruschetta app. Just kindly mention that you'll give a smaller portion since you didn't partake. Asking for your own check at the beginning of the night may be an easier solution to avoiding an awkward situation when the bill arrives.

Attending parties and potlucks

You don't have to avoid your gluten-eating friends or starve when enjoying your college party scene. Here are some simple ideas for surviving social gatherings:

- Eat before you go. You can look for veggies and other safe foods to munch on at the gathering, but you won't be famished if you can't find safe options.

- Keep your expectations low if you aren't bringing any food.

- Check with the host to make sure it's okay to bring a dish. Find easy and delicious recipe ideas in Parts II and III. You never need to mention you're gluten-free!

- For potlucks, bring two dishes — a main dish and a side or dessert that you and others can enjoy — to give yourself more choices.

Gluten-free dining card

Make a copy of this information to take with you to restaurants to explain your dining needs:

I would be grateful for your help in choosing a meal that I can safely enjoy.

- I cannot eat wheat, barley, rye, or oats or foods related to them, such as wheat flour, breadcrumbs, flour tortillas, gravies and sauces made with flour, beer, soy sauce, bread, or croutons.

- Please check to see that my order is prepared without wheat, barley, rye, or oats and check the labels of ingredients such as marinades, flavored rice, spice mixes, sauces, dips, and toppings.

- Please check to make sure that nothing in my order is fried with other flour-coated items.

- I can always eat fresh vegetables and fruits, fresh meat, corn tortillas, salt, sugar, oil, plain rice, potatoes, beans, cheese, many sauces, eggs, avocado, pure spices, and most dairy products.

Thank you!

Even if you're over 21, steer clear of beer unless it's specifically marked gluten-free. See Chapter 1 for a list of alcoholic beverages that are gluten-free.

Considering catered events

Your college years may be filled with formals, weddings, and catered gatherings. Don't let your gluten-free restrictions keep you away from these fun events! A few minutes of prep work can make it easy for you to enjoy festive meals with your friends and family.

 One of my best suggestions for setting yourself up for a great night out is to ask the host who's catering the party. Ask him whether he minds if you call the caterer and arrange for a gluten-free meal. Most caterers are well aware of what this entails, but a quick conversation can ensure you get safe fare. This special request usually doesn't cost the host extra money because it's often just a matter of leaving off sauces and making sure that side dishes are free of croutons, breadcrumbs, and sauces.

On the night of the event, find the catering event manager when you arrive and alert her that you ordered a gluten-free version of the meal. You probably won't get a gluten-free version of the dessert, but maybe you can snag some after-dinner fruit or a cup of coffee.

Overcoming the Trials of Traveling

Planes, trains, and automobiles can all offer successful travel fare — even for the gluten-free! In fact, most cruise lines have great gluten-free choices now. So do some research before a trip and find out what (if anything) you need to do to keep your travel drama-free and nourishing. If you're wondering which foods to pack for a trip, how to find gluten-free meals along the way, and how to manage your diet in an airport, read on.

Packing for road trips

Road trips are the easiest kind of travel to manage in terms of avoiding gluten. Just stock your car with your favorite snacks and bring a cooler for perishables. You're in control of what you have available and where you stop, and that makes gluten-free car travel a breeze!

Here are some good road-trip snacks that are easy to pack in a bag or cooler:

- ✔ Sandwiches on gluten-free bread
- ✔ Fresh fruit and veggies
- ✔ Dried fruit
- ✔ String cheese and yogurt
- ✔ Nuts and seeds
- ✔ Homemade or store-bought gluten-free trail mix
- ✔ Gluten-free cereals and granola bars
- ✔ Chips and gluten-free crackers and pretzels
- ✔ Gluten-free cookies or brownies

Researching your route and destination

Before you pull out of town, check online for gluten-free restaurants along your route. Most fast food restaurants have gluten-free/allergen menus.

You can also load smartphone apps to help you find restaurants in the cities and towns you'll pass through. One favorite app is Find Me Gluten Free. It lists links to gluten-free menus of popular chains and also shows you where to eat gluten-free near where you are at any given moment. Easy! If you're super prepared, you can even print menus and bring a stack with you. See Appendix A in this book for more recommendations on websites, guides, and apps.

If you're visiting a theme park or resort, a list of the gluten-free offerings is likely available online. Most places have a guest services phone number to call for gluten-free information as well.

Enjoying gluten-free airport fare

Are you flying any time soon? If so, chances are that you plan to depart from a major airport and may even stop at one or two along the way. If you find yourself searching for something to eat, rest assured that you can find good gluten-free food — from grab-and-go fare to gourmet cuisine — at most airports. You just need to know what to look for.

Studying abroad

Planning to study abroad while on a gluten-free diet? It may be easier than you think! Many countries are way ahead of the U.S. in terms of providing gluten-free fare in stores and restaurants.

Which country do you think is most challenging for gluten-free travel? If you say Italy, it's not a problem. Gluten-free pasta, fresh seafood, and vegetables abound. If you guess India, keep in mind that rice and chicken are great gluten-free options.

As usual, I advise you do some research online about your potential food choices before you travel internationally, but don't let your diet limit your college experiences! Check out these two blogs from college students who studied abroad while gluten-free:

✔ **Julie Goes to Rome:** Julie went gluten-free in Rome and elsewhere, including Italy, Spain, Scotland, and more. Visit: `http://juliegoes torome.wordpress.com/`.

✔ **Celiacs at College:** Stephanie did a Semester at Sea and visited more than ten countries and navigated gluten-free eating on the ship, too! See her blog at `http://www.celiacsatcollege.com/studyabroad.htm`.

 When you're in the mood for a snack, keep your eyes peeled for fresh fruit, frozen yogurt (watch the toppings, though), nuts, some candy, dried fruit, many bagged chips, cheese, salads (no croutons), and coffee, including some coffee specialty drinks. Always check labels before you buy.

Corn chips and potato chips are generally gluten-free unless they have wheat in the spices, like a taco flavor or sometimes barbecue flavor. It's pretty safe to stick with salted chips, but check the labels. Some cool chip versions may be available at the airport as well; sweet potato chips, rice chips, bean chips, or veggie chips. On candy, watch out especially for malt and wheat in the ingredient list. Steer clear of anything with a cookie crunch or licorice. Did you know one of the main ingredients in Twizzlers is wheat flour? Find out what exactly to look for on food labels in Chapter 5.

When you need a bit more substance, look for national chain restaurants that have gluten-free menus. Most airports have their restaurants and stores listed on their websites, so you can make a plan before you take off. But in every setting involving food, stay vigilant about asking questions and using good judgment based on how you see employees handling things.

A couple of airlines offer a gluten-free meal for a fee if you call at least 72 hours in advance, but it's safer to bring food on board. Mistakes happen, and you could end up with nothing to eat on a long flight if you're not prepared with your own gluten-free stash. Often, there's nothing gluten-free on airplanes, but hopefully that will change as more travelers stop consuming gluten.

All U.S. airports allow you to bring food through security unless it's in liquid form. You must purchase drinks inside the airport after you pass security. Anything from leftovers to trail mix should make it through security, although international flight security may restrict you from carrying fruits and vegetables. Check the latest rules and regulations online before planning what to pack if overseas travel is in your plans.

Chapter 5

Savvy Gluten-Free Shopping

. . . .

In This Chapter

▶ Getting ready to go to the store

▶ Saving some money while shopping

▶ Decoding the label lingo

. . . .

Shopping. The thought of it probably sends shivers down your spine. Either you love it, or you hate it; not many people feel neutral about grocery shopping. And when it comes to navigating the aisles in search of the best-tasting gluten-free items, it's more like a hunting expedition than a shopping trip. But making the right choices is important because stocking up on gluten-free ingredients, especially when you're first getting started, can get expensive. Wasting food in any situation is a bummer; when you don't have tons of dough to throw around, tossing expensive ingredients in the can feels extra bad.

In this chapter, I point out why it's smart to prepare for grocery trips and how to get ready. I also explain how to find gluten on food labels. Here, too, are tips for stretching your food budget to ensure you get the most meals for the money you spend — and maybe even find yourself with a little extra for those concert tickets you've had your eye on.

Preparing to Stock Up

Doing a little preparation before your grocery run pays big dividends. How many times have you stood in front of a pantry or fridge that's full of food and walked away hungry or headed out the door for fast food because nothing looked good? Buying things that you can put together into an appealing meal is key to avoiding waste in your food budget.

Take these five steps before you walk out your door:

✓ **Clear the shelves.** Before beginning your gluten-free diet, get rid of all gluten-containing foods. Give them to your roommates or donate unopened cans and boxes to a local homeless shelter or food bank. Also check expiration dates and throw out anything that's gone bad.

✓ **Plan some meals.** Check out the recipes in this book and plan out a few days' worth of meals. Try to pick main dishes and sides that use some of the same ingredients, especially if a recipe calls for a pricier item. Don't forget to include fruits and vegetables; you want some nutritional balance in your meals. (Find meal-planning tips in Chapter 16.)

✓ **Make a list.** Create a grocery list of foods you need for your menu as well as snack foods and other items you want to pick up. This can help you stay focused and ensure you don't forget any key ingredients. Flip to Chapter 6 for a list of basic foods to include in your pantry and fridge.

✓ **Take inventory.** Figure out what you already have and make sure you have enough for your recipe. Find smart food storage tips in Chapter 6.

✓ **Find deals.** Check manufacturers' websites for coupons on key ingredients you know you want to pick up during your grocery run. Also look up local grocery ads online and download store apps to your smartphone to see what's on sale.

If you have a health food or natural foods store nearby, great! These stores tend to be ahead of the game and have been carrying specifically gluten-free products for many years. Some major grocery chains are just beginning to add small gluten-free sections. Also use your search engine to check for gluten-free bakeries in your town. They're popping up all over the place.

Stretching Your Dough

You're likely to experience sticker shock when buying gluten-free specialty items on your first few shopping trips. A tiny loaf of bread without gluten can be two or three times the cost of a gluten-filled one! Some easy tricks and planning can help you stretch your food budget a little further.

In this section, I cover how to save at your local store and offer tips for buying at a discount online.

Getting the most from local stores

If you need specialty products, buying them from a local grocery store may be the most cost-effective way to go. But you can save a ton of money by preparing meals on your own and forgoing some of the outrageously priced convenience foods. Use these tips to save money when purchasing food at your local grocery store:

- **Buy naturally gluten-free groceries.** Skip the convenience foods. Processed and packaged foods are usually more expensive than plain meat, fresh produce, and other whole foods. Look for store specials and visit farmers' markets to stock up on naturally gluten-free foods such as potatoes, rice, fruit, vegetables, dairy products, eggs, meats, fish, and poultry.

- **Check ads online.** Many stores put their weekly grocery ads online. Visit the store website, click on the grocery ad, enter your zip code, choose your store, and see what's on sale.

- **Use club and loyalty cards.** Sign up for your local store's savings card to take advantage of special pricing, sales, and rewards. Just register your card online and enjoy savings at the checkout.

- **Special-order by the case.** When you need to purchase expensive gluten-free food, especially canned or nonperishable items, consider buying by the case from your grocery store or health food store. Many stores will give you a 10 percent discount on bulk orders, making this a win/win. You don't pay for shipping, and the grocer doesn't need to find shelf space for products that may not sell.

- **Buy major national brands instead of specialty brands.** Food companies are becoming increasingly allergy friendly, so many products are made on dedicated lines to help prevent cross-contamination with common allergens. Confirming a company's process by e-mail or a phone call can put your mind at ease and enable you to buy less-expensive gluten-free products.

  Among the large companies that offer gluten-free options — and that issue coupons — are Betty Crocker, Boar's Head, General Mills, Zatarains, Kraft, Frito Lay, Chex Cereals, Progresso, and Heinz.

- **When buying specialty brands, become a fan.** Many specialty gluten-free food manufacturers, including Udi's Gluten Free and Rudi's Gluten-Free, post discount coupons on their websites and Facebook pages, and most companies send alerts about their special promotions if you give them your e-mail address or Like their Facebook page.

✔ **Shop at large chain stores.** Trader Joe's and Whole Foods Market carry a wide variety of gluten-free foods. If you don't have one of these stores nearby, then Target, Wal-Mart, Costco, and other large chain stores also offer some gluten-free items.

✔ **Explore ethnic groceries.** Some people swear by Asian stores for cheap rice and rice noodles. Don't overlook this great option if you have a specialty grocery nearby.

Shopping online

Shopping online may be a good solution for getting that great gluten-free bread you read about. Maybe you're in a spot where stores that carry gluten-free goods are hard to come by. Or maybe you tried a favorite somewhere and it's only available online.

Unfortunately, Internet shopping can be really expensive. If you buy just a couple of products online, shipping costs can be more than your order. And if you need your products delivered quickly, the costs can skyrocket!

Try the following tricks to help keep prices reasonable:

✔ Buy from websites that have no shipping charge when possible — or buy a lot at once to save on shipping. Many sites offer free shipping if you purchase a certain amount in one order, and some have a very small fixed shipping charge.

If you can't afford to buy in large enough quantities to make shipping fees manageable — or if you can't use that much food before it goes bad — consider sharing an order with friends and splitting the shipping costs.

✔ Utilize gluten-free deal sites such as http://glutenfree deals.com and www.glutenfreesaver.com. With these sites, you buy a voucher for a product at a discount and then redeem the voucher at a store or online.

✔ Look for "Deal of the Day" specials for many gluten-free products on company sites like www.julesglutenfree. com/dealoftheday.asp.

✔ Compare prices of gluten-free products using search engines such as Google. On the Shopping tab of the search engine, type in a product and look at the price comparison. Search-engine comparisons often even tell you whether the shipping is free. I conducted this search for Bob's Red Mill Almond Meal/Flour and found a 1-pound bag for $8.99, about $4 less than it was on other sites. Score!

Turning a flop into a favorite

A solid bet for stretching your food money, whether you're gluten-free or not, is never to throw away food that's still within the expiration period (and that isn't moldy, rancid, or burnt beyond recognition). For example, your stale bread can turn into breadcrumbs, croutons, or an awesome French Toast Casserole (see Chapter 8 for the recipe). Too-flat cookies can turn into pie crust or ice cream toppings. Just crunch them up and toss 'em in the freezer until you're ready to use them.

A bland casserole can be the beginning of a fantastic soup. I recently turned a leftover gluten-free chicken pot pie and some leftover cauliflower into one of the best soups I've ever made. Flip to Chapter 16 for some more tips for using all the food you buy.

Decoding Food Labels

It's no secret that the gluten-free lifestyle takes a fair amount of research and a lot of diligence. If you're just starting, try not to get overwhelmed; it does get easier with time.

Knowing what to look for on a food label is huge. Deciphering labels for gluten-free status is even trickier when you've never heard of the items on the label! Gluten isn't a required ingredient to list in the U.S. If you see wheat, barley, or rye listed on the allergen statement or the ingredient list, then gluten's in there. (See Chapter 1 for a list of other names for these grains.) But even if these grains aren't included in a product's ingredient list, gluten may still be in the food. Use the tips in this section to figure out whether the food behind the label is gluten-free.

Making sense of what a label says — and doesn't say

If you're gluten-free due to a medical condition, then you need to be extra vigilant about avoiding every bit of gluten.

You may find conflicting information on the gluten-free status of some ingredients, so purchasing a list of known gluten-free brands in book or app form can help (find a list of resource recommendations in Appendix A). Some grocery stores have a list of gluten-free foods they carry at the customer service desk, so start there.

Things change, so even with a guide, you need to check the labels of the food you buy to confirm gluten-free status.

Some ingredients have been controversial in gluten-free circles because myth and misinformation perpetuate rumors that they're not gluten-free. In the United States and Canada, the ingredients listed here are not typically derived from wheat; if they are, the word "wheat" should be included in the allergy statement. This means, unless otherwise stated, these ingredients are gluten-free and safe to consume on a gluten-free diet:

- Caramel color
- Cyclodextrin
- Dextrin
- Dextrin palmitate
- Hydrolyzed plant protein
- Hydrolyzed vegetable protein
- Maltodextrin
- Modified starch or modified food starch
- Vanilla extract
- Vinegar (with the exception of malt vinegar, which does contain gluten)

A particularly puzzling ingredient is wheatgrass. If you're in a fitness or health food store, you may see protein drinks and protein bars that are labeled gluten-free but contain wheatgrass. Wheat contains gluten, so how can wheatgrass be gluten-free? The fact is that wheat's seeds, not its grass, contain gluten, and the grass can be around for a few weeks before developing seeds. If you're sensitive to wheat or allergic to it, steer clear of wheatgrass, but if gluten is your issue, wheat grass is gluten-free and safe. That said, I personally stay away from anything made with wheat — even if it is gluten-free — but that's a personal choice.

Just because a product *doesn't* say it's gluten-free in big bold letters on the front doesn't mean it's not. Many products are naturally gluten-free and don't call attention to it. In fact, many companies use a lot of legal jargon to refuse verifying that a product is absolutely gluten-free, even though it is, because they're afraid of being sued if a consumer with celiac disease or gluten allergy happens to get sick after consuming it. This is when guidance for the gluten-free community is especially helpful.

Considering contamination

Gluten-free labeling is currently unregulated in the United States (although final labeling standards are expected soon). At this point, companies can say their products are gluten-free even if they contain significant amounts of gluten due to contamination in processing. No federal labeling standard exists for gluten.

This means that *gluten-free* doesn't necessarily mean that a food product is fully free of gluten. The fact is that even naturally gluten-free foods can pick up trace amounts of gluten in processing and manufacturing.

Some companies use the same equipment to manufacture or package several different products. For example, a potato chip company may run chips with gluten-containing flavorings on the same conveyor belts as plain potato chips, causing the plain ones to be contaminated with gluten. Laws require cleaning between runs, and many companies run gluten-containing products on different days from gluten-free products. They clean equipment well between runs and observe other safe practices.

Still, some people choose to eat only gluten-free foods that have been produced on totally separate lines or separate facilities altogether if gluten makes them severely sick — just to be on the safe side. You can call specific companies to confirm the processes used to manufacture and package the foods you question.

The Food and Drug Administration (FDA) has proposed that when gluten-free labeling requirements are implemented, only foods that test less than 20 parts of gluten per million will be able to claim to be gluten-free. According to most celiac experts, that trace amount is safe for people who must avoid gluten altogether, even after several servings throughout a day.

Making decisions

Here are some tips for avoiding gluten in your groceries by paying attention to labels:

- ✔ **Look for a seal from a third party that verifies an item is gluten-free.** The three main certification organizations are the Gluten-Free Certification Organization (GFCO), the National Foundation for Celiac Awareness (NFCA), and the Celiac Sprue Association (CSA).

✔ **Find out all the different names for glutenous ingredients.** If you think you may forget all the words you're looking for, like *malt,* take a list with you to the store until you're confident that you've got it (see Chapter 1).

✔ **Read the label, review the ingredients, and read it all again.** Even if you've purchased a product dozens of times, check the label each time. Companies sometimes switch suppliers or change their formulas.

✔ **Contact the manufacturer, if needed.** If you've done your research and know what to avoid, you've read the label, and you still can't figure out whether a product is safe, call the manufacturer. Almost all packages and company websites list a customer service phone number or e-mail, and reputable companies are happy to talk with customers about their ingredients and processes.

✔ **When in doubt, leave it out.** If your reaction to gluten is fairly mild and you're unsure whether a food is gluten-free, a bite for experimentation's sake may be worth the discomfort. But people with a severe reaction to gluten need to stay away from all foods that aren't certifiably gluten-free. It's just not worth it!

Do oats contain gluten?

Oats are one of those puzzling ingredients that fall in the gray area between gluten-containing and gluten-free. Some sources of information say that oats are not safe for people who are gluten-free for medical reasons, and some argue that oats are fine. Many people have difficulty digesting oats, but do oats contain gluten?

Naturally, oats are gluten-free, but this food is often processed on the same equipment as wheat and gluten-containing foods, which contaminates it. Oats may also be grown in a field that was used for growing wheat in the previous season, and some wheat seeds may sprout with the oats. So the answer is maybe so, maybe no.

The American Dietetic Association says that oats are safe for people with celiac disease and others on gluten-free diets as long as the oats are labeled gluten-free and cleaned and packaged in a plant without wheat.

Finding a brand of oats that's labeled gluten-free is imperative because this designation means that special care was taken to grow and process the oats away from wheat, barley, and rye in order to retain the oats' gluten-free status.

Chapter 6

Prepping Your Space for Gluten-Free Cooking

. . . .

In This Chapter

▶ Sharing the kitchen with gluten

▶ Picking perfect pots, pans, and gadgets

▶ Stocking your kitchen with basic foods

▶ Keeping fruits and vegetables fresh

. . . .

*T*he recipes and advice in this book make it easier to prepare and enjoy safe, gluten-free meals that don't require a great deal of space or equipment. But avoiding cross-contamination can be tricky if you're sharing your cooking space with roommates who eat gluten, whether you're living in a small apartment or a dorm with only a tiny cooking area or you're fortunate enough to have a massive kitchen in a large house that you share with a gaggle of others.

In this chapter, I offer advice for keeping your food gluten-free in a shared kitchen, suggest some basic tools for cooking, and point out staple ingredients that can make gluten-free meal prep easy and convenient.

You don't need to have all the best gadgets and to know everything there is to know to begin living gluten-free. An adventurous spirit and a willingness to experiment with cooking and eating are the most important components. With time, you'll pick up new tips and tricks for avoiding gluten, but refining this way of life takes time. Getting started is easy.

Sharing the Kitchen with Gluten

To avoid cross-contaminating food with gluten, my family eventually made everything in our kitchen gluten-free. But in your shared-housing situation, a totally gluten-free kitchen may not be possible, so you need to take some precautions to ensure that you don't accidentally consume gluten.

If you're gluten-free for health reasons, then avoiding all gluten — down to and including the crumbs — in your food storage areas, all the prep and cooking surfaces you use, and your eating spaces is crucial. With the plans and precautions I describe in this section, it's totally doable.

Storage: Going for the top shelf

Keeping your food separate from gluten-containing items is important to gluten-free living. So hopefully, your shared kitchen affords you a shelf in the pantry and in the fridge that you can call your own. If you have your pick, choose the shelf at the top. That way, your food is safe from the bits of crackers, cookies, and breadcrumbs that fall from your roommates' shelves.

If space is super limited and you're forced to mix and mingle food items in a shared area, purchase a small cabinet or shelf that you can position away from the other food. Even a lidded basket or plastic bin can work great in the pantry or the fridge. Label it prominently with your name and with the very important words "Gluten-Free!"

Keeping your gluten-free goodies away from others also tames their temptation to eat your food when the other supply is running low or gone. Your groceries are likely more expensive than traditional brands and, believe me, those gluten-free cookies are appealing — even to those who've never thought twice about cutting out gluten. College food has a tendency to walk away when you're not looking, so the farther away yours is from hungry eyes, the better.

Claiming your stuff

Make sure everyone knows that your food is exclusively yours. Keep a marker in the kitchen and label everything that's yours either with your initials or a big "GF." Or take a lesson from my father, who used to draw a skull and crossbones on the Twinkie box to keep the rest of the family away.

Hoarding your condiments is especially important when you're avoiding gluten. The butter dish, the peanut butter jar, the jelly — they're probably all full of crumbs in a typical kitchen. After the knife touches regular bread, it can't go back into the container; otherwise, the entire container becomes contaminated to some degree with gluten.

Don't trust your housemates to remember your instructions, even if they mean well. Buy — and label — your own containers of dips and spreads, especially these items (opt for squeezable bottles if you can find them):

- ✔ Butter or margarine
- ✔ Jelly or jam
- ✔ Mayonnaise
- ✔ Mustard
- ✔ Peanut butter

Food preparation: Keeping it clean

You've heard the saying, "Cleanliness is next to healthiness," right? Okay, that's not exactly how it goes, but if you're gluten intolerant, that's the deal. Cleanliness is the name of the game for avoiding cross-contamination in a shared kitchen. A clean workspace when you're cooking or rummaging around for a snack is imperative to your health.

Even if you don't see crumbs on your countertop, a light layer of dust from flour that your roommate may have whipped into the air while making cookies hours earlier can be all it takes to trigger a health crisis for you.

Chances are pretty good that those in your house who aren't gluten intolerant care much less about the cleanliness of the space than you should. That's why you need to take matters of cleanliness into your own hands and make sure your cooking space doesn't end up making you sick.

Use this guidance to avoid the gluten in your kitchen when you prepare your own food:

✔ Always wipe down the countertop before you begin to prepare your food. Use your own clean plate or cutting board. You can also lay out a piece of plastic wrap or foil to cover the area. A silicone pastry mat is ideal for this purpose, as it can keep any surface free of contamination while you work.

Use paper towels to clean countertops and dry dishes. Crumb-filled towels and sponges sabotage your effort to keep your kitchen clean.

✔ Buy and use your own cutting board and toaster. It's almost impossible to keep these items crumb-free.

Toaster bags can protect your bread from the toaster environment. You can get some online for a couple of dollars and reuse them many times.

✔ Use your own judgment on sharing toaster ovens. If a crumb makes you sick, definitely skip it! If you choose to share, make sure you cover the bottom pan with fresh aluminum foil every time you use it.

✔ If you're making dinner for the house and you're the only gluten-free diner, prepare the gluten-free food before making the gluten-containing items. Be sure to use your own colander for gluten-free pasta draining — and using your own cookware isn't a bad idea, either. That way, you can make sure it's clean each time you cook.

Remain vigilant for cross-contamination threats. No matter whose turn it is to clean the kitchen, be diligent about keeping your counters, shelves, and drawers gluten-free. Don't expect others to do it for you.

Equipping Your Kitchen

With a few well-chosen resources and tools, you can safely feed yourself and follow the recipes in this book. The following sections list the essentials — and a few nice-to-have items — to get you started.

You can share utensils with gluten-eaters if the utensils are very clean each time you cook — but not within the same meal. Don't flip gluten-free and gluten-filled pancakes with the same spatula or use the same pan. Keep everything separate for cooking and serving. Make sure gluten-free dishes have their own serving utensils, and watch that utensils that have been in gluten-containing food never make their way into the gluten-free stuff.

Before outfitting your kitchen, check with your parents to see what they have. They may be thrilled to hand over their perfectly good kitchen gadgets — and appreciate the excuse to upgrade.

Resources

The most important tool in your kitchen is your head. It tells you what to cook, whether your food looks right, how to avoid dangerous crumbs, and so on. Of course, having some food-related reference materials on hand helps, too.

Here are some helpful resources for a gluten-free kitchen:

- ✔ **Cookbooks:** An easy gluten-free cookbook (you've got that one covered!) and favorite recipe websites can be lifesavers when you don't know what to cook for yourself. Be sure to have some gluten-free bread recipes on hand so you're ready to address that unavoidable bread or cookie craving when it hits.

- ✔ **Friends and family:** Do you have gluten-free friends or family? They're a great resource for advising you on cooking issues that may arise. Even if Mom and Dad aren't gluten-free, they may have some great cooking tips to share with you.

- ✔ **Restaurant options:** Keep a list of gluten-free offerings from local restaurants. Find out which gluten-free foods a restaurant offers by looking at menus online and asking the manager when you visit.

Cookware and bakeware

Having a small kitchen filled with too much stuff can be frustrating, so try to avoid having too many pot and pan choices. You can share pans with gluten-eaters if you wash thoroughly; however, it's always easier to have your own set if a trace of gluten can make you ill. You can get by easily with the following pots, pans, and baking dishes:

- ✔ **Pans:** Get one small (8-inch) and one medium (10-inch) nonstick skillet.

- ✔ **Pots:** Be sure to have a small (2-quart) and a medium (3-quart) nonstick saucepan along with a pot large enough to cook pasta (6-quart).

If the pots you may use have been used to cook glutenous foods before and they have any deep scratches, buy new pots.

✔ **Bakeware:** Choose glass, metal, or ceramic bakeware in these sizes: a square 8-x-8-inch baking pan and a rectangular 9-x-13-inch pan. A 9-inch pie plate, a muffin tin, and two cookie sheets are also helpful.

Electrics

Buy these few appliances, and you're in business to cook in the modern world:

✔ **Toaster/toaster oven:** Many gluten-free breads are better toasted, and the toaster oven affords a quick way to heat up a meal or broil something topped with cheese. See Chapter 9 for recipes and broiling tips.

✔ **Microwave:** This appliance offers the quickest way to cook a potato or a bowl of soup or reheat a refrigerated or frozen meal.

✔ **Electric mixer:** See Chapter 15 for some great dessert ideas that use a mixer. You don't necessarily need a fancy, expensive one. A hand mixer does the job just fine.

✔ **Blender:** A blender is a college necessity. Use a blender for quick smoothies. Even a small hand blender (see Figure 6-1) can do the trick. Flip to Chapter 7 for quick breakfast drinks you can blend up.

✔ **Can opener:** Buy a good quality can opener. Especially for premade soups and other ingredients, you'll want a reliable way to get at the goods inside the can. A small, inexpensive electric can opener can make your life much easier.

IMMERSION
BLENDER

Figure 6-1: You can use a hand blender to make sauces, puree soups, and blend drinks.

Essential dorm appliances

If your school allows you to have a few appliances in the dorms, here are some helpful things to have:

✔ **Toaster:** Make a quick breakfast with your gluten-free bread or frozen waffles and French toast.

✔ **Microwave:** Heat some soup, cook potatoes, pop popcorn, or reheat leftovers.

✔ **Mini fridge/freezer:** Store your basics.

✔ **Rice cooker:** A rice cooker is great for rice and pasta in a hurry.

✔ **Electric grill/panini maker:** Make grilled cheese or a quick chicken breast and grilled veggies. Carry this appliance into the kitchen down the hall or onto a patio or balcony before cooking to avoid a food smell in your room.

Many dorms are old buildings and have restrictions on how powerful your appliances can be in order to cut down on fire danger. Some schools even tell you where you can order approved appliances, so check school policies before you buy. This information is often located in the freshman housing section FAQ of your university website.

If you can't get all of these for your dorm room, plan ahead to get these for your first apartment.

Other tools

If you're in a house or apartment, the following kitchen tools allow you to chop, measure, stir, flip, scrape, mash, and otherwise prepare and serve your food:

✔ **Mixing bowls:** You need three mixing bowls: small, medium, and large.

✔ **Serving bowls:** Be sure to have two to three serving bowls.

✔ **Knives and cutting boards:** Keep your own cutting boards to make sure they're used only for gluten-free items. Use one board for raw meat and fish and another for everything else.

✔ **Measuring cups and spoons:** These are must-haves for baking!

✔ **Spatulas:** Get a large spatula and a small one for flipping and serving.

✔ **Whisk:** A whisk is a great way to make sure things are mixed well without having to pull out a blender or mixer.

✔ **Large spoons:** You need big spoons for stirring as well as serving.

✔ **Vegetable peeler:** Use a vegetable peeler for peeling all sorts of produce, especially apples, carrots, and potatoes.

✔ **Potato masher:** Use a potato masher to make mashed potatoes and to mash up ingredients in soups while they're cooking.

✔ **Colander:** A colander drains your pasta or veggie water after boiling. It's tough to get each little hole cleaned out, so have one dedicated to gluten-free food prep.

✔ **Potholders:** Grab a potholder before grabbing your hot pots and cookware. These can get crumbs on them, so it's best to have a dedicated set for gluten-free reaching.

Gathering Basic Foods

Here's a handy list of gluten-free items you should keep in your fridge or pantry. Check all the labels to make sure you're buying gluten-free versions.

Filling the pantry

I recommend these gluten-free baking supplies for your pantry:

✔ All-purpose gluten-free flour mix

✔ Baking powder

✔ Baking soda

✔ Cooking spray, nonstick

✔ Cornmeal

✔ Cornstarch (use to thicken sauces, soups, and gravies and in dessert and dinner recipes; see Chapter 13 for some delicious, hearty soup recipes using cornstarch)

✔ Oats (marked gluten-free)

✔ Parchment paper, aluminum foil

✔ Sugar (granulated, brown, and powdered/confectioners)

✔ Pure vanilla extract

✔ Xanthan gum

Playing with your food (kind of)

Here's a fun use for cornstarch that has nothing to do with cooking, but you may remember it from your childhood chemistry classes. Mix 2 parts cornstarch with 1 part water to make *Oobleck*, a type of goo that acts as both solid and liquid, depending on how you apply pressure to it. It also creeps around like something alive if you put it on a subwoofer and play low frequencies — look up "non-Newtonian fluid" and you'll find videos online. Oobleck isn't food, but it's made of edible stuff and is gluten-free. College students should know about gluten-free food-like stuff to play with, too, right?

Stock up on the following packaged ingredients, making sure you check them for gluten-free status:

- ✔ Cereals
- ✔ Coffee and tea
- ✔ Crackers
- ✔ Pasta
- ✔ Rice
- ✔ Bread
- ✔ Breadcrumbs (either homemade or purchased)
- ✔ Mixes: brownie, cake, cookie
- ✔ Potato flakes, instant (great for coatings, thickening soups, and a quick side)
- ✔ Tortillas
- ✔ Ready-made gluten-free snacks (see Chapter 19 for suggestions)

Look for these cans, bottles, and jars:

- ✔ Beans
- ✔ Soups, including broth or stock and bouillon
- ✔ Tomatoes
- ✔ Pasta sauce
- ✔ Olive oil and vegetable oil
- ✔ Balsamic vinegar
- ✔ Peanut butter
- ✔ Jam, jelly, or preserves

Look for the following herbs and spices. Buy small jars so you can use them up while they're most flavorful. Spice mixes often contain wheat, so stick with single spices and read labels.

- ✔ Salt and pepper
- ✔ Chili powder
- ✔ Garlic salt
- ✔ Italian seasoning (or oregano and basil)
- ✔ Dried parsley flakes

Look for the following gluten-free sauces, dressings, condiments, and other flavorings. Buy squeeze bottles when possible, and remember to mark your containers with your initials or a big "GF" so your roommates don't stick a crumby knife into your crumb-free products:

- ✔ Ketchup
- ✔ Mustard
- ✔ Mayo
- ✔ Barbecue sauce
- ✔ Salad dressings
- ✔ Gluten-free soy sauce (tamari) and teriyaki sauce

When purchasing soy sauce and teriyaki sauce, be vigilant in looking for the gluten-free status. These products are often made with wheat, but gluten-free versions are available. The gluten-free version of soy sauce is usually called *tamari*.

Filling the fridge

Some products must be refrigerated. Pick up the following produce, meat, eggs, and dairy products:

- ✔ Butter
- ✔ Cheese
- ✔ Eggs
- ✔ Fresh fruit and vegetables
- ✔ Fresh meat
- ✔ Milk
- ✔ Yogurt

Unless you plan to use fresh raw meat, fish, and poultry within a day or two, put individual servings into freezer bags and freeze what you don't plan to use right away. Fresh fish, chicken, and turkey should be rinsed and patted dry with a paper towel before packaging and freezing.

 Cut up carrots, pineapple, and other favorite produce and keep these foods in the fridge for a quick and naturally gluten-free snack or side. See the section "Storing Produce" later in this chapter for tips on keeping your fruit and veggies fresh.

Packing the freezer

Frozen foods have a longer shelf life than fresh and refrigerated foods, making them smart buys for college students in many cases. For instance, if you like to make spur-of-the-moment smoothies, you can stock up on frozen berries; they're every bit as nutritious as fresh, and they're much easier to store and find out of season.

Here are some other gluten-free foods to keep in the freezer so they're available when you need them:

- Breads, such as sandwich bread, buns, waffles, pancakes, French toast, and muffins (gluten-free breads spoil quickly on the counter, so keep them frozen for best results)
- Ready-made pizza and pizza crust
- Frozen fruits and veggies
- Steak, chicken, and fish
- Microwaveable meals

 Make your own heat-and-eat meals by packaging your leftovers into individual serving sizes and popping them into the freezer! Find more ideas for repurposing leftovers in Chapter 16.

Stocking Shortcuts

Who doesn't love shortcuts? In this section, I point out products that can make your gluten-free food prep much simpler and quicker, especially when compared to assembling all the ingredients to make certain foods from scratch. But shortcuts usually cost you, and gluten-free food-prep shortcuts are no exception. Consider the savings in time these products can provide you to decide whether they're worth the higher price.

Using an all-purpose gluten-free flour blend

When you begin a gluten-free diet, you may be surprised by how many different kinds of flour are used in baking. Most people assume that eliminating gluten means less flour, but the reality is that your one all-purpose wheat flour is replaced by many specialty flours, which can include white rice flour, brown rice flour, tapioca starch, potato starch, potato flour, and sorghum flour — just to name a few. Buying an all-purpose gluten-free flour blend saves you the space of stocking the different flours; the mixing is done for you and it's all placed in one little bag, ready to go.

Brands vary greatly in taste and texture, depending on which flours the blend features. Try out a few different kinds to find the one you prefer.

 Some brands of all-purpose gluten-free flour come with xanthan gum included. Xanthan gum, along with a mixture of flours, makes gluten-free baked goods come as close as possible to traditional versions. The gum simulates the gooey gluten that binds ingredients in traditional baked goods. Add about a teaspoon per cup of flour. Xanthan gum is pretty expensive for a tiny little bag, so I recommend paying a bit extra for a flour blend that includes it.

Purchasing polenta

Try polenta. This naturally gluten-free cornmeal porridge makes great toppings and crusts for main dishes and can be used in tasty side dishes. You can buy polenta in a bag or box in instant form, or you can buy it precooked in a roll.

Polenta is an affordable and quick-to-cook food that can be pre-pared in many ways and used in a wide range of meals and snacks. Polenta is a staple for gluten-free cooking for many people. Use it instead of rice, pasta, or bread.

If you've never cooked with polenta, now's a great time to give it a try. Here are some ideas for using polenta:

- ✔ Serve instant polenta, either plain or with herbs or cheese, as a side dish.
- ✔ Serve polenta instead of pasta or rice as an accompaniment to stew, stir-fry, or chili.

✔ Use polenta in a vegetarian main dish, topped with sauce or sautéed vegetables.

✔ Try instant polenta as a hot breakfast cereal, either sweet (topped with fruit, nuts, cinnamon, and milk) or savory (served with cheese and eggs).

✔ Use baked, fried, or grilled polenta rounds as a base for appetizers or hearty snacks and lunches.

✔ Use instant polenta in casseroles or as a casserole crust.

✔ Use polenta to replace the biscuit or pastry topping on potpies.

Find polenta recipes in Chapters 8, 9, 11, and 13.

Baking with mixes

Gluten-free baking has come a long way. Your results can be far tastier and less gritty and crumbly than in the past.

Mixes differ from gluten-free flour blends in that they have many of the ingredients you need already mixed in. In fact, foods made with gluten-free baking mixes are often better than what you can make from scratch. Better yet, using a commercial mix is quicker, saving you the time and effort of experimenting with different flours to get a tasty finished product.

Here are some mixes to try:

✔ **All-purpose gluten-free baking mix:** Use this mix as a coating for fried and baked meats and vegetables as well as for gravies and in basic cake and cookie recipes. Different brands use different mixes of flours, so test out a few options to find a brand you like.

✔ **Biscuit and bread mix:** These mixes also work for coating meats and veggies, but (as their name implies) they're especially great for making biscuits and breads. Recipes in Chapter 12 and Chapter 13 utilize biscuit mix for a bready casserole crust and biscuits.

✔ **Brownie mix:** You can make gluten-free brownies that are every bit as good as their gluten-containing counterparts, especially with the help of this kind of mix. See Chapter 15 for some great ideas for customizing your brownie mix.

✔ **Cake mix:** Store-bought gluten-free cake mixes are usually awesome, and they (ahem) take the cake for making it quick and easy to celebrate a birthday or other festivity. Personalize your cakes using some of the ideas in Chapter 15.

Keep in mind that cupcakes tend to come out a bit lighter and less crumbly than full-sized cakes when baking gluten-free. Cupcakes are easier to store, too! Just seal the extras in plastic wrap and toss them in the freezer to really make them last.

✔ **Cookie dough and mix:** Gluten-free cookie dough (frozen or refrigerated) and cookie mixes can help you get a batch of freshly baked cookies in no time.

✔ **Muffin mixes:** Gluten-free muffin mixes come in a wide variety of flavors — blueberry, apple, pumpkin spice, and more — so you can use them to get your fix for pretty much any kind of muffin you want. Muffin mix is also great for quick breads.

✔ **Pancake and waffle mix:** Every gluten-free pancake mix I've tried is great. There are even some dairy-free ones on the market. These mixes also usually include a few other recipes on the package, including directions for muffins and biscuits.

To find out how to prepare delicious gluten-free breads, muffins, and other baked goods from scratch, check out *Gluten-Free Baking For Dummies*.

Using premade products

The single easiest — and healthiest — way to follow a gluten-free diet is to stick to naturally gluten-free foods, such as plain meats, fresh fruit and veggies, and gluten-free grains. Another way to simplify your life on a gluten-free diet is to buy some of the wonderful premade products, especially ones that aid in recipe preparation.

Here are some premade foods that are pretty easy to find, and most brands are really tasty, too:

✔ **Breads:** Bagels, muffins, baguettes, rolls, English muffins, and tortillas are all available gluten-free. Try a few brands until you find the ones you like best. I list my favorites in Chapter 19.

✔ **Breakfast cereals:** A few major cereal brands are becoming gluten-free, often by removing barley malt as a sweetener in a corn or rice cereal. You can usually find at least a few gluten-free cereals in any grocery store, but be sure to check the natural foods section to weigh all the options.

✔ **Crackers:** Not long ago, recipes for gluten-free crackers were pretty popular. But with so many great cracker choices available now, many people are forgoing the time and effort required for the homemade versions.

✔ **Pasta:** Unless you're feeling really ambitious, you'll likely want to buy gluten-free pasta instead of making your own. Most stores offer several choices. Check Chapter 19 for my favorites.

✔ **Pie crust:** Find great pie crust mixes, frozen pie shells, and frozen and refrigerated ready-made foldout crusts at your local grocery store. Or if your store doesn't carry the brand you want, try using crushed gluten-free cookies or graham crackers to make a delicious crust. See Chapter 15 for directions on making crumb crusts.

✔ **Pizza and pizza crust:** Several brands of awesome gluten-free frozen pizzas are available. You can also find premade crusts and crust mixes in many stores.

✔ **Tortillas:** Corn tortillas are usually gluten-free as long as they aren't made from a mix of corn and wheat. You can also buy large tortillas made from other gluten-free grains. See Chapter 19 for brand recommendations, and find out how to make your own corn tortillas in Chapter 11.

Storing Produce

In general, buy small amounts of fresh fruit and vegetables so you can use them up quickly before they begin to droop. To prevent spoilage, be sure you store produce in the right place to begin with. In this section, I offer some advice for storing fruits and vegetables to keep your produce fresh and cut down on food waste.

Wash your fruits and vegetables right before you use them, not in advance. Figure 6-2 shows some washing techniques.

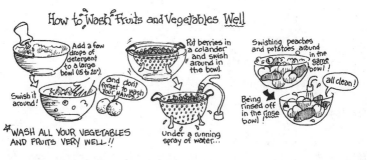

Figure 6-2: Wash fruits and vegetables well.

Deciding to let your veggies chill or hang out

These vegetables are best stored in the refrigerator:

- ✔ Lettuce, spinach, other leafy vegetables
- ✔ Carrots, celery, beets
- ✔ Broccoli, cauliflower, cabbage
- ✔ Corn
- ✔ Green beans, asparagus, artichokes, peas, okra
- ✔ Parsley, cilantro
- ✔ Mushrooms
- ✔ Sprouts
- ✔ Zucchini, yellow squash

 Store vegetables separately from fruits, in different drawers, because ethylene, a gas from fruits that encourages ripening, can build up in the fridge, causing other foods to spoil.

Keep produce in perforated plastic bags in the produce drawer of the refrigerator so moisture doesn't build up and cause rotting or mold. To perforate bags, punch tiny holes in the bag with a sharp object.

 To store fresh herbs, snip off the ends, store them upright in a glass of water, and cover them with a plastic bag. Or store the herbs in a ventilated plastic bag in your refrigerator's veggie drawer. Wash the herbs just before you use them.

Store these veggies and herbs on the countertop:

- ✔ Tomatoes
- ✔ Basil
- ✔ Cucumbers
- ✔ Eggplant
- ✔ Garlic, ginger

Store these ingredients in a cool, dry place, such as a dark pantry:

- ✔ Onions (away from potatoes)

- ✔ Potatoes and sweet potatoes (away from onions and out of the sun)

- ✔ Pumpkin, spaghetti squash, acorn squash, and butternut squash

Figuring out what to do with fruit

Fresh fruit doesn't usually last long. The best idea is to buy it as you think you'll eat it, not buying too much at once.

Keeping fruit on the countertop can be a nice decorator touch and can also encourage you to eat it when you see it. Store the following uncut fruit on the countertop, out of direct sunlight:

- ✔ Bananas

- ✔ Oranges, lemons, limes, grapefruit

- ✔ Mangoes, papayas

- ✔ Pineapple

- ✔ Pomegranates

- ✔ Watermelon

Have some bananas that are about to go bad? Peel the ripe bananas, break or cut them into chunks, and pop them in the freezer. Use frozen bananas in the Peanut Butter Cup Soft Serve recipe in Chapter 15, or throw them in the Banana Oat Smoothie from Chapter 7.

Leave these fruits on the counter to ripen; then refrigerate them:

- ✔ Avocados

- ✔ Peaches and nectarines

- ✔ Pears

- ✔ Plums

- ✔ Kiwi

Store these fruits in the fridge:

- ✔ Any cut fruit
- ✔ Apples
- ✔ Apricots
- ✔ Berries
- ✔ Cantaloupe, honeydew
- ✔ Figs

Part II
Preparing Gluten-Free Goodies

In this part . . .

- ✔ Check out gluten-free recipes that get you fed and out the door in less than 10 minutes.

- ✔ Find out how to prepare more elaborate meals when you have extra time to spend in the kitchen.

- ✔ Discover recipes for comforting home-cooked casseroles.

- ✔ Get grilling for easy meals that can make you a tailgating hero.

Chapter 7

5 Minutes or Less: Grab-and-Go Breakfasts

In This Chapter

▶ Fixing no-cook breakfasts
▶ Starting the day with smoothies
▶ Making quick-cook breakfasts

*Y*ou've probably heard your mother say that breakfast is the most important meal of the day. She's right — again! A healthy breakfast revs up your metabolism and gives your brain and body the fuel they need to operate throughout the day. And with so many quick and satisfying options for this refueling process, there's no need to skip breakfast — even if you're in a rush. To prove it, in this chapter, I offer more than a dozen recipes for delicious gluten-free breakfast foods you can make in 5 minutes or less.

Throwing Together No-Cook Breakfasts

If you think only of grain-based foods like cereal, donuts, pancakes, toast, oatmeal, and bagels when you envision breakfast, you may wonder what a gluten-free soul can eat. The truth is you don't have to cut out those day-starter favorites; you just need to find gluten-free versions.

But you may find that you really enjoy other kinds of satisfying foods in the morning, too. For grab-and-go breakfasts, consider yogurt, fresh fruit, dried fruit and nuts, cottage cheese with fruit, or hard-boiled eggs (see the "Boiling the perfect egg" sidebar). If you have a few minutes to assemble something for breakfast, try the no-cook recipes that follow.

Boiling the perfect egg

Boiled eggs are great as a snack or part of a quick meal. They provide protein and other nutrients, are versatile, taste great, and come in their own convenient packages. Keep a few ready to go in the fridge, or pack them up for a snack or part of a lunch on the go. Here's how to make them:

1. **Gently place the eggs in a small pot with enough water to cover them completely.**

2. **Bring the water to a boil over medium-high heat.**

3. **Reduce the heat to low and cook for 5 minutes.**

4. **Turn off the heat, cover the pot, and let the eggs sit in the hot water for about 10 minutes.**

5. **Remove the pot from stovetop, drain the water, place the pot in the sink, and run cold water over the eggs until they're cooled.**

Strawberry and Yogurt Parfait

Prep time: 5 min • **Yield:** 1 serving

Ingredients	Directions
1 cup yogurt, any flavor ½ cup gluten-free granola 4 sliced strawberries	*1* In a large glass, layer half the yogurt, half the granola, and half the berries. Repeat the layers and eat with a spoon.

Per serving: Calories 491 (From Fat 118); Fat 13g (Saturated 3g); Cholesterol 12mg; Sodium 162mg; Carbohydrate 76g (Dietary Fiber 6g); Protein 19g.

Note: Granola that's not labeled gluten-free is often made with oats that have probably been contaminated with wheat or other glutenous grains in processing. Be sure to use granola that is specifically marked gluten-free.

Vary It! Use any kind of fruit you have or substitute any cereal marked gluten-free in place of granola.

Vary It! For a dairy-free option, try yogurt made from coconut.

Pumpkin Pecan Parfait

Prep time: 5 min • **Yield:** 1 serving

Ingredients	*Directions*
1 cup plain yogurt **2 tablespoons pumpkin puree**	**1** In a small bowl, stir together the yogurt, pumpkin, and cinnamon.
¼ teaspoon cinnamon **¼ cup chopped pecans** **1 tablespoon honey**	**2** In a large drinking glass, layer half the yogurt mixture, half the pecans, and half the honey. Repeat.

Per serving: Calories 436 (From Fat 228); Fat 25g (Saturated 4g); Cholesterol 15mg; Sodium 174mg; Carbohydrate 42g (Dietary Fiber 5g); Protein 16g.

Note: Make sure you purchase plain pumpkin puree and not pumpkin pie filling for this recipe. And if you're wondering what to do with the leftover pumpkin, see Chapters 8 and 15 for more pumpkin recipes.

Vary It! To make this dairy-free, try almond yogurt.

Vary It! Use vanilla-flavored yogurt and cut the honey to ½ tablespoon or just a drizzle.

Banana Split Breakfast

Prep time: 5 min • **Yield:** 1 serving

Ingredients	Directions
1 banana	*1* Slice the banana lengthwise and place it in a bowl.
½ cup plain Greek yogurt	
2 tablespoons 100% fruit preserves	*2* Spoon the yogurt onto the banana.
¼ cup fresh berries	*3* Warm the preserves in the microwave for about 10 seconds. Spoon them over the yogurt and banana.
2 tablespoons slivered almonds	
	4 Top the banana and yogurt with fresh berries and almonds.

Per serving: Calories 357 (From Fat 88); Fat 10g (Saturated 2g); Cholesterol 8mg; Sodium 34mg; Carbohydrate 58g (Dietary Fiber 7g); Protein 14g.

Vary It! Instead of preserves, warm up a touch of nut butter or your favorite chocolate hazelnut spread and top your banana split breakfast with these decadent alternatives.

Vary It! If you have trouble with dairy, make this with Greek yogurt made with almond milk.

Apple, Raisin, and Nut Butter Sandwich

Prep time: 5 min • **Yield:** 2 servings

Ingredients	Directions
1 tart apple, such as Granny Smith 4 tablespoons almond or peanut butter 2 tablespoon raisins	*1* Core the apple and slice it into ¼-inch to ½-inch thick rings (see Figure 7-1). Use four slices.
	2 Spread a tablespoon of nut butter onto each apple slice, like a sandwich.
	3 Top the nut butter with raisins and put a couple of apple slices together — filling on the inside. Make two sandwiches.

Per serving: Calories 274 (From Fat 173); Fat 19g (Saturated 2g); Cholesterol 0mg; Sodium 5mg; Carbohydrate 26g (Dietary Fiber 4g); Protein 5g.

Tip: If you don't have an apple corer, cut the apple into ¼-inch thick rings and then cut the seeds out of the middle of each slice.

Tip: If you don't end up sharing this breakfast or eating the extra slices of apple right away, you can put them in a small plastic bag with a few drops of lemon juice (so they don't turn brown). Save them in the fridge, separately from the other sandwich ingredients, or take all the fixin's with you for a between-classes snack.

CUTTING APPLE RINGS

Figure 7-1: Cutting apple rings.

Banana Breakfast Tortilla

Prep time: 5 min • **Yield:** 2 servings

Ingredients	Directions
2 large brown rice tortillas **4 tablespoons nut butter** **1 banana, sliced in half lengthwise** **2 tablespoons honey**	*1* Warm the tortillas in the microwave for a few seconds on high to soften them. Then warm the nut butter in the microwave for a few seconds.
	2 Spread the nut butter on the tortilla.
	3 Add a banana half to each tortilla.
	4 Top each banana half with 1 tablespoon honey.
	5 Roll up the tortillas and enjoy!

Per serving: Calories 451 (From Fat 195); Fat 22g (Saturated 2g); Cholesterol 0mg; Sodium 165mg; Carbohydrate 62g (Dietary Fiber 5g); Protein 8g.

Note: Rudi's Gluten-Free Bakery makes large and pliable gluten-free tortillas in several flavors that I love. Find this product in the freezer section of your local grocery store. Find other brand recommendations in Chapter 19.

Tip: Hazelnut spread is a delicious type of nut butter that makes a sweet version of this delicious roll up.

Vary It! Use cream cheese instead of nut butter on the tortilla and top it with fruit and nuts for a new twist on this morning favorite. Try dairy-free cream cheese to make this recipe fit into a dairy-free gluten-free diet.

Getting a Smooth Start with Breakfast Beverages

Whipping up a high-protein breakfast on your way out the door is easy and takes almost no time at all! Make a satisfying smoothie with fruit juice or milk — or try coconut, rice, or almond milk instead of the traditional dairy type.

Be creative with other ingredients, too, to give your smoothie the perfect taste and texture. Use yogurt, peanut butter, gluten-free oats, a splash of coffee, chocolate chips, spinach leaves, flax or chia seeds, cocoa powder, frozen berries, fresh fruit, or other favorites to start your day just right. Try the smoothie ideas in this section and then make 'em your own. You're limited only by your imagination — well, and the ingredients you have on hand.

Add a scoop of protein powder to your breakfast smoothie, especially if you're an athlete, you're trying to increase your body weight, or you're vegetarian and need more protein sources! Tons of gluten-free protein powders are available with different types of protein, including whey (milk solids), soy, rice, and egg. Find vegetarian, dairy-free, sugar-free, low-calorie, high-calorie, flavored, and unflavored varieties, too.

For a refreshing and pleasantly chunky smoothie, throw frozen fruit in your blender with the other ingredients. Just be sure to peel your bananas *before* tossing them in the freezer, because peeling a frozen banana is nearly impossible. Might be fun to watch someone try, though! And don't worry if you don't have frozen bananas or berries; just add 1 cup of ice to the goodies in the blender to chill and thicken your breakfast treat.

To make less noise in the morning, use a hand blender (find a picture of this handy gadget in Chapter 6) or just pulse your regular blender a few times instead of putting it on high. You'll get similar results, and your sleeping roommates will thank you . . . or at least not startle awake and want to kick you.

That's right, you don't need a big, expensive blender to make a smoothie. A small hand blender can get the job done, too. This tool blends the smoothie right in the cup, so there's no extra container to wash. Plus, they're affordable and easy to store.

Banana Oat Smoothie

Prep time: 5 min • **Yield:** 1 serving

Ingredients	*Directions*
1 banana, frozen	**1** Combine the banana, yogurt, oats, milk, honey, cinnamon, and almonds in a blender.
¼ cup plain Greek yogurt	
¼ cup gluten-free oats	
½ cup skim milk	**2** Blend the ingredients on high for 30 seconds or until they're smooth.
1 tablespoon honey	
¼ teaspoon cinnamon	
1 tablespoon sliced almonds	

Per serving: Calories 442 (From Fat 64); Fat 7g (Saturated 2g); Cholesterol 6mg; Sodium 82mg; Carbohydrate 82g (Dietary Fiber 9g); Protein 18g.

Vary It! Replace the yogurt and skim milk with a full cup of almond milk, rice milk, coconut milk, or soy milk for a dairy-free version. Or use nondairy coconut Greek yogurt.

Note: Thin this smoothie with a touch more milk if the oats make it thicker than you like.

Berry Delicious Smoothie

Prep time: 5 min • **Yield:** 1 serving

Ingredients	*Directions*
½ **banana, frozen**	*1* Combine the banana, berries, apple juice, and yogurt in a blender.
½ **cup mixed berries, frozen**	
1 cup 100% apple juice	*2* Blend the ingredients on high for 30 seconds or until they're smooth.
½ **cup lowfat vanilla yogurt**	

Per serving: Calories 316 (From Fat 21); Fat 2g (Saturated 1g); Cholesterol 6mg; Sodium 93mg; Carbohydrate 70g (Dietary Fiber 4g); Protein 7g.

Tip: Buying frozen berries can save you money. They're usually less expensive than fresh, and they ensure that you'll always have this sweet and nutritious ingredient ready for smoothies. Just throw them in your blender. Simple and delicious.

Vary It! Use dairy-free yogurt if you prefer to avoid dairy.

Piña Colada Smoothie

Prep time: 5 min • **Yield:** 1 serving

Ingredients	*Directions*
1 cup refrigerated coconut milk	**1** Combine the coconut milk, pineapple chunks, honey, and ice cubes in a blender.
½ cup pineapple chunks	
2 tablespoons honey	**2** Blend the ingredients on high for 30 seconds or until they're smooth.
1 cup ice cubes	

Per serving: Calories 284 (From Fat 46); Fat 5g (Saturated 5g); Cholesterol 0mg; Sodium 33mg; Carbohydrate 62g (Dietary Fiber 1g); Protein 2g.

Mocha Coconut Smoothie

Prep time: 5 min • **Yield:** 1 serving

Ingredients	*Directions*
1 cup refrigerated coconut milk	**1** Combine the coconut milk, coffee, chocolate sauce, and ice cubes in a blender.
½ cup coffee, prepared	
2 tablespoons chocolate sauce	**2** Blend the ingredients on high in a blender for 30 seconds or until they're smooth.
1 cup ice cubes	

Per serving: Calories 185 (From Fat 49); Fat 5g (Saturated 5g); Cholesterol 0mg; Sodium 52mg; Carbohydrate 31g (Dietary Fiber 1g); Protein 2g.

Cooking Quick Breakfasts

Five minutes is all you need to throw together a quick, warm breakfast using a toaster, microwave, toaster oven, or oven broiler. These recipes also make fabulous late-night study snacks when you need a fast pick-me-up to carry you through a few more hours.

Eating a healthy breakfast aids memory, attention span, and cognitive skills. For the best nutrition and to feel full longer, try to include both protein and fiber in your breakfasts. To strike the right balance, choose one option in each of the following categories.

Fiber-packed foods:

❑ Fresh and dried fruit

❑ Energy bars

❑ Oatmeal

❑ Whole-grain cereal and granola

❑ Whole-grain muffins and breads

❑ Waffles and pancakes

❑ Quinoa

Protein sources:

❑ Eggs

❑ Cheese

❑ Dairy, almond, or soy milk

❑ Yogurt

❑ Meat

❑ Quinoa

❑ Protein powder

❑ Nuts

DIY convenience breakfast foods

Make your own convenience foods — they tend to be cheaper than ready-made products, the ingredients are less suspect, and the taste is great. Here are some breakfast ideas that go beyond obvious things like homemade muffins and granola:

✔ **Yogurt cups:** Buy plain yogurt and stir in berries or preserves or the homemade jam that you wheedled from Mom during your last visit home. You can save mixing, serving, and cleaning time in the morning by storing individual servings in the fridge; mix and store the last cup in the jam jar or yogurt container to avoid dirtying another dish.

✔ **Instant oatmeal packets:** Throw gluten-free oats, brown sugar, dried fruit, and any other favorite mix-ins into zippered sandwich bags. To prepare, dump the oat mix in a bowl, add water, and microwave. Regular oats take only a minute or so longer to nuke than store-bought instant-oatmeal packets.

✔ **Frozen gluten-free waffles and pancakes:** Freeze leftover homemade waffles or pancakes. For a crisp texture, defrost them in the microwave and then crisp them in the toaster oven.

✔ **Gluten-free pancake mix:** Find a pancake recipe. Stir together the dry ingredients. Store the mix in an airtight container, label the contents, and put the rest of the recipe directions on the lid.

Nut Butter Banana Toast

Prep time: 5 min • **Yield:** 2 servings

Ingredients	Directions
2 slices gluten-free sandwich bread	*1* Toast the bread.
2 tablespoons peanut or almond butter	*2* Spread a tablespoon of nut butter on each slice of toast.
1 banana, sliced	
1 tablespoon honey	*3* Place the banana slices on the nut butter and drizzle the honey on top.

Per serving: Calories 321 (From Fat 133); Fat 15g (Saturated 2g); Cholesterol 0mg; Sodium 85mg; Carbohydrate 45g (Dietary Fiber 3g); Protein 6g.

Vary it! Try chocolate hazelnut spread instead of peanut or almond butter and leave out the honey for a chocolaty treat.

Strawberry Cream Cheese Bagel

Prep time: 5 min • **Yield:** 1 serving

Ingredients	*Directions*
1 gluten-free bagel	*1* Toast the bagel.
2 tablespoons cream cheese	
3 strawberries, sliced	*2* Spread cream cheese on the toasted bagel and top it with strawberries.

Per serving: Calories 438 (From Fat 181); Fat 20g (Saturated 7g); Cholesterol 32mg; Sodium 676mg; Carbohydrate 53g (Dietary Fiber 5g); Protein 11g.

Note: If you're watching your figure, try O'Doughs 100-calorie bagel thins for this recipe.

Vary It! If you don't have fresh strawberries, this morning meal is also delicious with a drizzle of honey.

Vary It! Try dairy-free cream cheese if you're looking for a dairy-free breakfast!

Maple Raisin Oatmeal

Cook time: 5 min • **Yield:** 1 serving

Ingredients	Directions
½ **cup gluten-free oats** **1 cup water**	**1** Combine the oats and water in a microwave-safe bowl.
2 tablespoons raisins **2 tablespoons maple syrup**	**2** Cover the bowl and microwave on high for 1 to 2 minutes.
	3 Stir in the raisins and maple syrup. Enjoy!

Per serving: Calories 320 (From Fat 24); Fat 3g (Saturated 1g); Cholesterol 0mg; Sodium 8mg; Carbohydrate 70g (Dietary Fiber 5g); Protein 7g.

Vary It! Mix in brown sugar and cinnamon or honey instead of maple syrup to change the sweetness of this cozy morning meal.

Vary It! If you don't like raisins or forgot to pick them up during your last shopping trip, use cranberries, almonds, or even white chocolate chips to flavor your oatmeal instead.

Tip: Thin the oatmeal with milk or water, if necessary.

Breakfast Tacos

Prep time: 5 min • **Cook time:** 5 minutes • **Yield:** 2 servings

Ingredients	Directions
2 eggs 1 tablespoon shredded pepper Jack cheese	*1* Spray a small frying pan with nonstick cooking spray. Heat the pan on the stove over medium heat.
1 tablespoon real bacon bits 2 corn tortillas	*2* Crack the eggs into a bowl and whisk them together.
1 tablespoon salsa Salt to taste Black pepper to taste	*3* Add the eggs to the hot pan. Stir the eggs slowly and continually in the pan until they're no longer runny. While stirring, add the cheese and bacon bits.
	4 Heat the tortillas in the microwave for 10 to 15 seconds on high to soften. Put half the egg mixture on each tortilla.
	5 Add salsa and salt and pepper to taste. Fold the tortillas in half and eat your tacos.

Per serving: Calories 163 (From Fat 67); Fat 7g (Saturated 3g); Cholesterol 192mg; Sodium 429mg; Carbohydrate 14g (Dietary Fiber 1g); Protein 10g.

Vary It! To make this dairy-free, replace the pepper Jack cheese with rice, almond, or soy cheese.

Note: Check the gluten-free status of your bacon bits, especially if they are imitation.

Broiled Grapefruit

Prep time: 1 min • **Cook time:** 5 min • **Yield:** 1 serving

Ingredients	Directions
1 grapefruit, cut in half 2 tablespoons brown sugar	**1** Section out the grapefruit, carefully cutting between the membranes with a sharp knife between the membranes.
	2 Place the two halves of the grapefruit on a baking sheet lined with aluminum foil.
	3 Sprinkle brown sugar on top of each grapefruit half and broil in the oven or toaster oven until bubbly, about 5 minutes. If you use a toaster oven, this dish cooks a little faster because the food is closer to the heat. Watch to make sure your grapefruit isn't browning too quickly.

Per serving: Calories 194 (From Fat 2); Fat 0g (Saturated 0g); Cholesterol 0mg; Sodium 13mg; Carbohydrate 51g (Dietary Fiber 3g); Protein 1g.

Hard-Boiled Egg Melt

Prep time: 5 min • **Yield:** 1 serving

Ingredients	Directions
2 slices gluten-free sandwich bread	*1* Toast the bread and spread half the butter on each slice.
1 teaspoon butter	
1 hard-boiled egg	*2* While the bread is toasting, crack, peel, and slice the egg.
2 slices American cheese	
Salt to taste	*3* Put half the egg on each slice of bread and top it with a slice of cheese.
Black pepper to taste	
	4 Microwave on high until the cheese is bubbly, about 20 seconds.

Per serving: Calories 527 (From Fat 287); Fat 32g (Saturated 12g); Cholesterol 223mg; Sodium 727mg; Carbohydrate 43g (Dietary Fiber 1g); Protein 17g.

Tip: Find an egg slicer in the kitchen gadget row in the grocery store. With this tool, you just put your peeled hard-boiled egg in the middle and bring down the slicer for perfect slices every time. I use mine on mushrooms, too.

Vary It! To make this dish dairy-free, replace the American cheese with rice, almond, or soy cheese and use a butter substitute or dairy-free margarine instead of butter.

Tip: Keep hard-boiled eggs in your fridge so they're always ready for a quick high-protein breakfast, snack, or salad topping. Crack them just before using them. Take note of the sell-by date on the carton, and use your eggs — cooked or raw — within a couple of weeks of that.

Chapter 8

20 Minutes 'til Mealtime: Hearty Breakfasts

In This Chapter

▶ Indulging your morning sweet tooth
▶ Enjoying savory breakfasts

Setting aside 20 minutes to prepare breakfast before heading for class may seem impossible, but research shows that students who eat breakfast are better able to pay attention, concentrate, and remember things. So avoid hitting your snooze button that final time; instead, get up and into the kitchen.

Most of the recipes in this chapter take less than 20 minutes to go from idea to table, and you can make many of them in advance for an even quicker serving time. Other dishes may become weekend favorites. Either way, I hope you'll see that a good breakfast is more doable than you think.

Here, I offer step-by-step prep for sweet breakfasts as well as savory choices — from the classics to first-meal ideas that you may not have considered for breakfast.

Cooking Up Sweet Comfort Fare

Many people enjoy a bit of sweetness in the morning, and the recipes in this section offer just that. The following breakfasts provide a dose of sweet to satisfy your taste buds while offering lasting nutrition. Find recipes here for morning favorites like delicious gluten-free pancakes and French toast.

Keep in mind that consuming too much sugar at any time of day can create a quick burst of energy that leaves you crashing just a short time later. Use syrup in moderation, substitute with 100-percent fruit preserves occasionally, and add lots of naturally sweet fresh fruit when it's available.

Here are a few cooking tips for making sweet gluten-free breakfasts:

✔ When a recipe calls for oats, use uncooked oats that are marked gluten-free.

✔ Check labels for malt flavorings if you're not using pure maple syrup. Using pure maple syrup ensures that you won't have to check for gluten and mess with ingredients like high-fructose corn syrup.

✔ Use nonstick cooking spray, not baking spray. "Baking" spray often contains flour. All other varieties of nonstick spray tend to be gluten-free. Check labels.

✔ To measure a dry ingredient like flour, scoop it into a measuring cup and level it off with the back of a knife.

Maple Pecan Pancake Bites

Prep time: 5 min • **Cook time:** 15 min • **Yield:** 6 servings (2 mini muffins each)

Ingredients	Directions
1 cup gluten-free pancake mix **1 egg, beaten** **¼ cup maple syrup** **½ cup water** **12 pecan halves**	*1* Preheat the oven to 375 degrees. In a medium bowl, stir together the pancake mix, egg, maple syrup, and water until the ingredients are thoroughly combined.
	2 Spray a 12-cup mini muffin pan with nonstick cooking spray or place paper muffin liners in the pan. Fill each cup with batter about three-quarters of the way up.
	3 Top each muffin with a pecan half.
	4 Bake the pancake bites for 12 to 14 minutes, or until they're golden.

Per serving: Calories 138 (From Fat 28); Fat 3g (Saturated 0g); Cholesterol 31mg; Sodium 183mg; Carbohydrate 25g (Dietary Fiber 1g); Protein 1g.

Tip: Make these regularly and keep them on hand to enjoy whenever you need a quick breakfast or a sweet snack or dessert. After they cool completely, cover them with plastic wrap and save them on the counter or in the fridge for a few days. Reheat them in the microwave for about 20 seconds if you prefer a warm treat. Pack them up for the perfect camping or road trip food as well!

Tip: Dip these in a touch of maple syrup for a special treat.

Note: I use Pamela's Baking & Pancake Mix for these. Nondairy gluten-free pancake mixes are available as well.

Perfect Pancakes

Prep time: 5 min • **Cook time:** 15 min • **Yield:** 5 servings (2 pancakes each)

Ingredients	Directions
1¼ cups all-purpose gluten-free flour	**1** In a medium bowl, mix together the flour, sugar, baking powder, baking soda, and salt.
½ tablespoon sugar	
1 teaspoon baking powder	**2** Add the eggs, butter or oil, milk, and vanilla to the flour mixture. Stir to thoroughly combine the batter.
½ teaspoon baking soda	
¼ teaspoon salt	**3** Spray a flat pan or griddle with nonstick cooking spray and heat the pan over medium to medium-high heat.
2 eggs, beaten	
2 tablespoons melted butter or vegetable oil	**4** For each pancake, ladle ¼ cup batter onto the hot pan. When the pancakes begin to puff, form small bubbles, and become lightly browned on the edges (after about a minute), flip the pancakes over with a spatula and cook the other side.
1 cup milk	
½ teaspoon vanilla extract	
Butter for serving	
Maple syrup for serving	
	5 Serve the pancakes with butter and a touch of maple syrup.

Per serving: Calories 206 (From Fat 83); Fat 9g (Saturated 5g); Cholesterol 93mg; Sodium 368mg; Carbohydrate 26g (Dietary Fiber 3g); Protein 7g.

Tip: Make your own pancake mix by measuring and mixing the dry ingredients (Step 1) and storing them in a plastic bag. Be sure to write the rest of the ingredients and directions on the bag.

Vary It! Throw a handful of fresh blueberries or mini chocolate chips into the batter while mixing to sweeten your cakes. Or add the mix-ins to individual pancakes in the pan, and you can make multiple variations from a single batch.

Note: Leftover pancakes save well in the refrigerator or freezer. After they cool, layer the pancakes with plastic wrap and seal them in a plastic bag. Reheat them in the microwave or toaster oven when you're ready to enjoy the leftovers.

Classic French Toast

Prep time: 5 min • **Cook time:** 10 min • **Yield:** 2 servings (2 slices each)

Ingredients	*Directions*
1 egg	*1* In a wide bowl, beat together the egg, milk, and cinnamon with a fork.
¾ cup lowfat milk	
½ teaspoon cinnamon	*2* Spray a flat pan or griddle with nonstick cooking spray. Heat the pan on the stove over medium heat until the spray begins to sizzle just a bit.
4 slices gluten-free bread	
Maple syrup and/or powdered sugar for serving	
	3 Dip a slice of the bread in the egg mixture, using a fork to flip the bread and cover both sides. Let the excess egg mixture drip back into the bowl.
	4 Place the egg-soaked bread in the hot pan.
	5 Flip the bread with a spatula when the bottom side is toasted. When the second side is golden brown, move the French toast to a plate. It should take a couple of minutes on each side.
	6 Serve the French toast with a touch of syrup and/or powdered sugar.

Per serving: Calories 356 (From Fat 128); Fat 14g (Saturated 2g); Cholesterol 97mg; Sodium 78mg; Carbohydrate 50g (Dietary Fiber 4g); Protein 10g.

Tip: Don't throw out your stale bread! It works great for this recipe!

Vary It! Warm some preserves or frozen berries to replace the maple syrup on this breakfast goodie, or serve the French toast with fresh fruit slices.

Vary It! If you're feeling fancy, turn this into Peach-Stuffed French Toast. Mix ½ cup Greek yogurt (plain or vanilla) and 1 cup diced peaches and put it between two pieces of French toast.

Apple French Toast Pie

Prep time: 5 min • **Cook time:** Less than 15 min • **Yield:** 8 servings

Ingredients	Directions
10 slices gluten-free bread 2 eggs, beaten ¾ cup milk ¼ cup brown sugar ¼ cup (4 tablespoons) unsalted butter, melted 1 teaspoon vanilla 1 medium apple, peeled and cut into chunks 2 tablespoons finely chopped walnuts 1 teaspoon cinnamon Maple syrup for serving	**1** Preheat the oven to 375 degrees. Spray a 9-inch pie plate with nonstick cooking spray.
	2 Cut the bread into ½-inch cubes (with or without crust). Place the bread cubes in the pie plate.
	3 In a medium bowl, mix the eggs, milk, brown sugar, butter, and vanilla. Pour the mixture over the bread.
	4 Stir the bread cubes until the liquid is mostly absorbed.
	5 Top the bread mixture with apple chunks, nuts, and cinnamon.
	6 Bake for 15 to 20 minutes, or until the pie is firm in the center and looks lightly toasted.
	7 Serve with a touch of maple syrup.

Per serving: Calories 306 (From Fat 141); Fat 16g (Saturated 5g); Cholesterol 65mg; Sodium 31mg; Carbohydrate 39g (Dietary Fiber 3g); Protein 5g.

Vary It! Top this delicious breakfast pie with raisins, berries, or yogurt instead of syrup for a burst of natural sweetness.

Note: Share with friends or save leftovers covered in the fridge. Reheat a piece in the microwave for 30 to 45 seconds.

Vary It! Try leftovers for dessert with a drizzle of chocolate or caramel!

Tip: To make this dish ahead, prepare it through Step 5 and refrigerate it in a sealed container overnight. When you're ready to bake, allow the mixture to warm to room temperature and then put it in your preheated 375-degree oven.

Fruit-and-Nutty Granola

Prep time: 5 min • **Cook time:** 20 min • **Yield:** 6 servings (½ cup each)

Ingredients	Directions
⅓ cup honey	*1* Preheat the oven to 325 degrees.
¼ cup vegetable oil	
1 teaspoon vanilla extract	*2* In a large bowl, stir together the honey, oil, and vanilla.
3 cups gluten-free rolled oats (not instant)	
3 tablespoons brown sugar	*3* Add the oats, brown sugar, cinnamon, nuts and seeds, and salt to the honey mixture. Stir until everything is well-coated.
½ teaspoon cinnamon	
½ cup chopped raw unsalted nuts and seeds	*4* Spread the mixture in a single layer on a baking sheet with a rim.
¼ teaspoon salt	
½ cup diced dried fruit	*5* Bake for 15 minutes, stir, and cook for another 5 minutes, until the granola is lightly toasted.
	6 Remove the granola from the oven and mix in the dried fruit.
	7 Cool and store the granola in a plastic bag or airtight container.

Per serving: Calories 429 (From Fat 166); Fat 19g (Saturated 2g); Cholesterol 0mg; Sodium 104mg; Carbohydrate 62g (Dietary Fiber 6g); Protein 9g.

Tip: Cover the baking sheet with parchment paper or aluminum foil before adding the oat mixture to keep it from sticking and for easy clean-up.

Tip: If you choose to use salted nuts instead of unsalted, omit the ¼ teaspoon salt in the ingredient list.

Note: Enjoy the granola in a bowl with milk or yogurt for breakfast or toss a bagful into your backpack before you hit the road! It makes a great nutritious study snack, too!

Vary It! You can customize this easy and delicious not-too-sweet granola. Add more cinnamon, less sugar, extra nuts — whatever you like.

Baked Chocolate Lava Oatmeal

Prep time: 5 min • **Cook time:** 25 min • **Yield:** 12 servings

Ingredients	Directions
2 cups gluten-free rolled oats (not instant)	*1* Preheat the oven to 375 degrees.
¼ cup butter	*2* Combine the oats, butter, brown sugar, eggs, milk, vanilla, and baking powder in a microwave-safe dish. Stir until well mixed.
½ cup brown sugar	
2 eggs	
2 cups milk	*3* Microwave the oatmeal mixture on high for 4 minutes.
1 teaspoon vanilla	
1 teaspoon baking powder	*4* Place 12 paper muffin cups in a regular muffin pan. Fill each paper cup halfway with the oatmeal mixture.
¼ cup (12 teaspoons) chocolate hazelnut spread	
1 banana, sliced into 12 pieces	*5* On top of each muffin cup of oatmeal, place 1 teaspoon of the chocolate hazelnut spread and 1 slice of banana.
	6 Top each muffin cup with the remaining oatmeal mixture.
	7 Bake for 15 minutes.

Per serving: Calories 191 (From Fat 74); Fat 8g (Saturated 4g); Cholesterol 47mg; Sodium 69mg; Carbohydrate 25g (Dietary Fiber 2g); Protein 5g.

Vary It! Use jam, almond butter, or peanut butter instead of chocolate hazelnut spread for a different version of this decadent breakfast.

Tip! Freeze your leftovers. When you're ready to enjoy an oatmeal cup, reheat it in the microwave for about 1 minute.

Berry Nutty Quinoa

Prep time: 5 min • **Cook time:** 15 min • **Yield:** 2 servings

Ingredients	Directions
½ **cup milk**	**1** Combine the milk, water, cinnamon, pecans, and quinoa in a small saucepan.
½ **cup water**	
1 teaspoon cinnamon	**2** Heat the quinoa mixture on the stove over high heat until the mixture comes to a boil.
¼ **cup chopped pecans**	
½ **cup quinoa, rinsed**	
1 tablespoon honey	**3** Cover the saucepan, reduce the heat to low or medium-low, and simmer the quinoa for 10 to 15 minutes, or until most of the liquid is absorbed. Stir in the honey.
½ **cup berries**	
	4 Divide the mixture into two bowls and top each serving with half the berries.

Per serving: Calories 361 (From Fat 139); Fat 15g (Saturated 2g); Cholesterol 8mg; Sodium 31mg; Carbohydrate 49g (Dietary Fiber 7g); Protein 11g.

Note: Quinoa (KEEN-wah) is a versatile nutty-tasting gluten-free grain that resembles couscous.

Tip: If you're eating alone, prepare the extra serving through Step 3. Store the extra in the fridge, covered, for up to a few days. When ready to enjoy this dish, reheat it in the microwave and add the toppings.

Note: This breakfast also makes a nice side dish for lunch or dinner, too!

Pumpkin Pecan Breakfast Cookies

Prep time: 10 min • **Cook time:** 12 min • **Yield:** 8 servings (2 cookies each)

Ingredients	Directions
1 cup gluten-free quick oats	**1** Preheat the oven to 375 degrees.
½ cup canned pumpkin puree	
½ cup unsweetened applesauce	**2** Combine the oats, pumpkin, applesauce, raisins, pecans, vanilla, and cinnamon in a medium bowl. Stir well.
½ cup raisins	
¼ cup chopped pecans	**3** Set a timer and allow the batter to sit for 5 minutes.
1 teaspoon vanilla	
1 teaspoon cinnamon	**4** Lightly coat a cookie sheet with nonstick cooking spray. Drop the dough by teaspoonfuls a couple of inches apart onto the cookie sheet.
	5 Flatten the dough balls just a bit with a fork.
	6 Bake the cookies for 10 minutes for a softer cookie or 12 minutes for a crisper cookie.

Per serving: Calories 109 (From Fat 31); Fat 3g (Saturated 0g); Cholesterol 0mg; Sodium 3mg; Carbohydrate 19g (Dietary Fiber 3g); Protein 3g.

Vary It! Use this recipe to make Cranberry Almond Breakfast Cookies. Just replace the pumpkin with two mashed bananas, use raisins instead of dried cranberries, and substitute almonds for the pecans for a whole new flavor.

Note: These cookies provide a soft and not-too-sweet breakfast. Grab a few on your way out the door.

Tip: Lining your cookie sheet with parchment paper before baking has a few advantages: Cookies slide right off the pan, and no washing is required. Just throw away the paper when you're done and put your cookie sheet back in the cabinet.

Tip: Store these breakfast cookies on a covered plate or in a sealed plastic bag in the fridge. Or put single servings in small freezer bags, pop them in the freezer, and defrost as needed.

Getting an Egg Up with Savory Breakfasts

A high-protein breakfast helps you feel full longer, causing you to eat less throughout the day. So although a breakfast of meat and eggs may feel like a splurge, it can help you curb your appetite for snacks throughout the day.

Here are some helpful tips for cooking breakfast meats:

✔ Dispose of bacon and sausage grease by wiping it out of the pan with a paper towel after it cools and throwing it away. Pouring grease down the drain can clog the pipes.

✔ Buy precooked microwavable bacon and nuke it for about 30 seconds on a paper towel–lined plate, and you've got crispy bacon with almost no grease. This type of bacon lasts longer in the fridge than raw, too.

✔ Use lower-fat cheese, bacon, and sausage options to reduce grease and calories at the same time.

Omelets are a great way to eat your eggs and give yourself a big dose of protein and veggies before heading out to class in the morning. Omelets are also an inexpensive and filling lunch or dinner option! Plus, you only need a bowl, a whisk, a narrow spatula, and a good, small nonstick pan for making omelets (see how to make an omelet in Figure 8-1). In this section, find many ways to prepare and enjoy eggs as well as other protein-packed breakfasts.

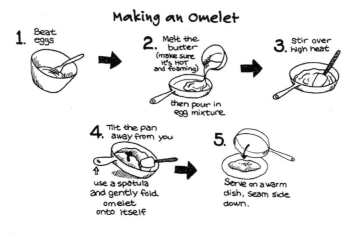

Making an Omelet

1. Beat eggs

2. Melt the butter (make sure it's HOT and foaming) then pour in egg mixture.

3. Stir over high heat

4. Tilt the pan away from you — use a spatula and gently fold omelet onto itself

5. Serve on a warm dish, seam side down.

Figure 8-1: Making a folded omelet.

TECHNICAL STUFF

Checking out egg nutrition

Eggs have gotten a bit of a bad rap over the years. Here are some egg facts that may surprise you:

- Egg yolks contain nutrients that are great for your eyes! Recent studies show that they may even help prevent macular degeneration and lower the risk of developing cataracts.

- Studies show that, contrary to their reputation, eggs may actually lower the risk of stroke, blood clots, and heart attacks when consumed regularly.

- Regular consumption of two eggs a day does not raise cholesterol as previously thought, according to new research.

- Eggs may prevent breast cancer. In one study, women who consumed at least six eggs per week lowered their risk of breast cancer by 44 percent.

Sausage Breakfast Burrito

Prep time: 5 min • **Cook time:** 10 min • **Yield:** 1 serving

Ingredients	Directions
¼ **cup packaged hash browns**	**1** Heat a small skillet over medium-high heat. Cook the hash browns and sausage together until the sausage is no longer pink and the hash browns are beginning to brown, about 5 minutes. Transfer the meat and potatoes to a bowl.
¼ **cup breakfast sausage**	
2 eggs, beaten	
1 large brown rice tortilla	
2 tablespoons shredded cheddar cheese	**2** Wipe the skillet clean with a paper towel, return the sausage and potatoes to the skillet, and put the skillet back on the burner. Add the eggs to the sausage mixture in the pan. Gently stir continuously until the eggs are completely cooked, about 5 more minutes.
	3 Microwave the tortilla for 10 to 15 seconds, until it's just warm and pliable. Start with 10 seconds and add an extra few seconds if needed.
	4 Spread the sausage-and-egg mixture down the center of the tortilla. Top the mixture with cheese. Fold in the two ends of the tortilla and roll it into a burrito.

Per serving: Calories 510 (From Fat 257); Fat 29g (Saturated 10g); Cholesterol 416mg; Sodium 844mg; Carbohydrate 35g (Dietary Fiber 3g); Protein 26g.

Tip: This breakfast burrito is delicious with salsa and a dab of sour cream.

Tip: Use Rudi's Gluten-Free tortilla for this recipe if it's available at your grocery. You can find it in the freezer section.

Brunch Pizza

Prep time: 10 min • **Cook time:** 20 min • **Yield:** 8 servings

Ingredients	Directions
8 eggs	**1** Preheat the oven to 400 degrees. Spray a 14-inch pizza pan with nonstick cooking spray (or use any similar size of low-rimmed, oven-safe pan).
20-ounce package refrigerated hash browns	
A dash of salt	
A dash of black pepper	**2** In a medium bowl, beat 1 egg and then stir in the hash browns. Spread the hash browns in the prepared pizza pan all the way to the edges. Pat down the hash-brown crust with the back of a spoon. Sprinkle the crust with a dash of salt and pepper and bake it for 15 minutes.
½ cup milk	
1½ cups shredded cheddar cheese	
¼ cup chopped green bell peppers	
¼ cup sliced mushrooms	**3** While the crust is baking, whisk together the remaining 7 eggs and the milk in a microwave-safe bowl. Cook the eggs in the microwave on high for 3 minutes. Stir. Cook an additional 3 minutes. Stir the eggs again.
¼ cup bacon (a couple of slices), cooked and crumbled	
¼ cup chopped ham, fully cooked	
¼ cup cooked spinach	**4** When the crust is baked, remove it from the oven and spread the egg mixture evenly over the crust.
	5 Top the eggs with cheese, bell peppers, mushrooms, bacon, ham, and spinach. Return the pan to the oven and bake for another 5 minutes, or until the cheese is melted. Cut the pizza into 8 wedges.

Per serving: Calories 188 (From Fat 92); Fat 10g (Saturated 4g); Cholesterol 200mg; Sodium 310mg; Carbohydrate 12g (Dietary Fiber 1g); Protein 12g.

Tip: I use refrigerated Simply Potatoes shredded hash browns for this recipe. If using frozen hash browns, check them for gluten-free status and defrost them before using them.

Tip: If you want to soften the bell peppers and mushrooms, cook them quickly with a touch of oil in a pan heated to medium-high — a quick sauté. Stir and cook them until they reach your desired softness and then toss them on the pizza in Step 5.

Vary It! Use any toppings that sound good. Try green onions, tomatoes, sausage, and broccoli.

Note: A pizza pan and a pizza cutter are helpful for this recipe, but you can make a rectangular version on a cookie sheet and cut the pizza with a knife.

Note: This pizza provides plenty to share with friends or roommates. If you're saving the extras for yourself, seal up the leftovers in plastic wrap or a zipper bag and store them in the fridge. Reheat a slice in the microwave on high for about 45 seconds.

Vary It! Use egg substitute or egg whites (see Figure 8-2) if you want to reduce fat and calories: 2 egg whites = 1 whole egg or 2 egg yolks = 1 whole egg or ¼ cup egg substitute = 1 whole egg.

How to Separate an Egg

1. Hold the egg in one hand over two small bowls.

2. Crack the shell on the side of one bowl.

3. Let the white fall into one of the bowls.

4. Pass the yolk back & forth, each time releasing more white.

5. When all the white is in the bowl, drop yolk in the other bowl.

Figure 8-2: Separating an egg yolk from the white.

Mushroom Swiss Omelet

Prep time: 5 min • **Cook time:** 10 min • **Yield:** 1 serving

Ingredients	Directions
3 eggs	**1** Whisk the eggs and milk in a small bowl until they're a little frothy. Add the mushrooms to the egg mixture.
1 tablespoon milk	
3 mushrooms, sliced or chopped	**2** In an 8-inch nonstick skillet, heat the butter on medium-low. When the butter is melted, add the egg mixture.
1 teaspoon butter	
2 tablespoons shredded Swiss cheese	**3** Increase the heat to high.
Salt to taste	**4** As the bottom of the eggs begins to cook, gently lift an edge with a thin spatula and tilt the pan to send the uncooked eggs to the bottom. Sprinkle cheese over the surface of the eggs. Fold the omelet in half to cover the cheese filling (see Figure 8-3). Continue to cook the omelet until the cheese melts, about another minute.
Black pepper to taste	
	5 Slide your omelet off the pan and onto a plate.

Per serving: Calories 331 (From Fat 209); Fat 23g (Saturated 10g); Cholesterol 583mg; Sodium 412mg; Carbohydrate 5g (Dietary Fiber 1g); Protein 25g.

Tip: Add another egg and cut the finished omelet in half to serve two. No need to add more mushrooms or cheese, but you can if you want.

Vary It! Add any veggies, meats, and cheeses you like to make your favorite omelet combinations!

Mini Frittatas

Prep time: 10 min • **Cook time:** 20 min • **Yield:** 12 servings

Ingredients	Directions
6 slices bacon, cooked crispy and crumbled ¼ cup chopped green onion	**1** Preheat the oven to 375 degrees. Spray a 12-cup muffin pan with nonstick cooking spray.
½ cup shredded Parmesan cheese 4 eggs	**2** Divide the bacon, green onion, and cheese evenly among the 12 muffin cups.
1½ cups milk ½ to ⅔ cup Bisquick Gluten Free mix	**3** Whisk the eggs and milk together in a small bowl. Stir in the Bisquick. Pour the egg mixture into the 12 muffin cups, dividing the mixture evenly.
	4 Bake for 20 minutes, or until the eggs are completely cooked.

Per serving: Calories 95 (From Fat 48); Fat 5g (Saturated 2g); Cholesterol 72mg; Sodium 192mg; Carbohydrate 6g (Dietary Fiber 0g); Protein 6g.

Note: This recipe makes enough to share with friends. You can place any extra frittatas on a plate lined with a paper towel, cover them, and store them in the refrigerator for up to 3 or 4 days. Reheat one in the microwave for about 1 minute on high.

Vary It! Use ham, sausage, or Canadian bacon instead of the bacon. Or leave out meat altogether and add veggies such as steamed broccoli or mushrooms.

Veggie Scramble

Prep time: 5 min • **Cook time:** 10 min • **Yield:** 2 servings

Ingredients	Directions
2 teaspoons butter	**1** In a medium skillet, melt the butter over medium heat.
¼ of a medium white onion, chopped	
¼ cup chopped broccoli	**2** Add the onion, broccoli, and mushrooms to the skillet. Cook the veggies until they're tender, about 5 minutes.
¼ cup sliced mushrooms	
4 eggs	**3** In a medium bowl, whisk the eggs with the salt and pepper.
Salt to taste	
Black pepper to taste	
¼ cup diced tomato	**4** Add the tomato and eggs to the skillet. Gently stir and heat the eggs until they're completely cooked, about 5 minutes.

Per serving: Calories 196 (From Fat 126); Fat 14g (Saturated 6g); Cholesterol 382mg; Sodium 277mg; Carbohydrate 4g (Dietary Fiber 1g); Protein 13g.

Tip: Serve this scramble with gluten-free tortillas or toast.

Vary It! Replace the onion, broccoli, mushrooms, and tomato with any vegetables you have handy.

Vary It! Substitute garlic salt for the regular table salt for an extra zing.

Southwest Sausage Scramble

Prep time: 5 min • **Cook time:** 10 min • **Yield:** 2 servings

Ingredients	*Directions*
½ **cup chorizo sausage**	*1* In a medium skillet, cook the sausage, onion, and bell peppers over medium-high heat until the veggies are tender and the sausage is no longer pink, about 5 minutes. Drain any extra grease from the pan.
¼ **of a medium white onion, diced**	
¼ **cup diced green or red bell pepper**	
4 eggs	*2* In a medium bowl, whisk together the eggs and salt and pepper.
Salt to taste	
Black pepper to taste	*3* Add the tomato and the egg mixture to the pan of veggies, cooking and gently stirring until the eggs are completely cooked.
¼ **cup diced tomato**	
¼ **cup shredded cheddar or pepper Jack cheese**	*4* Top the eggs with cheese and a dash of hot sauce.
Dash of hot sauce	

Per serving: Calories 380 (From Fat 256); Fat 28g (Saturated 11g); Cholesterol 418mg; Sodium 803mg; Carbohydrate 5g (Dietary Fiber 1g); Protein 25g.

Tip: Serve this scramble with gluten-free tortillas or toast.

Note: Check the chorizo sausage for gluten-free status.

Vary It! Feel free to replace the chorizo with any breakfast sausage. Just remember to verify that the brand you use is gluten-free. Also, you can use any vegetables you have handy in addition to or in place of the onion, bell pepper, and tomato.

Egg-cellent Breakfast Sandwich

Prep time: 5 min • **Cook time:** 20 min • **Yield:** 1 serving

Ingredients	*Directions*
1 slice Canadian bacon	*1* Preheat the oven to 375 degrees.
1 egg 1 tablespoon shredded cheese	*2* In a regular muffin pan, place the Canadian bacon in one of the cups.
1 gluten-free bagel thin Salt to taste Black pepper to taste	*3* Crack one egg and place it on top of the Canadian bacon. Sprinkle cheese on top of the egg.
	4 Bake for 20 minutes, or until egg is completely cooked.
	5 Scoop the egg out with a spoon and serve it on a gluten-free bagel thin, toasted if you prefer. Add salt and pepper to taste.

Per serving: Calories 238 (From Fat 110); Fat 12g (Saturated 4g); Cholesterol 207mg; Sodium 775mg; Carbohydrate 15g (Dietary Fiber 1g); Protein 16g.

Note: You can make enough for one sandwich or as many as 12 all at once. Just fill as many muffin cups as you want. Store the leftovers in the refrigerator. Warm each one in the microwave for 30 to 45 seconds. Toast your bread when you're ready to eat.

Note: Store these sandwiches covered or in a plastic bag in the fridge. Reheat a sandwich for about 1 minute in the microwave when you want one. They even freeze well; reheat for about 2 minutes, or just until warm.

Vary It! Instead of Canadian bacon, use ham, sausage, or bacon. You can also replace the bagel thin with a gluten-free English muffin, sandwich bread, or bun, depending on what you have and feel like eating. Or even enjoy it with no bread at all.

Easy Breakfast Quesadilla

Prep time: 5 min • **Cook time:** 10 min • **Yield:** 1 serving

Ingredients	Directions
1 slice bacon 1 egg, lightly beaten 2 corn tortillas ¼ cup shredded reduced-fat cheddar cheese ½ tablespoon salsa ½ tablespoon fat-free sour cream	*1* Microwave the slice of bacon on a paper towel–lined plate until crisp (about 30 seconds if it's precooked microwave bacon or about 1 minute if it's raw bacon). Crumble the bacon.
	2 Add the egg to the crumbled bacon in a medium skillet over medium heat, cooking and gently stirring until the mixture is completely set.
	3 Meanwhile, heat another small skillet over medium heat. When the eggs are ready, put one tortilla in the skillet. Top the tortilla with half the cheese, the egg mixture, and then the other half of the cheese. Place the second tortilla on top.
	4 Cook the quesadilla for 2 to 3 minutes on each side, or until the tortilla is lightly browned. Flip the quesadilla carefully.
	5 Cut the quesadilla into four wedges. Top it with salsa and sour cream.

Per serving: Calories 319 (From Fat 140); Fat 16g (Saturated 7g); Cholesterol 212mg; Sodium 301mg; Carbohydrate 28g (Dietary Fiber 3g); Protein 19g.

Vary It! Add onions, mushrooms, tomatoes, bell peppers, fresh chopped cilantro, or any other fresh veggies or herbs that sound good to you.

Perfect Savory Breakfast Polenta

Prep time: 5 min • **Cook time:** 10 min • **Yield:** 1 serving

Ingredients	Directions
¼ cup yellow polenta (corn grits) 1 cup water	**1** In a medium saucepan, whisk together the polenta, water, butter, and garlic salt. Bring the polenta to a boil over high heat.
2 tablespoons butter ¼ teaspoon garlic salt	**2** Reduce the heat to low and continue to stir the mixture until it's thick and the liquid is absorbed, about 1 or 2 minutes.
1 tablespoon shredded cheddar cheese 1 slice bacon, cooked crispy and crumbled	**3** Pour the polenta into a small bowl and stir in the cheese. Top it with crispy bacon.

Per serving: Calories 426 (From Fat 254); Fat 28g (Saturated 17g); Cholesterol 74mg; Sodium 388mg; Carbohydrate 36g (Dietary Fiber 4g); Protein 8g.

Tip: Add a few snips of fresh chives for flavor if you have them.

Note: This little bowl of goodness is much more filling than it looks. It's perfect for a cold winter morning, whether you're heading out to class or relaxing in your pj's.

Vary It! Serve the polenta with a fried egg if you want an even heartier meal. Crack the egg into a small pan with melted butter. Flip the egg when the clear part of the egg has turned white. Cook the egg about 1 minute on the other side, until the egg white is firm but the yolk is slightly runny.

Chapter 9

5 Minutes or Less: Quick Lunches

In This Chapter

▶ Cool no-cook lunches
▶ Quick heat-it-and-eat-it lunches

*I*t's lunchtime! Chances are you have a few minutes between classes to grab something quick. You can stop by the cafeteria and attempt to find something filling and gluten-free, or you can swing by your house or apartment and make something that's nearly effortless as well as healthy and delicious. I vote for the apartment!

Even if your digs are a dorm room instead of an apartment, this chapter has some great ideas for you if you have a bit of refrigerator storage space and a few small appliances.

I provide 20 speedy recipes here for a midday meal that takes less than 5 minutes to prepare! The recipes in the first half of the chapter are no-cook options. A clever arrangement of the right ingredients makes for a great fast lunch. Refer to the list of gluten-free kitchen staples in Chapter 6 to be sure you're well-stocked with the basics.

The second half of the chapter contains recipes that require a little heat from the stove, toaster, or microwave, but any of them can be prepared in about 5 minutes. For days when you have more time to spare or want to be extra creative with your sandwich ingredients, flip to Chapter 10 for a couple dozen great sandwich, pizza, and Tex-Mex lunch ideas. Find tips on prepping ingredients ahead of time to make meal-time effort quick and easy in Chapter 16.

Staying Cool with No-Cook Lunches

Don't fall into the trap of grabbing a bag of chips or swinging through the drive-through when you're short on time. When you hear "no-cook lunch," you may instantly think peanut butter and jelly sandwich or some equally ordinary option. And sure, you can have one of those using sliced gluten-free bread, but the following recipes may just make you rethink how simple and delicious no-cook options can be.

You can do a lot with 5 minutes and a few basic ingredients. Get adventurous in your variations, and you'll no doubt come up with lots of other ideas. For example, you can turn any wrap into a salad, quesadilla, or sandwich with a few simple changes. And if these recipes are a bit too minimal for your inner chef, feel free to spice them up with extra sauces, veggies, and sides. I was careful to use only multipurpose and easily accessible ingredients for these recipes because exotic spices can be pricey and tough to find in some areas.

Most corn tortillas are acceptable on a gluten-free diet, but check the ingredients to confirm that wheat isn't in there, too. Several companies make good wraps made of alternative gluten-free grains as well. See Chapter 19 for my recommendations. Or make your own corn tortillas sometime by following the instructions in Chapter 11.

When reading these recipes, keep in mind that commercial gluten-free tortillas come in two sizes: small and large. The large tortillas tend to be more pliable than the small (often corn) tortillas. Look for gluten-free tortillas in your grocer's freezer or refrigerator section; they're usually not with the regular tortillas.

Tuna in a Tomato Cup

Prep time: 5 min • **Yield:** 1 serving

Ingredients	Directions
1 medium ripe tomato	*1* Slice off the top of the tomato. Hollow out the tomato to make a cup.
1 teaspoon Dijon mustard	
2 tablespoons Greek yogurt or mayonnaise	*2* Stir together the mustard, yogurt, lemon juice, garlic salt, and pepper in a small bowl. Add the tuna, cucumber, and avocado and mix well.
1 teaspoon lemon juice	
Dash of garlic salt	
Dash of black pepper	*3* Spoon the tuna mixture into the tomato cup.
3-ounce can tuna in water, drained	
¼ cup peeled and diced cucumber	
¼ cup chopped avocado	

Per serving: Calories 225 (From Fat 72); Fat 8g (Saturated 2g); Cholesterol 27mg; Sodium 489mg; Carbohydrate 13g (Dietary Fiber 3g); Protein 27g.

Vary It! To change the pace of this dish a bit, make a sandwich on gluten-free bread or serve the tuna on a bed of lettuce.

California Roll Bowl

Prep time: 5 min • **Yield:** 1 serving

Ingredients	*Directions*
1 cup cooked rice ½ **cup spinach leaves**	**1** If your rice is leftover, microwave it for 15 seconds to warm it.
½ **cup salmon or tuna (pouch or can), drained** ¼ **cup avocado chunks** ¼ **cup peeled and diced cucumber** **1 tablespoon gluten-free soy sauce**	**2** Combine the rice, spinach, fish, avocado, cucumber, and soy sauce in a bowl. Stir gently to mix.

Per serving: Calories 384 (From Fat 107); Fat 12g (Saturated 2g); Cholesterol 45mg; Sodium 1,242mg; Carbohydrate 49g (Dietary Fiber 3g); Protein 21g.

Tip: Imitation crab (used in many California rolls) is usually made with wheat, so use salmon or tuna for this sushi-inspired dish.

Tip: Leftover rice from a Chapter 11 stir-fry is perfect for this recipe.

Vary It! Stir ½ tablespoon rice vinegar or cider vinegar and a little sugar into the rice for a more authentic flavor.

Turkey Tortilla Wrap

Prep time: 5 min **Yield:** 1 serving

Ingredients	*Directions*
1 large rice tortilla	*1* Spread mustard on the tortilla.
1 tablespoon mustard	
3 slices turkey breast	*2* Top the tortilla with turkey, cheese, and lettuce.
2 slices Swiss cheese	
2 lettuce leaves	*3* Roll up the wrap and slice it in half.

Per serving: Calories 402 (From Fat 182); Fat 20g (Saturated 11g); Cholesterol 67mg; Sodium 958mg; Carbohydrate 28g (Dietary Fiber 3g); Protein 28g.

Vary It! Add a spoonful of salsa to spice up your wrap.

Greek Salad Wrap

Prep time: 5 min • **Yield:** 1 serving

Ingredients	Directions
8 sliced Kalamata olives	**1** Combine the olives, cucumber (See Figure 9-1), tomato, feta cheese, oil, and vinegar in a small bowl.
¼ of a cucumber, chopped	
¼ of a tomato, chopped	
¼ cup feta cheese, crumbled	**2** Spread cream cheese on one side of the tortilla.
1 teaspoon olive oil	
1 teaspoon balsamic vinegar	**3** Put the salad mixture on the tortilla. Roll up the wrap.
1 large gluten-free tortilla	
2 tablespoons cream cheese	

Per serving: Calories 462 (From Fat 298); Fat 33g (Saturated 14g); Cholesterol 65mg; Sodium 1,156mg; Carbohydrate 31g (Dietary Fiber 3g); Protein 10g.

Vary It! Use any kind of olives you have.

CHOPPING A CUCUMBER

1. WASH AND PEEL THE CUCUMBER USING A VEGETABLE PEELER (OPTIONAL).
2. SLICE OFF ABOUT ½" OF THE ENDS OF THE CUCUMBER
3. TO CHOP CUCUMBER INTO SMALLER PIECES, FIRST CUT LENGTHWISE. SLICE EACH HALF INTO SEVERAL LONG STRIPS, THEN SLICE THE STRIPS INTO PIECES.

Figure 9-1: Chop the cucumber into small pieces.

Fruity Chicken Lettuce Wrap

Prep time: 5 min • **Yield:** 1 serving

Ingredients	Directions
2 teaspoons honey	**1** To make the dressing, stir together the honey and almond butter in a small bowl.
2 teaspoons almond butter	
½ cup chopped, cooked chicken	**2** Add the chicken, grapes, apples, and almonds to the bowl. Stir until everything is coated with the dressing.
2 tablespoons chopped grapes	
3 tablespoons chopped apple	**3** Put the mixture on a lettuce leaf and wrap it up.
2 teaspoons sliced almonds	
1 or 2 large romaine lettuce leaves	

Per serving: Calories 297 (From Fat 124); Fat 14g (Saturated 2g); Cholesterol 62mg; Sodium 64mg; Carbohydrate 22g (Dietary Fiber 2g); Protein 23g.

Vary It! Switch out the almond butter for Greek yogurt for a cooler, creamier wrap.

Chicken Caesar Wrap

Prep time: 5 min • **Yield:** 1 serving

Ingredients	Directions
Dash of lemon juice	*1* Stir the lemon juice and mayonnaise together in a small bowl.
1 tablespoon mayonnaise	
½ cup chopped, cooked chicken	*2* Place the chicken, Parmesan cheese, mayonnaise mixture, and salt and pepper on the lettuce leaves.
¼ cup shredded Parmesan cheese	
Salt to taste	*3* Roll up the wraps.
Black pepper to taste	
1 or 2 large romaine lettuce leaves	

Per serving: Calories 328 (From Fat 200); Fat 22g (Saturated 7g); Cholesterol 86mg; Sodium 652mg; Carbohydrate 2g (Dietary Fiber 1g); Protein 11g.

Vary It! Replace the mayonnaise with Greek yogurt to reduce the fat.

Vary It! For a more traditional Caesar version, add a touch of garlic powder and gluten-free Worcestershire sauce.

Vary It! Replace the salt in Step 2 with garlic salt and put everything on gluten-free bread to create a delicious Chicken Caesar Sandwich.

Nutty Banana Dog

Prep time: 5 min • **Yield:** 1 serving

Ingredients	Directions
1 gluten-free hot dog roll	**1** Soften the roll by heating it for 5 to 7 seconds in the microwave.
2 tablespoons peanut or almond butter	
1 banana	**2** Spread peanut or almond butter on the roll.
1 teaspoon honey	
	3 Place the whole banana in the roll. Drizzle honey over the top.

Per serving: Calories 609 (From Fat 264); Fat 29g (Saturated 4g); Cholesterol 0mg; Sodium 150mg; Carbohydrate 82g (Dietary Fiber 8g); Protein 11g.

Tip: This sandwich is just as great for a quick breakfast as it is for lunch!

Tip: Gluten-free rolls really need to be heated a few seconds — fresh or not. They're just better a little warm.

PBJ Smoothie

Prep time: 5 min • **Yield:** 1 serving

Ingredients	Directions
1 cup cold milk	*1* Combine the milk, banana, peanut butter, oats, and preserves in a blender.
1 banana, fresh or frozen, cut into chunks	
2 tablespoons peanut butter	*2* Blend until smooth, about 15 to 20 seconds.
2 tablespoons gluten-free oats or granola	
1 teaspoon 100% fruit preserves	

Per serving: Calories 505 (From Fat 226); Fat 25g (Saturated 9g); Cholesterol 33mg; Sodium 269mg; Carbohydrate 58g (Dietary Fiber 7g); Protein 19g.

Tip: Blend in a few ice cubes for a colder and chunkier shake.

Tip: Keep a few peeled and sliced bananas in the freezer so you're ready for a smoothie at any time.

Note: Use dairy or nondairy milk for this smoothie.

Note: This filling smoothie is great for breakfast or a late-night snack!

Rice, Bean, and Veggie Salad

Prep time: 5 min • **Yield:** 1 serving

Ingredients	Directions
½ cup cooked brown rice	**1** In a medium serving bowl, combine the rice, beans, corn, and bell pepper.
¼ cup canned black beans, drained	
¼ cup canned corn, drained	**2** Stir in the cilantro, lime juice (see Figure 9-2), and olive oil.
¼ of a red or yellow bell pepper, chopped	
½ tablespoon cilantro	**3** Add the salt and pepper to taste.
½ tablespoon lime juice	
1 tablespoon olive oil	
Salt to taste	
Black pepper to taste	

Per serving: Calories 327 (From Fat 138); Fat 15g (Saturated 2g); Cholesterol 0mg; Sodium 584mg; Carbohydrate 41g (Dietary Fiber 7g); Protein 7g.

Tip: Make a few of the recipes that use a portion of canned vegetables at the same time or within a few days to use up your entire can. Check out Chapter 10 for a Southwest Black Bean and Turkey Burger.

Vary It! Add a few drops of salsa or hot sauce for an extra kick.

How to Juice a Lime

Cut a lime in half, across the middle.

Hold a half in one hand at an angle. Use a fork to apply pressure and squeeze out the juice!

Figure 9-2: Juicing a lime.

Making a Heat-and-Eat Meal

Even if you only have a few minutes for lunch, resist grabbing one of the many unhealthy or unsatisfying options available to you. Instead, take a few minutes to heat and eat something great that gives you energy to make it through your afternoon lab or lecture.

If you plan ahead, you can package your leftovers from larger-yield meals into individual servings and store them in the refrigerator (if you plan to use them fairly quickly) or in the freezer. Then simply heat and enjoy them when you're ready for a quick and healthy no-prep lunch.

Check out Chapter 12 to find out how to make casseroles that freeze well. Find recipes for soups that you can freeze in Chapter 13, and gather other ideas on using up leftovers and getting ahead with food prep in Chapter 16.

In this section, I include recipes that may require you to toast, microwave, or broil something, but all these sandwiches, pizzas, and Tex-Mex favorites can be ready to eat in about 5 minutes.

Broiling to perfection

Broiling is one of the easiest ways to produce a crunchy, melty, warm topping on any dish in a toaster oven or regular oven. With *broiling,* the upper heating element in your oven cooks your food from above.

This high-heat cooking method is quick and easy, but the cooking times vary depending on your food, its distance from the heat, and your particular oven or toaster oven. Here are a few tips to help you broil to perfection:

✔ No need to preheat your oven or toaster oven, but after you turn the knob to "broil," stay nearby and watch whatever you're cooking. Broiling may take a bit longer in the oven than a toaster oven, but after your food begins to toast, not much time is needed to complete the task. Be ready to remove your dish quickly from the oven when it's toasted and melted perfectly to your liking. The only way you can fail at broiling is by being distracted and walking away during cooking.

✔ Make sure your food isn't touching the toaster oven coil, or your food will burn.

✔ You can move your oven rack up to its top position to speed the broiling time. If you leave your oven rack in the middle, broiling still works, but it takes a couple minutes longer.

Open-Faced Hummus Avocado Melt

Prep time: 5 min • **Cook time:** Less than 1 min • **Yield:** 1 serving

Ingredients	*Directions*
2 slices gluten-free multigrain bread	*1* Toast the bread.
2 tablespoons hummus 2 tomato slices 4 avocado slices	*2* On a microwave-safe plate, layer each slice of bread with half the hummus, avocado (see Figure 9-3), tomato, and cheese.
2 slices provolone cheese	*3* Microwave the sandwiches for about 30 seconds, until the cheese is bubbly.

Per serving: Calories 493 (From Fat 266); Fat 30g (Saturated 11g); Cholesterol 39mg; Sodium 910mg; Carbohydrate 44g (Dietary Fiber 8g); Protein 20g.

How to Pit and Peel an Avocado

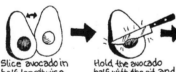

Slice avocado in half lengthwise and pull apart.

Hold the avocado half with the pit, and firmly strike the pit with a chef's knife in your other hand.

Lift the pit out with a gentle twist of the knife.

GENTLY scoop out the meat with a spoon.

Chop or slice according to your recipe.

Figure 9-3: Peeling and pitting an avocado.

Open-Faced Luau Sandwich

Prep time: 5 min • **Cook time:** Less than 5 min • **Yield:** 1 serving

Ingredients	Directions
2 slices gluten-free multigrain bread	*1* Toast the bread.
2 slices canned pineapple 4 slices ham	*2* Top each piece of bread with pineapple, ham, and cheese.
2 slices American cheese	*3* Broil the sandwich until the cheese is melted.

Per serving: Calories 493 (From Fat 202); Fat 22g (Saturated 10g); Cholesterol 67mg; Sodium 2,288mg; Carbohydrate 45g (Dietary Fiber 5g); Protein 28g.

Vary It! If you like mustard, spread on a few teaspoons! Its flavor combines nicely with the pineapple.

Note: This recipe makes two open-faced sandwiches. Enjoy them both as one serving!

Note: Check the ham for gluten-free status.

5-Minute Tasty Tostada

Prep time: 5 min • **Cook time:** Less than 5 min • **Yield:** 2 servings

Ingredients	Directions
4 corn tortillas	**1** Broil the tortillas in the oven until they're crispy.
½ cup fat-free refried beans	
½ cup shredded cheddar cheese	**2** Spread 2 tablespoons beans and 2 tablespoons cheddar cheese on each tortilla.
1 cup shredded lettuce	**3** Broil the bean-and-cheese-topped tortillas for another minute.
1 cup salsa	
	4 Top each tortilla with lettuce and salsa.

Per serving: Calories 364 (From Fat 96); Fat 11g (Saturated 6g); Cholesterol 30mg; Sodium 1,269mg; Carbohydrate 51g (Dietary Fiber 6g); Protein 17g.

Tip: Keep an eye on your tortillas while they're broiling so the tortillas don't burn.

Portobello Pepperoni Pizza

Prep time: 2 min • **Cook time:** 2 min • **Yield:** 1 serving

Ingredients	Directions
1 portobello mushroom (4 to 5 inches in diameter)	**1** Wash the mushroom, remove the stem, and hollow out the mushroom cap with a spoon.
¼ cup marinara (tomato) sauce	**2** Fill the mushroom cap with marinara sauce and pepperoni. Top it with cheese, garlic salt, and Italian seasoning.
5 slices gluten-free pepperoni, chopped	
¼ cup shredded part-skim mozzarella cheese	**3** Place your portobello pizza on a paper towel on a microwave-safe plate and microwave on high for about 2 minutes, until the cheese is melted and mushroom is soft.
½ teaspoon garlic salt	
½ teaspoon Italian seasoning	

Per serving: Calories 273 (From Fat 162); Fat 18g (Saturated 8g); Cholesterol 38mg; Sodium 1,436mg; Carbohydrate 12g (Dietary Fiber 3g); Protein 16g.

Tip: Hormel Turkey Pepperoni is lowfat and marked gluten-free on the package.

Vary It! If you're not a fan of mushrooms — or you're fresh out — try this recipe with zucchini. Just slice a medium zucchini into about 8 slices, place it on a baking sheet, and top it with sauce, pepperoni, cheese, and spices. Broil it in the oven or toaster oven until the cheese is bubbly. Mmm . . .

Pesto Mushroom Polenta Cakes

Prep time: 5 min • **Cook time:** 5 min • **Yield:** 4 servings

Ingredients	*Directions*
18-ounce roll precooked polenta	*1* Spray a baking sheet with nonstick cooking spray.
¼ **cup pesto**	
4 or 5 mushrooms, sliced	*2* Slice the polenta into ½-inch slices (about 10) and arrange them on the prepared baking sheet.
½ **cup Swiss or Monterey Jack cheese**	
	3 Top the polenta with pesto, mushroom slices, and cheese.
	4 Broil the polenta cakes until the cheese is bubbly and the polenta is heated, about 5 minutes.

Per serving: Calories 222 (From Fat 98); Fat 11g (Saturated 4g); Cholesterol 17mg; Sodium 550mg; Carbohydrate 21g (Dietary Fiber 2g); Protein 10g.

Macho Nachos

Prep time: 5 min • **Cook time:** Less than 5 min • **Yield:** 4 servings

Ingredients	Directions
25 corn tortilla chips	*1* Spread the chips on a microwave-safe plate.
15-ounce can black or refried beans	*2* Layer the beans, olives, jalapeño slices (see Figure 9-4), and cheese over the chips.
3-ounce can black olives	
1 jalapeño, sliced	*3* Heat the nachos in the microwave until the cheese is melted and the beans are warm, about 1 minute on high. If the nachos aren't ready after a minute, check the nachos after each 30 additional seconds of cooking time.
½ cup shredded cheddar or pepper Jack cheese	
½ cup salsa	
½ cup sour cream	*4* Top the hot nachos with salsa, sour cream, and guacamole.
½ cup guacamole	

Per serving: Calories 613 (From Fat 209); Fat 23g (Saturated 8g); Cholesterol 28mg; Sodium 650mg; Carbohydrate 87g (Dietary Fiber 12g); Protein 19g.

Tip: Homemade guacamole is always better than packaged, in my book! Find a recipe in Chapter 14.

Vary It! Throw on some leftover beef or chicken to make this dish heartier.

Vary It! Leave out the sour cream and swap out the corn chips for a tortilla if you're looking for a more respectable — and lower-fat — lunch.

Seeding a Jalapeño

Figure 9-4: Seeding a jalapeño pepper.

Easy Italian Sausage and Lentils

Prep time: 5 min • **Cook time:** 5 min • **Yield:** 1 serving

Ingredients	Directions
1 Italian sausage link (about 4 ounces)	*1* Slice the sausage or remove the sausage from its casing and crumble it.
1 cup canned lentils, drained	
10 cherry tomatoes, halved	*2* Cook the sausage in a small or medium skillet over medium-high heat until the sausage is completely browned. Drain the grease from the skillet.
1 tablespoon balsamic vinegar	
1 teaspoon dried basil or Italian seasoning	
½ teaspoon garlic salt	*3* Add the lentils, tomatoes, vinegar, and basil to the cooked sausage, and cook the mixture another minute, until it's warm.
1 teaspoon grated Parmesan cheese	
	4 Top the mixture with Parmesan cheese.

Per serving: Calories 443 (From Fat 144); Fat 16g (Saturated 6g); Cholesterol 46mg; Sodium 1,364mg; Carbohydrate 46g (Dietary Fiber 20g); Protein 30g.

Tip: To drain grease, tip the pan slightly toward an empty jar while using a large spoon to keep food in the pan; let the grease harden, seal the container, and throw it in the trash. Or remove the pan from the heat for a couple of minutes and use a paper towel to wipe up the extra grease. Do not dump grease down the drain — it can harden and clog the pipes.

Note: Enjoy this dish with a side salad, or add some greens to the pan after the sausage has browned.

Quick Leftover Fried Rice

Prep time: 5 min • **Cook time:** 5 min • **Yield:** 1 serving

Ingredients	Directions
1 tablespoon butter	*1* Melt the butter in a medium-sized skillet over medium-high heat.
1 cup cooked rice	
¼ cup sliced green onions	*2* Add the cooked rice, green onion, and carrots to the skillet and sauté until the rice is warm, about 3 minutes.
½ carrot, grated	
1 egg, lightly beaten	
Gluten-free soy sauce	*3* Push the rice to one side of the pan and add the beaten eggs to the pan.
	4 Stir the egg continuously until it's cooked. Then stir the egg into the rice and veggies.
	5 Sprinkle the rice with soy sauce and serve.

Per serving: Calories 407 (From Fat 152); Fat 17g (Saturated 9g); Cholesterol 217mg; Sodium 167mg; Carbohydrate 51g (Dietary Fiber 2g); Protein 12g.

Vary It! Use any leftover, frozen, or canned veggies you may have in addition to (or instead of) green onion and carrots. Broccoli or a mixture of peas and carrots is an excellent choice.

Tip: Defrost frozen veggies in warm water or the microwave while sautéing the green onion in the skillet.

Note: You can also use oil in the pan instead of butter if you're dairy-free or just prefer it. I like the flavor of butter in this dish.

Cheesy Chili Dog

Prep time: 5 min • **Cook time:** 5 min • **Yield:** 1 serving

Ingredients	Directions
1 hot dog	*1* In a small saucepan or skillet over medium heat, heat the whole hot dog and chili for a couple of minutes, until they're warm.
1 gluten-free hot dog roll	
3 tablespoons chili	
2 tablespoons shredded cheddar cheese	*2* Heat the hot dog roll in the microwave for about 5 to 7 seconds to soften it.
	3 Put the hot dog and chili in the warm roll and top it with cheese.

Per serving: Calories 580 (From Fat 329); Fat 37g (Saturated 11g); Cholesterol 59mg; Sodium 859mg; Carbohydrate 47g (Dietary Fiber 2g); Protein 16g.

Vary It! Top the chili dog with chopped onion, mustard, and/or other cheese for extra flavor.

Tip: Gluten-free buns are best when they're slightly heated and softened.

Note: Check the chili and hot dog for gluten-free status.

Doggone Good Reuben

Prep time: 5 min • **Cook time:** Less than 1 min • **Yield:** 1 serving

Ingredients	Directions
1 tablespoon Thousand Island or Russian dressing	**1** Spread the salad dressing on a gluten-free hot dog roll.
1 gluten-free hot dog roll	
4 slices corned beef or pastrami	**2** Place the corned beef, cheese, and sauerkraut on the roll on a microwave-safe plate.
1 slice Swiss cheese	**3** Microwave on high for 30 seconds, until the sandwich is warm.
¼ cup sauerkraut	

Per serving: Calories 602 (From Fat 335); Fat 37g (Saturated 11g); Cholesterol 86mg; Sodium 1,040mg; Carbohydrate 46g (Dietary Fiber 3g); Protein 21g.

Vary It! Add a bit of rye-bread flavor without the gluten of rye by sprinkling about ½ teaspoon caraway seeds on top.

Vary It! If you don't have a gluten-free hot dog roll, make this a Reuben panini. Just butter two pieces of gluten-free bread, assemble the sandwich (butter side out), and toast it — grilled-cheese style — in a skillet over medium-high heat, pressing to flatten the sandwich while cooking.

Note: Check the meat and salad dressing for gluten-free status.

All-American Quesadilla

Prep time: 5 min • **Cook time:** Less than 5 min • **Yield:** 1 serving

Ingredients	Directions
¼ cup shredded cheddar cheese 2 large gluten-free tortillas ¼ cup cooked chicken ½ of a small apple, thinly sliced	*1* Place half the cheese on a tortilla. Layer on the chicken, apple (see Figure 9-5), and remaining cheese. Top with the other tortilla. *2* Place the quesadilla in a skillet over medium heat. Heat the quesadilla for a couple of minutes, or until the cheese is melted, turning the quesadilla over once during cooking. *3* Cut the quesadilla into quarters.

Per serving: Calories 472 (From Fat 154); Fat 17g (Saturated 7g); Cholesterol 61mg; Sodium 526mg; Carbohydrate 56g (Dietary Fiber 5g); Protein 21g.

Vary It! Microwave the quesadilla 15 to 30 seconds, until cheese is melted, instead of cooking in a skillet.

HOW TO CORE AND SLICE AN APPLE

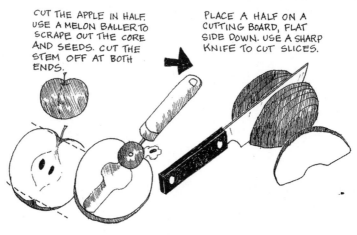

CUT THE APPLE IN HALF. USE A MELON BALLER TO SCRAPE OUT THE CORE AND SEEDS. CUT THE STEM OFF AT BOTH ENDS.

PLACE A HALF ON A CUTTING BOARD, FLAT SIDE DOWN. USE A SHARP KNIFE TO CUT SLICES.

Figure 9-5: Coring and slicing an apple.

Spinach Mushroom Quesadilla

Prep time: 5 min • **Cook time:** Less than 5 min • **Yield:** 1 serving

Ingredients	Directions
¼ cup shredded Monterey Jack cheese 2 large gluten-free tortillas ¼ cup spinach leaves ¼ cup sliced mushrooms 2 tablespoons sliced black olives	**1** Place half the cheese on a tortilla. Layer on the spinach, mushrooms, black olives, and remaining cheese. Top with the other tortilla.
	2 Put the quesadilla in a skillet over medium heat. Heat the quesadilla for a couple of minutes, or until cheese is melted, turning it over once during cooking.
	3 Cut the cooked quesadilla into four equal pieces.

Per serving: Calories 391 (From Fat 139); Fat 15g (Saturated 6g); Cholesterol 25mg; Sodium 625mg; Carbohydrate 50g (Dietary Fiber 5g); Protein 12g.

Vary It! You can microwave the quesadilla 15 to 30 seconds, until cheese is melted, instead of cooking in a skillet.

Chapter 10

25 Minutes 'til Mealtime: Satisfying Sit-Down Lunches

In This Chapter

▶ Munching on meal-sized salads and rice bowls

▶ Grabbing great burgers and hearty sandwiches

*Y*ou may be tempted to skip over this chapter when you see that these lunch recipes may take up to 25 minutes. But don't do it! You can whip up most of these foods in less than 25 minutes — you can hardly get to a fast food place and back in less time! And isn't a safe, healthy, and affordable homemade meal preferable to a super-processed lunch with mystery ingredients?

This chapter contains recipes that are great for lunch or a light dinner, including meal-sized salads and vegetable dishes, burgers, and hearty sandwiches. (If you're still concerned about time, flip to Chapter 16 for tips on getting ahead with food prep.)

Serving Up Salads and Vegetables

Munching on meal-sized salads can be super satisfying, and these meals are really fast to prepare, especially if you use precooked meat. Leave out the meat altogether to make your salad vegetarian or extra thrifty. This section has some snazzy salads that taste like much more work than they are. Just don't expect lots of lettuce here. These are creative and satisfying meals that can fill you up!

Pasta Salad Italiano

Prep time: 10 min • **Cook time:** Less than 15 min • **Yield:** 2 servings

Ingredients	Directions
1 cup gluten-free rotini pasta ¼ cup diced salami or pepperoni	**1** Cook the pasta according to the directions on the package. Drain the pasta, rinse it in cold water, and place it in a medium bowl.
¼ cup diced tomato 2 tablespoons sliced black olives	**2** Add salami or pepperoni, tomato, olives, bell pepper, pine nuts, and beans to the pasta.
2 tablespoons diced green bell pepper	**3** Refrigerate the salad for about 10 minutes.
2 tablespoons pine nuts ¼ cup canned cannellini beans, drained	**4** Add mozzarella cheese and Italian dressing to the salad and mix well.
¼ cup diced mozzarella cheese ¼ cup Italian dressing Parmesan cheese for garnish	**5** Top with a few sprinkles of Parmesan cheese. Serve immediately.

Per serving: Calories 465 (From Fat 280); Fat 31g (Saturated 8g); Cholesterol 27mg; Sodium 796mg; Carbohydrate 33g (Dietary Fiber 3g); Protein 13g.

Tip: Slightly undercook your gluten-free pasta to keep it firm. Overcooked, it tends to get mushy and fall apart. Rinse the pasta in cold water after boiling it to wash off extra starch.

Vary It! Instead of pasta, try quinoa for a nuttier, more rustic flavor, or use brown rice for a lighter but filling version.

Note: Check the meat and salad dressing for gluten-free status.

Note: Gluten-free pasta isn't great the next day, so if you don't think you'll eat it all in one sitting, cut the amount of ingredients to make a smaller salad.

Cashew Roasted Chicken Salad

Prep time: 10 min • **Yield:** 1 serving

Ingredients	Directions
2 tablespoons plain Greek yogurt	*1* In a medium bowl, stir together the yogurt, lemon juice, salt, and pepper. Add the cooked chicken, celery, parsley, and capers. Mix well.
1 teaspoon lemon juice	
Salt to taste	
Black pepper to taste	*2* Place the mixture on a bed of two or three leaves of lettuce.
1 cup shredded cooked chicken	
1 stalk celery, finely chopped	*3* Sprinkle chopped cashews on top.
1 tablespoon chopped flat-leaf parsley	
1 teaspoon capers	
2 or 3 leaves of lettuce, torn	
½ cup chopped cashews	

Per serving: Calories 696 (From Fat 385); Fat 43g (Saturated 10g); Cholesterol 127mg; Sodium 570mg; Carbohydrate 28g (Dietary Fiber 4g); Protein 55g.

Tip: You can easily make this salad into two chicken salad sandwiches with some sliced gluten-free bread.

Note: Capers are small, green, berry-like flower buds that add a nice, tangy flavor that pairs well with lemon. You can find them in small jars near the olives in the grocery store. You can skip this ingredient if you don't have any, but I like to add them to dishes with lemon for an extra zing.

Note: Store leftovers covered in the fridge for a day or two.

Warm Chicken Teriyaki Quinoa Salad

Prep time: 5 min • **Cook time:** Less than 15 min • **Yield:** 2 servings

Ingredients	Directions
1 cup water 1 gluten-free chicken bouillon cube	**1** In a medium saucepan, bring 1 cup water to a boil over high heat. Add the bouillon cube and stir until it dissolves.
½ cup quinoa, rinsed 1 boneless, skinless chicken breast (about 4 to 5 ounces), cut into 1-inch cubes	**2** Lower the heat to a simmer and add the quinoa. Cook uncovered until all the water is absorbed, about 10 minutes.
1 green onion, chopped ½ cup gluten-free teriyaki sauce 12-ounce can mandarin oranges, drained	**3** While the quinoa is cooking, spray nonstick cooking spray in a small skillet and place it over medium heat. Add the chicken to the hot skillet, stirring the chicken after it begins to brown.
1 tablespoon sliced almonds	**4** Add the green onions to the chicken. Continue to stir every minute or 2 until the chicken is lightly browned on all sides and is no longer pink in the middle, about 5 minutes.

5 Turn off the heat to the chicken, add teriyaki sauce to the skillet, and stir about 30 seconds until the sauce is just warm.

6 In a medium bowl, combine the cooked quinoa, the chicken mixture, and the mandarin oranges.

7 Top with sliced almonds.

Per serving: Calories 365 (From Fat 51); Fat 6g (Saturated 1g); Cholesterol 40mg; Sodium 3,650mg; Carbohydrate 54g (Dietary Fiber 4g); Protein 26g.

Note: Most teriyaki sauces list wheat as a major ingredient, but gluten-free Asian sauces are available in many grocery chains. If you can't find gluten-free teriyaki sauce, you can use gluten-free soy sauce and a tablespoon of honey instead.

Vary It! Rice is a great option with this recipe if you don't have quinoa on hand.

Vary It! Refrigerate leftovers and enjoy the salad cold for a cool, quick quinoa lunch.

Vary It! Make this recipe vegetarian by using a vegetable bouillon cube (or 1 cup vegetable broth and no water) and substituting 1 cup cubed tofu for the chicken.

MAKING A MOUNTAIN OF LETTUCE

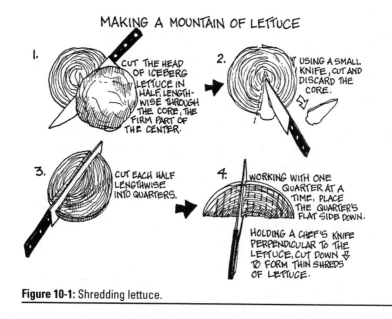

1. CUT THE HEAD OF ICEBERG LETTUCE IN HALF, LENGTHWISE THROUGH THE CORE, THE FIRM PART OF THE CENTER.

2. USING A SMALL KNIFE, CUT AND DISCARD THE CORE.

3. CUT EACH HALF LENGTHWISE INTO QUARTERS.

4. WORKING WITH ONE QUARTER AT A TIME, PLACE THE QUARTER'S FLAT SIDE DOWN.

HOLDING A CHEF'S KNIFE PERPENDICULAR TO THE LETTUCE, CUT DOWN TO FORM THIN SHREDS OF LETTUCE.

Figure 10-1: Shredding lettuce.

Taco Salad

Prep time: 5 min • **Cook time:** Less than 10 min • **Yield:** 2 servings

Ingredients	Directions
1 cup (about 3 ounces) ground beef	**1** Heat a small skillet over medium heat. Brown the ground beef with garlic salt and chili powder, breaking apart the meat with a large spoon or spatula as it cooks.
1 teaspoon garlic salt	
1 teaspoon chili powder	
3 cups shredded lettuce	**2** Drain any fat from the pan. Pat the beef with a paper towel to absorb any remaining grease.
1 tomato, diced	
1 avocado, diced	**3** In a medium bowl, combine the cooked beef, shredded lettuce (see Figure 10-1), tomato, avocado, olives, corn, cilantro, cheese, and salsa.
2 tablespoons sliced black olives	
¼ cup canned corn, drained	
2 tablespoons fresh cilantro	**4** Top the salad with crushed tortilla chips and add a drizzle of ranch dressing.
¼ cup shredded cheddar cheese	
½ cup salsa	
1 cup crushed corn tortilla chips	
Drizzle of ranch dressing	

Per serving: Calories 442 (From Fat 237); Fat 26g (Saturated 8g); Cholesterol 30mg; Sodium 1,222mg; Carbohydrate 38g (Dietary Fiber 13g); Protein 20g.

Tip: Turn this into a no-cook recipe by using leftover meat in this salad.

Tip: Heat things up by using a hot salsa, hot sauce, or a dash of cayenne pepper.

Vary It! Use cooked chicken instead of beef for a spicy chicken taco twist, or leave out the meat altogether.

Steak and Baked Potato Salad

Prep time: 5 min • **Cook time:** 7 min • **Yield:** 2 servings

Ingredients	Directions
2 small white potatoes	*1* Microwave the potatoes on high for 4 minutes on a microwave-safe plate. Test for tenderness with a fork. Microwave another minute if the potato is still hard. The potatoes should be soft all the way through. Place the cooked potatoes in a medium bowl.
2 slices bacon	
3 slices deli roast beef	
2 cups lettuce	
5 cherry or grape tomatoes, cut in half	*2* Cook the bacon on a microwave-safe plate lined with a paper towel until the bacon is crisp, approximately 1½ to 2 minutes on high. Crumble the cooked bacon.
¼ cup feta or Monterey Jack cheese	
¼ teaspoon garlic salt	
¼ teaspoon Italian seasoning	*3* Slice the roast beef into strips and add it to the bowl with the potatoes. Add the bacon, lettuce, tomatoes, and cheese.
2 tablespoons olive oil	
1 tablespoon balsamic vinegar	
	4 Stir together the garlic salt, Italian seasoning, oil, and vinegar in a small bowl or measuring cup. Pour this dressing over the salad ingredients and toss to coat.

Per serving: Calories 400 (From Fat 200); Fat 22g (Saturated 7g); Cholesterol 41mg; Sodium 805mg; Carbohydrate 35g (Dietary Fiber 4g); Protein 17g.

Tip: Use a leftover baked potato half in place of the white potatoes. Simply cut it into chunks and toss it in!

Vary It! Replace the roast beef with leftover steak if you have it.

Note: Check the roast beef for gluten-free status.

Veggie Rice Bowl

Prep time: 5 min • **Cook time:** Less than 15 min • **Yield:** 1 serving

Ingredients	Directions
¼ cup uncooked rice	**1** Follow the directions on the rice package for cooking one serving in the microwave or on the stovetop.
1 cup frozen stir-fry vegetables (without sauce)	
1 teaspoon sesame seeds	**2** While the rice is cooking, place the frozen vegetables and 1 tablespoon water in a skillet sprayed with nonstick cooking spray. Stir and cook the vegetables over medium-high heat for 3 to 7 minutes. Add sesame seeds and cook for another minute or 2, until the vegetables are crisp but tender.
1 tablespoon gluten-free soy sauce	
	3 Spoon the rice into the bottom of a serving bowl. Top it with vegetables and soy sauce.

Per serving: Calories 268 (From Fat 15); Fat 2g (Saturated 0g); Cholesterol 0mg; Sodium 948mg; Carbohydrate 49g (Dietary Fiber 4g); Protein 10g.

Tip: Make this meal completely by microwave. Reheat ½ cup cooked rice if you have some on hand — or use a pouch of microwaveable rice — and microwave the veggies according to the package directions.

Tip: Cook extra rice and use it to make a California Roll Bowl or Quick Fried Rice the next day. You can find these recipes in Chapter 9.

Vary It! Use fresh veggies instead of frozen. Either buy a precut mix in the produce section or buy your favorite variety and do your own chopping.

Vary It! Add some leftover chicken or steak to make this bowl even heartier.

Vary It! Add 2 tablespoons of honey to the soy sauce for a teriyaki flavor.

California-Style Chicken Curry Salad

Prep time: 15 min • **Cook time:** Less than 10 min • **Yield:** 2 servings

Ingredients	Directions
1 boneless, skinless chicken breast (about 4 to 5 ounces)	*1* Spray a small skillet with nonstick cooking spray and place it over medium heat.
1 celery stalk, chopped	
5 red grapes, halved	*2* Cut the chicken into ½-inch cubes. Put them in the hot skillet, stirring the chicken after it begins to brown.
¼ cup plain Greek yogurt	
¼ cup pecan halves	*3* Stir the chicken every minute or 2, cooking until it's lightly browned all the way around and is no longer pink in the middle, about 5 minutes.
½ teaspoon curry powder	
1 medium avocado	
	4 In a medium bowl, combine the cooked chicken, celery, grapes, yogurt, pecans, and curry. Stir well. Refrigerate the mixture for 10 to 15 minutes.
	5 Cut an avocado in half and remove the pit.
	6 Place half of the chicken salad mixture on each avocado half. Share one cup of chicken salad with your roommate, or store the chicken salad covered in the fridge for a day or two without the avocado.

Per serving: Calories 341 (From Fat 221); Fat 25g (Saturated 4g); Cholesterol 41mg; Sodium 67mg; Carbohydrate 14g (Dietary Fiber 10g); Protein 21g.

Tip: Air causes avocados to brown quickly. To save half an avocado, squirt a little lemon juice over the surface and keep the pit attached. Or you can wrap the avocado with plastic wrap touching the inside with no air in the middle. With either of these storage methods, your leftover avocado should last about a day without browning.

Vary It! Make two sandwiches with this chicken salad on gluten-free toast. Or enjoy one serving in an avocado half now and one as a sandwich later.

Building Better Burgers and Sandwiches

No need to settle for a PB&J or a takeout burger when you want a great sandwich. With a few extra minutes and ingredients, you can make a restaurant-quality burger or sandwich in your apartment and if you're in a dorm and have an electric grill or panini maker, you're in business! Making your own burger or sandwich takes less time than going to pick one up, especially if you're looking for gluten-free options.

In this section, you find some interesting recipes for burgers and hearty sandwiches that are great for lunch and dinner. After you've figured out the bread, you're more than halfway to a great gluten-free sandwich! (See recommendations for great brands of gluten-free bread in Chapter 19.)

 Gluten-free breads stay freshest in the freezer. To defrost, heat the bread or bun in the microwave on high for about 20 seconds, or just toast your sandwich bread. You can also do sandwiches protein style (wrapped in lettuce leaves) or bundle your fillings with gluten-free tortillas.

Mozzarella Burger

Prep time: 5 min • **Cook time:** Less than 15 min • **Yield:** 1 serving

Ingredients	Directions
3 ounces lean ground beef ⅛ teaspoon garlic salt ¼ teaspoon Italian seasoning 1½ tablespoons shredded mozzarella cheese 1 gluten-free hamburger bun 1 tablespoon tomato sauce	**1** Add the ground beef, garlic salt, and Italian seasoning to a small bowl. Mix the meat and spices together with your hands. Form it into a patty about ½ inch thick and a little larger than your bun's diameter.
	2 Heat a small skillet over medium-high heat. Add the hamburger patty to the hot skillet.
	3 Cook the patty 3 to 5 minutes, flip it over, and cook it an additional 3 to 4 minutes for a well-done burger. During the final minute or 2 of cooking, top the patty with cheese.
	4 While the cheese is melting, heat your gluten-free bun in the microwave on high for about 20 seconds (if frozen) or 10 seconds (if thawed).
	5 Place the burger on the bottom half of the bun and spread the tomato sauce on the top bun. Join the two halves and enjoy.

Per serving: Calories 473 (From Fat 211); Fat 24g (Saturated 6g); Cholesterol 40mg; Sodium 318mg; Carbohydrate 42g (Dietary Fiber 2g); Protein 22g.

Note: Smushing your burger down or flipping too often dries out the burger.

Vary It! Don't have a gluten-free bun? Enjoy your burger on a bed of lettuce and tomato instead.

Tip: When buying ground beef for burgers, I find that 85 to 90 percent lean (ground round) works well. It's still juicy even though it's lean.

Tip: You don't need oil when cooking ground beef because it contains enough fat for cooking.

Southwest Black Bean and Turkey Burger

Prep time: 10 min • **Cook time:** 11 min • **Yield:** 1 serving

Ingredients	Directions
3 ounces lean ground turkey	**1** In a medium bowl, combine the turkey, beans, garlic salt, chili powder, and cumin. Form the mixture into a patty about ½ inch thick.
¼ cup canned black beans, drained and lightly mashed	
¼ teaspoon garlic salt	**2** Heat the oil in small skillet over medium heat. When the skillet is hot, place the patty in the skillet.
¼ teaspoon chili powder	
¼ teaspoon ground cumin	
1 teaspoon vegetable oil	**3** Cook the patty about 4 to 5 minutes on each side, or until it's no longer pink in the center. Make sure the patty is well done. Top the burger with cheese for the final minute or 2 of cooking, cooking until the cheese is melted.
1 slice pepper Jack cheese	
1 gluten-free hamburger bun	
3 avocado slices	
1 teaspoon fat-free sour cream	**4** Heat the bun in the microwave on high for 20 seconds (if frozen) or 10 seconds (if thawed).
1 teaspoon salsa	
	5 Slide the burger onto the bun and top it with avocado slices, sour cream, and a touch of salsa.

Per serving: Calories 679 (From Fat 345); Fat 38g (Saturated 9g); Cholesterol 80mg; Sodium 721mg; Carbohydrate 55g (Dietary Fiber 7g); Protein 31g.

Note: Lean turkey burgers can be dry. The beans add some moisture and make for a moist and delicious burger!

Tip: Add a little bit of oil when cooking lean turkey to ensure it doesn't stick to the pan.

Classic Egg Salad Sandwich

Prep time: 5 min • **Cook time:** 10 min • **Yield:** 2 servings

Ingredients	Directions
2 eggs 1 celery stalk, diced	*1* Boil the eggs for 10 minutes. Cool, peel, and chop them.
1½ tablespoons Greek yogurt or mayonnaise ¼ teaspoon garlic salt ¼ teaspoon black pepper	*2* In a medium bowl, combine the chopped eggs, celery, yogurt, garlic salt, and pepper.
4 slices gluten-free sandwich bread 2 large lettuce leaves 4 tomato slices	*3* Toast four slices of gluten-free bread. Assemble two sandwiches, topping the toast with the egg mixture, lettuce, and tomato.

Per serving: Calories 373 (From Fat 162); Fat 18g (Saturated 3g); Cholesterol 187mg; Sodium 232mg; Carbohydrate 43g (Dietary Fiber 2g); Protein 10g.

Note: Find out how to boil the perfect egg in Chapter 8.

Tip: You can store egg salad in a sealed container for a couple of days in the refrigerator.

Open-Faced Tuna Tarragon Melt

Prep time: 10 min • **Cook time:** 5 min • **Yield:** 1 serving

Ingredients	Directions
3-ounce can tuna packed in water, drained	**1** In a small bowl, stir together the tuna, celery, yogurt, lemon juice, and tarragon.
1 celery stalk, chopped	
1 tablespoon Greek yogurt or mayonnaise	**2** On a baking sheet, top the slice of bread with the tuna mixture, tomato, and cheese.
¼ teaspoon lemon juice	
½ teaspoon dried tarragon	**3** Broil in the oven or toaster oven until the cheese is melted and bubbly.
1 slice gluten-free sandwich bread	
2 thin tomato slices	
1 slice provolone cheese	

Per serving: *Calories 358 (From Fat 148); Fat 16g (Saturated 6g); Cholesterol 50mg; Sodium 582mg; Carbohydrate 25g (Dietary Fiber 2g); Protein 27g.*

Vary It! Don't have tarragon? Try basil or oregano.

Pilgrim Turkey Cranberry Panini

Prep time: 5 min • **Cook time:** 10 min • **Yield:** 1 serving

Ingredients	Directions
2 teaspoons butter 2 slices gluten-free sandwich bread 1 tablespoon Dijon mustard 1 tablespoon canned cranberry sauce 2 slices provolone cheese 3 thin slices turkey breast 5 spinach leaves	*1* Spread butter on one side of each slice of bread. Heat a medium skillet over medium heat. Place one slice of bread butter-side down in the skillet.
	2 Spread mustard and then cranberry sauce on the side of the bread that's facing up in the skillet.
	3 Layer one slice of cheese, all the turkey, all the spinach, and the second slice of cheese on the bread in the skillet.
	4 Top with other bread slice, butter-side up.
	5 Heat until the underside of the sandwich is toasted and the cheese begins to melt, about 3 minutes. Flip the sandwich over and repeat on the other side, pushing down with a spatula to flatten the sandwich.

Per serving: Calories 659 (From Fat 335); Fat 37g (Saturated 16g); Cholesterol 95mg; Sodium 961mg; Carbohydrate 51g (Dietary Fiber 3g); Protein 32g.

Tip: Put a slice of cheese next to each piece of bread with toppings in between to hold it all together!

Chapter 11

10 Minutes or Less: Eat-on-the-Go Dinners

- -

In This Chapter

▶ Fixing tantalizing 10-minute meals with tortillas

▶ Creating stir-fries

- -

*T*en-minute dinners? Believe it! You *can* put together speedy and nutritious meals — perhaps meals that even feel a little gourmet. These are grab-and-go recipes; some may not include a perfect balance of every food group, but they provide a healthy and filling meal in hardly any time at all.

If you use a little bit of free time to prepare a few ingredients ahead of time, you can cut even more time off these options. Check out time-saving tips for prepping ingredients in Chapter 16.

Tossing It in a Tortilla

Gluten-free diners are always looking for a good tortilla. Corn tortillas and taco shells are usually a safe gluten-free bet. But really, you can bundle taco fillings with just about anything. Aside from corn tortillas, you can sometimes find large brown rice tortillas, which are a little more pliable than corn, and lettuce leaves are terrific for a lighter, greener option.

A few great new brands of tortillas are beginning to show up online and on store shelves, too, making these convenient little wraps a great choice for the discerning gluten-free eater who happens to be in a hurry. Find a list of my favorite tortilla brands in Chapter 19.

Looking for new ideas for what to put in your tortillas? Try some of these combinations:

- Sautéed vegetables, such as zucchini and mushrooms
- Sautéed poblano chile, onion, and mashed potatoes
- Scrambled eggs, bacon, sausage, and cheese
- Barbecue beef and cole slaw
- Tofu, beans, and rice
- Salad with a dollop of salsa and guacamole

Making your own corn tortillas

If you're feeling adventurous — or just want a reason to take a long, food-producing homework break — you can try making your own corn tortillas. The only ingredients you need are water and some *masa harina,* a special corn flour treated with lime that you usually find with the other Mexican foods at the grocery.

To make tortillas, place 2 cups of masa flour in a large bowl. Add 1¼ cups warm water to the masa flour. Mix it in and let the dough sit for 5 minutes or so. Then work the dough with your hands for several minutes, like you're squeezing Play-Doh. Adjust the dough by adding a little more water if it seems dry and crumbly or more masa if it seems sticky and wet.

Shape pieces of dough into 16 to 18 balls, each about the size of a golf ball. Put a ball of dough between two pieces of wax paper — or use a cut-open plastic freezer bag — and roll out the dough super thin with a rolling pin. You can also flatten the dough with a heavy skillet or pie plate or tortilla press if you have one.

Now you're ready to cook! Heat a large skillet over high heat and spray it with nonstick cooking spray. One tortilla at a time, carefully remove one side of the wax paper. Place the tortilla in the pan while peeling off the other side of the wax paper. Cook the tortilla in the hot pan for 30 to 60 seconds on each side, until it's lightly browned and beginning to puff.

Wrap the stack of cooked tortillas in a towel or moist paper towels to keep them warm. If you don't eat all your tortillas right away, you can refrigerate them and reheat them later.

Salmon Tacos

Prep time: 10 min • **Yield:** 1 serving

Ingredients	*Directions*
2.5-ounce pouch salmon	*1* Place half the salmon in each tortilla. Microwave on high for 30 seconds.
2 corn tortillas	
1 tablespoon sour cream	*2* In a small bowl, stir together the sour cream, salsa, lime juice, and chili powder. Divide this mixture between the two tacos and top with avocado and lettuce.
1 tablespoon salsa	
½ teaspoon lime juice	
½ teaspoon chili powder	
¼ of an avocado, sliced	
¼ cup shredded lettuce or cabbage	

Per serving: Calories 321 (From Fat 130); Fat 14g (Saturated 4g); Cholesterol 45mg; Sodium 261mg; Carbohydrate 31g (Dietary Fiber 5g); Protein 19g.

Tip: Chicken of the Sea salmon in the pouch is gluten-free, fully cooked, and ready to go. Find this item near the tuna in the grocery store.

Vary It! If you're not a salmon fan, use a pouch or can of tuna instead of salmon. Salmon has a bit more vitamin B_{12} and B_6, but tuna has a bit more protein. Either one is a great, healthy choice.

Tuna and White Bean Tacos

Prep time: 5 min • **Yield:** 1 serving

Ingredients	Directions
2.5-ounce pouch or can of tuna, drained	**1** In a medium bowl, stir together the tuna, beans, corn, tomatoes, cilantro, lemon juice, oil, and salt and pepper.
¼ cup canned white beans, drained	
¼ cup white corn	**2** Heat the tortillas in the microwave on high for 10 seconds, or until they're warm.
6 cherry tomatoes, sliced	
½ teaspoon chopped fresh cilantro	**3** Divide the tuna mixture between the two tortillas.
Dash of lemon juice	
½ teaspoon olive oil	
Salt to taste	
Black pepper to taste	
2 corn tortillas	

Per serving: Calories 357 (From Fat 58); Fat 6g (Saturated 1g); Cholesterol 38mg; Sodium 697mg; Carbohydrate 52g (Dietary Fiber 8g); Protein 26g.

Vary It! Throw in any vegetables you have that sound good to you to boost the nutrition in these tasty tacos! How about some mushrooms and bell peppers?

Chicken and Black Bean Tacos

Prep time: 5 min • **Yield:** 1 serving

Ingredients	*Directions*
2 corn tortillas	**1** Heat the tortillas, chicken, and beans in the microwave on high for 10 seconds, or until they're warm.
½ cup cooked chicken	
¼ cup canned black beans, drained	
¼ cup shredded pepper Jack cheese	**2** Divide the chicken, beans, cheese, salsa, and cilantro between the two tortillas.
¼ cup salsa	
1 tablespoon fresh cilantro	

Per serving: *Calories 454 (From Fat 144); Fat 16g (Saturated 8g); Cholesterol 92mg; Sodium 864mg; Carbohydrate 42g (Dietary Fiber 6g); Protein 35g.*

Tip: Use leftover chicken, ready-made roasted chicken from the grocery store, or pregrilled chicken from the freezer or meat section of the store.

BLTA Tacos

Prep time: 10 min • **Yield:** 1 serving

Ingredients	Directions
2 corn tortillas	**1** Heat the tortillas in the microwave on high for 10 seconds, or until they're warm.
2 slices bacon, cooked	
½ cup chopped lettuce	**2** Divide the bacon, lettuce, tomato, avocado, and dressing between the two tortillas.
¼ of a tomato, thinly sliced	
4 thin slices avocado	
2 tablespoons ranch dressing	

Per serving: Calories 305 (From Fat 161); Fat 18g (Saturated 4g); Cholesterol 16mg; Sodium 470mg; Carbohydrate 31g (Dietary Fiber 5g); Protein 9g.

Vary It! Make this a wrap by swapping out the taco-sized tortillas for a burrito version and tossing in some precooked chicken.

Note: Most brands of ranch dressing are gluten-free, but check the label to be sure. If you see wheat or malt in the ingredient list, pick a different brand. I like the Classic Ranch flavor of Bolthouse Farms Creamy Yogurt Dressing — just 45 calories per serving. Look for this item in the produce refrigerator at your grocery store. Hidden Valley Ranch now labels their ranch dressings gluten-free as well.

Stuffed Beef Burrito

Prep time: 2 min • **Cook time:** Less than 10 min • **Yield:** 1 serving

Ingredients	*Directions*
½ **cup (4 ounces) lean ground beef**	**1** Heat a small skillet over medium heat. Add the ground beef, onion, salt, and pepper. Break apart the meat as you cook it, cooking until the ground beef is brown, about 5 minutes. Drain the grease from the pan.
2 tablespoons chopped onion	
Salt to taste	
Black pepper to taste	
1 brown rice tortilla or Rudi's Gluten-Free tortilla	**2** Layer the ground beef mixture, rice, beans, cheese, salsa, and sour cream in the middle of your tortilla. Fold one end of the tortilla toward the middle and then roll from one side to the other.
¼ **cup cooked rice**	
¼ **cup canned black beans or refried beans**	
2 tablespoons shredded cheddar cheese	**3** Place the burrito seam-side down on a microwave-safe plate and microwave it for about 1 minute on high, until warmed through.
2 tablespoons salsa	
1 tablespoon fat-free sour cream	

Per serving: Calories 475 (From Fat 137); Fat 15g (Saturated 6g); Cholesterol 46mg; Sodium 1,042mg; Carbohydrate 53g (Dietary Fiber 7g); Protein 29g.

Vary It! For a more classic taco beef flavor, toss 1 teaspoon of taco seasoning in the skillet while your beef is cooking instead of using salt and pepper. Go to Chapter 18 for a gluten-free taco seasoning recipe.

Tuna Spinach Wrap

Prep time: 5 min • **Yield:** 1 serving

Ingredients

1 large gluten-free	*Directions*
tortilla	**1** Heat the tortilla in the microwave on high for 10 seconds, or until it's warm.
½ tablespoon hummus	
½ cup fresh spinach leaves	**2** Spread the hummus on the warm tortilla and top it with spinach leaves and sliced tomato.
¼ of a tomato, thinly sliced	
2.5- to 3-ounce pouch or can of tuna, drained	
Salt to taste	**3** Spread tuna over the vegetables and add salt and pepper to taste.
Black pepper to taste	
	4 Roll the wrap tightly and enjoy it immediately, or wrap it in plastic wrap to take it to go.

Per serving: Calories 294 (From Fat 71); Fat 8g (Saturated 1g); Cholesterol 38mg; Sodium 831mg; Carbohydrate 34g (Dietary Fiber 4g); Protein 20g.

Sizzling Stir-Fries

You may think you need special equipment or expert cooking skills to make stir-fry at home, but you don't! Stir-fry meals are easy and healthy, and they take only a few minutes in front of the stove.

Stir-fry is a simple dish of vegetables and usually meat that's quickly cooked over high heat. You need only simple tools like a large skillet or wok and a spatula. And it doesn't really require constant stirring as the name would imply — it just takes a turn of the ingredients in the pan a few times until all sides are cooked.

Ingredients consist of a variety of vegetables, some protein, and a good gluten-free sauce. Inspiration can come from any type of cuisine, but check for gluten-free options from Kikkoman and La Choy. All of San-J's sauces are gluten-free, including Asian-inspired sauces like teriyaki sauce, soy sauce, and peanut sauce. Salad dressings and marinades can also make great stir-fry sauces.

Be aware that most Asian sauces include wheat as a main ingredient, so look for the ones marked gluten-free.

Here are a couple of stir-fry prep tips:

✔ Keep a bag of stir-fry veggies in the freezer to save shopping and chopping time. You may find fresh pre-cut stir-fry veggies in your produce section, too. Of course, cutting your own veggies isn't too difficult. Search online for a knife skills tutorial if you want to improve your speed and technique!

✔ A nice bed of rice, gluten-free noodles, or polenta makes a great base for your stir-fries. If you make these foods ahead, use leftovers, or buy instant versions, your stir-fry meal takes less than 10 minutes from start to finish.

One of the best plan-ahead moves I use is to cook a big pot of plain rice (any type) and freeze it in 1-cup servings. Voilà! Ready-made cooked rice for any recipe that calls for it — without the 20 minutes of cook time it normally takes. Just toss the cooled, cooked rice into plastic freezer bags. When you're ready to use it, dump it out and warm it up in the microwave on high for a minute or so.

There are many ways to stir-fry, but here are the simple steps to stir-fry just about anything:

1. **Cut the ingredients into thin strips of uniform size.**

2. **In a large skillet, add about a tablespoon of oil. Heat it over medium-high heat until anything placed in the pan sizzles.**

3. **Add the meat and spices in one layer in the bottom of the pan and let this food sear for about a minute.**

   Turn up the heat slightly if you don't hear sizzling.

4. **Stir the meat and add the vegetables. Cook for 1 to 2 minutes more.**

5. **Stir again and add the sauce. Cook another minute or so until the sauce is warm, the meat is no longer pink, and the vegetables are still crisp.**

The recipes in this section were inspired by many cuisines, including Japanese, Chinese, Indian, Thai, Italian, and American. After you get the hang of it, just use your own imagination and ingredients to make up a fresh, healthy meal on the spot anytime. (For a little international inspiration, check out the nearby sidebar for some flavor combinations to try.)

Surveying spices from around the world

Feeling adventurous? Maybe you just met a great new friend and want to cook something outside of your normal repertoire. Try some herbs, spices, and other flavorful foods that characterize different cuisines from around the world:

✔ **Chinese:** Bean paste, chile oil, garlic, gingerroot, green onions, hot red peppers, sesame oil, sesame seeds, soy sauce

✔ **Greek:** Cinnamon, dill, garlic, lemon, mint, nutmeg, olives, oregano

✔ **Indian:** Cardamom, chilies, coriander seeds, cumin, curry powder, garlic, gingerroot, mint, mustard seeds, red pepper, saffron, sesame seeds, turmeric, yogurt

✔ **Italian:** Anchovies, basil, bay leaves, fennel seeds, garlic, marjoram, onions, oregano, parsley, pine nuts, red pepper, rosemary

✔ **Japanese:** Mustard, Shichimi pepper, teriyaki sauce, wasabi

✔ **Mexican:** Bell peppers, chilies, cilantro, cinnamon, cocoa, coriander seeds, cumin seeds, garlic, lime, onions, oregano, vanilla

✔ **Thai:** Chilies, cumin, garlic, ginger, lemongrass, lime, mint, black pepper, shallots, turmeric

Chicken Teriyaki Stir-Fry

Prep time: 3 min • **Cook time:** Less than 7 min • **Yield:** 2 servings

Ingredients	*Directions*
1 teaspoon vegetable oil	*1* In a large skillet, add the oil. Heat on medium-high until anything placed in the pan sizzles.
6 to 8 ounces boneless, skinless chicken breast, cut into ½-inch strips	
1 small green bell pepper, cut into strips	*2* Add the chicken to the skillet in one layer and let it sear for about 1 minute. Turn up the heat slightly if you don't hear sizzling.
1 small red bell pepper, cut into strips	*3* Stir the chicken and add the green and red bell peppers (see Figure 11-1). Let the mixture cook for 1 to 2 minutes more.
½ cup pineapple chunks, drained	
½ cup gluten-free teriyaki sauce	*4* Stir again and add the pineapple chunks and teriyaki sauce. Cook about another minute, until the sauce is warm, the chicken is no longer pink, and the vegetables are still crisp.

Per serving: *Calories 230 (From Fat 41); Fat 5g (Saturated 1g); Cholesterol 47mg; Sodium 2,802mg; Carbohydrate 26g (Dietary Fiber 2g); Protein 22g.*

Vary It! Use canned mandarin oranges instead of pineapple for a slightly sweeter taste.

Tip: If you don't have teriyaki sauce, try ½ cup gluten-free soy sauce plus 2 tablespoons honey.

How to Core and Seed a Pepper

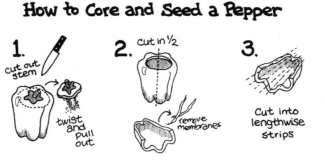

Figure 11-1: Coring and seeding bell peppers.

Peanut Chicken Stir-Fry

Prep time: 3 min • **Cook time:** Less than 7 min • **Yield:** 2 servings

Ingredients	*Directions*
1 teaspoon vegetable or peanut oil	**1** In a large skillet, add the oil. Heat on medium-high until anything placed in the pan sizzles.
½ teaspoon (about 1 clove) chopped or minced garlic	
6 to 8 ounces boneless, skinless chicken breast, cut into ½-inch strips	**2** Add the garlic and chicken to the skillet in one layer and let the chicken sear for about 1 minute. Turn up the heat slightly if you don't hear sizzling.
1 small green bell pepper, cut into strips	
1 small red bell pepper, cut into strips	**3** Stir the chicken and add the green bell pepper, red bell pepper, and mushrooms. Let them cook for 1 to 2 minutes more.
¼ cup sliced mushrooms	
¼ cup chicken broth	**4** Stir again and add the chicken broth, peanut sauce, and peanuts. Cook about another minute, until the sauce is warm, the chicken is no longer pink, and the vegetables are still crisp.
¼ to ½ cup gluten-free peanut sauce	
½ cup peanuts, halved or chopped	

Per serving: *Calories 443 (From Fat 276); Fat 31g (Saturated 5g); Cholesterol 48mg; Sodium 396mg; Carbohydrate 16g (Dietary Fiber 6g); Protein 32g.*

Tandoori Chicken Stir-Fry

Prep time: 3 min • **Cook time:** Less than 7 min • **Yield:** 2 servings

Ingredients	*Directions*
1 teaspoon vegetable or sesame oil	*1* In a large skillet, add the oil. Heat on medium-high until anything placed in the pan sizzles.
6 to 8 ounces boneless, skinless chicken breast, cut into ½-inch strips	
½ teaspoon (about 1 clove) chopped or minced garlic	*2* Add the chicken and garlic to the pan in one layer and let the chicken sear for about 1 minute. Turn up the heat slightly if you don't hear sizzling.
½ cup frozen sliced okra	
½ cup chopped red bell pepper	*3* Stir the chicken and add the okra and red bell pepper. Let the mixture cook for 1 to 2 minutes more.
¼ cup plain yogurt	
½ teaspoon lemon juice	
⅛ teaspoon cayenne pepper or red pepper flakes	*4* Stir again and add the yogurt, lemon juice, cayenne pepper, cumin, and soy sauce. Cook about another minute, until the sauce is warm, the chicken is no longer pink, and vegetables are still crisp.
¼ teaspoon ground cumin	
1 tablespoon gluten-free soy sauce	
1 tablespoon chopped fresh cilantro or basil	*5* Garnish with chopped cilantro or basil.

Per serving: *Calories 160 (From Fat 45); Fat 5g (Saturated 1g); Cholesterol 49mg; Sodium 817mg; Carbohydrate 8g (Dietary Fiber 2g); Protein 21g.*

Tip: Serve with basmati rice.

Vary It! Replace the okra with ½ cup fresh or canned asparagus spears.

Chicken Artichoke Stir-Fry

Prep time: 2 min • **Cook time:** Less than 8 min • **Yield:** 2 servings

Ingredients	Directions
1 teaspoon vegetable oil	**1** Heat the oil in a large skillet over medium-high heat.
6 to 8 ounces boneless, skinless chicken breast, cut into ½-inch strips	**2** When the oil is hot, add the chicken to the skillet in one layer and let it sear for about 2 minutes.
6-ounce jar marinated artichoke hearts, drained	
¼ cup sun-dried tomatoes packed in oil, drained	**3** Stir the chicken and add the artichoke hearts, sun-dried tomatoes, capers, lemon juice, garlic salt, Italian seasoning, and pepper.
½ tablespoon capers	
½ tablespoon lemon juice	
½ teaspoon garlic salt	**4** Let the mixture cook, stirring occasionally, until the chicken is no longer pink.
½ teaspoon Italian seasoning	
½ teaspoon black pepper	

Per serving: Calories 276 (From Fat 112); Fat 12g (Saturated 2g); Cholesterol 72mg; Sodium 655mg; Carbohydrate 14g (Dietary Fiber 4g); Protein 30g.

Vary It! Use sliced black, Kalamata, or green olives instead of capers.

Tip: Serve with rice or, for a restaurant-quality pasta dish, over gluten-free pasta.

Broccoli Beef Stir-Fry

Prep time: 3 min • **Cook time:** 10 min • **Yield:** 2 servings

Ingredients	Directions
1 teaspoon vegetable or sesame oil	**1** In a large skillet, add the oil. Heat on medium-high until anything placed in the pan sizzles.
½ teaspoon (about 1 clove) chopped or minced garlic	
¼ cup chopped onion	**2** Add the garlic, onion, and steak (see Figure 11-2) in one layer in the bottom of the pan and let the meat sear for about 1 minute. Turn up the heat slightly if you don't hear sizzling.
12-ounce flank steak, cut into ½-inch strips	
1 cup broccoli florets	
2 tablespoons gluten-free soy sauce	**3** Stir the steak and add the broccoli. Let the mixture cook for about 4 minutes more.
1 tablespoon sesame seeds	
	4 Stir again and add the soy sauce and sesame seeds. Stir the mixture continually about another minute until the sauce is warm, the meat is no longer pink, and the broccoli is still crisp.

Per serving: Calories 328 (From Fat 156); Fat 17g (Saturated 6g); Cholesterol 81mg; Sodium 1,033mg; Carbohydrate 4g (Dietary Fiber 1g); Protein 38g.

Cut your skirt or flank steak against the grain of the meat.

Figure 11-2: Slice a flank steak across the grain for more tender meat.

Thai Steak and Red Pepper Stir-Fry

Prep time: 3 min • **Cook time:** Less than 7 min • **Yield:** 2 servings

Ingredients	Directions
1 teaspoon vegetable or sesame oil	**1** In a large skillet, add the oil. Heat on medium-high until anything placed in the pan sizzles.
½ teaspoon (about 1 clove) chopped or minced garlic	
6 ounces flank steak or beef tenderloin, cut into ½-inch strips	**2** Add the garlic and steak to the pan in one layer and let the meat sear for about 1 minute. Turn up the heat slightly if you don't hear sizzling.
1 small red bell pepper, cut into strips	
¼ cup sliced mushrooms	**3** Stir the steak and add the bell pepper and mushrooms. Let the mixture cook for 1 to 2 minutes more.
½ cup chopped green onion	
2 tablespoons gluten-free Pad Thai sauce	**4** Stir again and add the green onion, Pad Thai sauce, and red pepper flakes. Stir about another minute, cooking until the sauce is warm, the meat is no longer pink, and the vegetables are still crisp.
½ teaspoon red pepper flakes	

Per serving: Calories 201 (From Fat 84); Fat 9g (Saturated 3g); Cholesterol 41mg; Sodium 456mg; Carbohydrate 12g (Dietary Fiber 2g); Protein 18g.

Tip: Serve with rice noodles or rice.

Philly Cheesesteak Stir-Fry

Prep time: 3 min • **Cook time:** Less than 7 min • **Yield:** 2 servings

Ingredients	Directions
1 teaspoon vegetable oil	*1* In a large skillet, add the oil. Heat on medium-high until anything placed in the pan sizzles.
6 ounces flank steak or beef tenderloin, cut into ½-inch strips	
Garlic salt to taste	*2* Add the steak to the pan in one layer and sprinkle the steak with garlic salt and pepper. Let the steak sear for 1 to 2 minutes. Turn up the heat slightly if you don't hear sizzling.
Black pepper to taste	
1 small onion, cut into strips	
1 small green bell pepper, cut into strips	*3* Stir the steak and add the onion, bell pepper, and mushrooms. Let the mixture cook for another 3 to 4 minutes, or until the meat is cooked thoroughly and no longer pink.
½ cup sliced mushrooms	
4 slices provolone cheese	
	4 Top with cheese when serving.

Per serving: Calories 366 (From Fat 214); Fat 24g (Saturated 13g); Cholesterol 80mg; Sodium 609mg; Carbohydrate 6g (Dietary Fiber 1g); Protein 32g.

Vary It! This recipe makes a great meal with rice, a hearty salad with lettuce, or a delicious sandwich on a gluten-free hot dog or sandwich bun. I toast the bun with a little butter and garlic salt.

Joe's Special Beef and Mushroom Stir-Fry

Prep time: 3 min • **Cook time:** 7 min • **Yield:** 2 servings

Ingredients	*Directions*
8 ounces lean ground beef ½ of a small onion, chopped ½ cup sliced mushrooms 1 tablespoon gluten-free Worcestershire sauce ¼ cup reduced-fat sour cream ½ teaspoon garlic salt 1 teaspoon Italian seasoning	*1* Heat a large skillet over medium-high heat. Cook the ground beef, onion, mushrooms, Worcestershire sauce, sour cream, garlic salt, and Italian seasoning until the meat is no longer pink, breaking up the ground beef chunks with a spatula as you go.
	2 Drain off any fat from the pan (pour the fat in an old jar and let the grease harden before throwing it away).
2 cups spinach leaves, stems removed	*3* Add the spinach and then stir, cooking the mixture about another minute.
¼ cup shredded Swiss or Jack cheese	*4* Remove the stir-fry from the heat and top it with cheese.

Per serving: *Calories 264 (From Fat 136); Fat 15g (Saturated 8g); Cholesterol 55mg; Sodium 472mg; Carbohydrate 9g (Dietary Fiber 2g); Protein 24g.*

Tip: Serve with rice or polenta.

Tip: Lea & Perrins Worcestershire sauce is gluten-free.

Italian Sausage Stir-Fry

Prep time: 3 min • **Cook time:** 10 min • **Yield:** 2 servings

Ingredients	Directions
1 teaspoon vegetable oil	**1** Heat a large skillet on medium-high until anything placed in the pan sizzles.
8 ounces Italian sausage links, cut into ½-inch slices	
1 small green bell pepper, cut into strips	**2** Add the sausage to the pan in one layer and let it sear for 3 to 4 minutes. Turn up the heat slightly if you don't hear sizzling.
½ of a small onion, cut into strips	
1 cup sliced mushrooms	**3** Stir the sausage and add the bell pepper, onion, and mushrooms. Let the mixture cook for about another 3 minutes.
¼ cup sliced black olives	
¾ cup tomato sauce	**4** Stir again and add the black olives, tomato sauce, garlic salt, and Italian seasoning. Cook about another 3 minutes, until the sauce is warm and the sausage is no longer pink. Sprinkle with Parmesan.
½ teaspoon garlic salt	
1 teaspoon Italian seasoning	
Parmesan cheese for sprinkling	

Per serving: Calories 292 (From Fat 181); Fat 20g (Saturated 6g); Cholesterol 47mg; Sodium 1,525mg; Carbohydrate 14g (Dietary Fiber 4g); Protein 16g.

Tip: Serve with gluten-free pasta or polenta.

BBQ Sausage Stir-Fry

Prep time: 3 min • **Cook time:** Less than 10 min • **Yield:** 4 servings

Ingredients	*Directions*
1 pound turkey polska kielbasa sausage, cut into ½-inch slices	*1* Spray a large skillet with nonstick cooking spray and heat the skillet over medium-high heat.
1 small green bell pepper, cut into strips	
½ of a small onion, cut into strips	*2* Add the sausage to the pan in one layer and let it sear for about 3 minutes.
¾ cup gluten-free barbecue sauce	*3* Stir the sausage and add the green bell pepper and onion. Let the mixture cook for another 3 or 4 minutes.
	4 Stir again and add the barbecue sauce. Cook another 1 to 2 minutes, until the sauce is warm.

Per serving: Calories 205 (From Fat 89); Fat 10g (Saturated 3g); Cholesterol 74mg; Sodium 1,382mg; Carbohydrate 10g (Dietary Fiber 1g); Protein 19g.

Tip: Serve with polenta or mashed potatoes.

Tip: I use Sweet Baby Ray's Sweet 'n Spicy barbecue sauce for this recipe. It's gluten-free.

Mixing up homemade barbecue sauce

Make your own barbecue sauce by combining ½ cup ketchup, ⅓ cup brown sugar, 1 tablespoon cider vinegar, 2 teaspoons gluten-free Worcestershire sauce, and 2 teaspoons gluten-free soy sauce. Store your sauce in a sealed glass container in the fridge and enjoy it as a dip and on anything from beans to burgers.

Chapter 12

30 Minutes 'til Mealtime: Dinner Entrees

*H*ome-cooked meals need not be a distant memory while you're a college student. Sure, Mom may be far away, but you can do your own home cooking with a little time, a few staple ingredients, and some basic know-how.

Some students take turns cooking with their roommates, and many of the recipes in this chapter are great for cooking with a few friends or for days when you have some spare time and want to cook ahead to have leftovers (see Chapter 16 for tips on storing and using leftovers). Even better, these recipes are so tasty that no one will even miss the gluten.

In this chapter, find simple recipes for pasta dishes, grilled entrees, and great main dishes that you can prepare in about a half hour. These foods call for just a handful of ingredients that you should have no trouble finding at your local grocery store.

Picking Pasta for Dinner

Yes, you can still have pasta on a gluten-free diet! You just need to look for alternatives to the old standard wheat pasta. Noodles made from rice and corn are usually gluten-free, and there's a wide and wonderful world of pastas made from other great grains, too. If your grocery doesn't have at least one or two gluten-free pasta choices — or if it doesn't carry the kind you like best — order a few packages online or ask your grocery's customer service department to order some. They usually will.

Everyone has different tastes in gluten-free pasta. My favorite is Tinkyada brand brown rice pasta. I dislike the goopy starch that comes from the corn pastas, but I know some people who love corn pasta. Quinoa pasta is another option that many people love; it's growing on me. A Japanese noodle called glucomannan is a soluble fiber with no calories, gluten, or carbs. You can even try spaghetti squash, a vegetable with an amazing pasta-like quality.

In this section, I give you some tips for preparing gluten-free pastas and spaghetti squash. Then on to recipes!

Cooking gluten-free pastas

Gluten-free pasta behaves a little differently from wheat pasta. Here are some things to keep in mind to make your pasta meals successful:

- ✔ Undercook gluten-free pasta; otherwise, it falls apart and gets mushy. Start taste testing for doneness at the minimum time noted on the package.

- ✔ Rinse gluten-free pasta immediately after cooking it to remove the extra starch.

- ✔ Don't plan to make extra gluten-free pasta. It keeps only about a day in the fridge before it turns to cardboard (figuratively, that is).

- ✔ Prepare to use extra sauce. Gluten-free pasta absorbs sauce like a sponge.

- ✔ Drain your pasta in your own designated gluten-free colander to avoid cross-contamination; getting all the wheat pasta bits out of every little hole is tough.

Be sure to cook pasta in its own fresh water. Don't cook it in water that's been used to cook gluten-containing pasta. When dining out, check with restaurants that offer gluten-free pasta to make sure they use fresh pasta water as well.

Preparing spaghetti squash

 When you're feeling extra creative, try using spaghetti squash instead of noodles for your favorite pasta dishes. Here's how to make it (see Figure 12-1):

1. **With some muscle and a large, sharp knife, cut the spaghetti squash in half.**

2. **Scrape the seeds and loose pulp fibers out of the squash with a fork and discard the seeds and pulp.**

3. **Place half the squash on a microwave-safe plate, flat side down, and microwave it on high for about 8 minutes.**

4. **Remove the squash from the microwave and let it cool for a couple of minutes.**

5. **Separate the strands of the squash with a fork to reveal the spaghetti-like texture.**

Spaghetti squash is especially tasty with marinara sauce — or just topped with a bit of butter and salt. It's also great as a side dish. It's not pasta, but it sure does look and taste like it! Half a large squash makes about 2 heaping cups of "spaghetti" and feeds two people as a main dish. Cook the whole squash and save half (wrapped tightly with plastic wrap) in the fridge for a few days.

Figure 12-1: Separate the strands of the spaghetti squash with a fork.

Spaghetti with Marinara Sauce

Prep time: 3 min • **Cook time:** 20 min • **Yield:** 2 servings

Ingredients	*Directions*
1 teaspoon plus ½ tablespoon olive oil 1 teaspoon (about 2 cloves) chopped or minced garlic ¼ of an onion, chopped	*1* Add 1 teaspoon of the oil and the garlic and onion to a medium-sized pot. Cook over medium heat, cooking and stirring until the onion is tender, about 5 minutes.
28-ounce can crushed tomatoes	*2* Add the entire can of crushed tomatoes, the salt, and the Italian seasoning.
1 teaspoon salt 1 teaspoon Italian seasoning 4 ounces gluten-free pasta	*3* Lower the heat to medium-low and partially cover the pot with a lid to minimize splatters. Don't cover the pot completely, or the sauce will become watery.
Parmesan cheese for serving	*4* While the sauce is simmering, cook the pasta according to the package directions.
	5 Drain and rinse the pasta. Serve with the sauce and top with a sprinkle of Parmesan.

Per serving: *Calories 412 (From Fat 68); Fat 8g (Saturated 1g); Cholesterol 2mg; Sodium 1,734mg; Carbohydrate 75g (Dietary Fiber 9g); Protein 11g.*

Note: This is the quick and easy version of the recipe from my Italian grandmother and mom. The other version of sauce (or "gravy," as the New York Italians call it) takes a whole day, but this one is super tasty and ready to go in less than 30 minutes!

Vary It! If you have some fresh basil and oregano, add it to the sauce a minute or so before you remove the sauce from the heat.

Date Night Chicken Carbonara

Prep time: 5 min • **Cook time:** 20 min • **Yield:** 2 servings

Ingredients	Directions
4 ounces gluten-free pasta **3 slices bacon** **6-ounce boneless, skinless chicken breast, cut into small chunks** **1 tablespoon butter** **¾ cup gluten-free chicken broth** **¾ cup sour cream** **½ cup Parmesan cheese** **1 cup peas** **½ teaspoon garlic salt** **½ teaspoon black pepper**	*1* Cook and drain the pasta according to the package directions. *2* While the pasta is cooking, add the bacon and chicken to a large skillet over medium heat. Stir the chicken and turn the bacon to cook all sides, heating until the chicken is no longer pink and the bacon is crispy. *3* Remove the chicken and bacon from the pan and set them aside on paper towels. Crumble the bacon. Wipe out any extra grease from the pan with a paper towel. *4* Add the butter, chicken broth, sour cream, and Parmesan cheese to the pan. Cook over medium-low heat until the butter is melted and the sauce is hot. *5* Add the peas and the cooked chicken and bacon to the sauce and cook about another minute. Stir in the garlic salt and pepper. *6* Pour the sauce over the pasta and serve it immediately.

Per serving: Calories 764 (From Fat 344); Fat 38g (Saturated 21g); Cholesterol 126mg; Sodium 1,296mg; Carbohydrate 60g (Dietary Fiber 5g); Protein 40g.

Tip: Cut the chicken with a sharp knife on a cutting board, holding the chicken in place with a fork. Using the fork ensures you don't have to touch the raw chicken with your hands.

Vary It! Use asparagus spears instead of peas. Cook them separately and then add them to the sauce in Step 5.

Tip: Use 2 cups precooked roasted or grilled chicken instead of cooking the raw chicken to speed up the meal prep.

Baked Ziti with Italian Sausage

Prep time: 5 min • **Cook time:** 25 min • **Yield:** 2 servings

Ingredients	Directions
4 ounces gluten-free ziti	*1* Preheat the oven to 400 degrees.
8 ounces Italian sausage links	*2* Cook and drain the pasta according to the package directions.
1½ to 2 cups marinara (tomato) sauce	
1 cup mozzarella cheese	*3* While the pasta is cooking, slice the sausage or remove it from its casing and crumble it. Cook the sausage in a medium-sized skillet over medium-high heat until the sausage is brown.
	4 Remove the sausage from the pan and drain it on paper towels.
	5 Combine the pasta, sausage, sauce, and cheese in an 8-x-8-inch baking dish. Bake it for about 10 minutes, until the cheese is bubbly.

Per serving: Calories 635 (From Fat 262); Fat 29g (Saturated 14g); Cholesterol 95mg; Sodium 1,879mg; Carbohydrate 59g (Dietary Fiber 3g); Protein 30g.

Vary It! Leave out the meat for a more economical and lower-fat meal.

Vary It! Cut the fat by using Italian chicken or turkey sausage.

Note: Check the sausage for gluten-free status.

Angel Hair Pasta with Creamy Sun-Dried Tomato Artichoke Sauce

Prep time: 5 min • **Cook time:** Less than 10 min • **Yield:** 2 servings

Ingredients	*Directions*
6 ounces gluten-free angel hair pasta	*1* Cook and drain the pasta according to the package directions.
¼ cup jarred sun-dried tomato paste	
¼ cup jarred artichoke hearts, drained and chopped	*2* In a medium-sized pot, stir together the sun-dried tomato paste, artichoke hearts, sour cream, chicken broth, garlic salt, Italian seasoning, and Parmesan cheese. Simmer the sauce over medium heat until it's warm, about 5 minutes.
½ cup sour cream	
½ cup gluten-free chicken broth	
½ teaspoon garlic salt	*3* Top the pasta with the sauce and serve.
1 teaspoon Italian seasoning	
¼ cup grated or shredded Parmesan cheese	

Per serving: Calories 540 (From Fat 146); Fat 16g (Saturated 10g); Cholesterol 34mg; Sodium 789mg; Carbohydrate 76g (Dietary Fiber 2g); Protein 15g.

Vary It! Instead of using Italian seasoning, add 1 tablespoon each of chopped, fresh basil and oregano to the sauce.

Chicken Pesto Parmesan Pasta

Prep time: 5 min • **Cook time:** 20 min • **Yield:** 2 servings

Ingredients	Directions
4 ounces gluten-free pasta 1 teaspoon olive oil	*1* Cook and drain the pasta according to the package directions.
6-ounce boneless, skinless chicken breast, cut into small chunks ¼ to ½ cup jarred pesto ¼ cup shredded Parmesan cheese	*2* While the pasta is cooking, add the olive oil and chicken to a medium skillet over medium heat. Turn the chicken chunks to cook all sides. Cook until the chicken is no longer pink in the middle, about 5 minutes.
	3 Add the pasta to the skillet and stir in the pesto. Cook until heated, about another 1 to 2 minutes. Add the Parmesan and stir. Taste the pasta and add a little more pesto if you prefer.

Per serving: Calories 519 (From Fat 195); Fat 22g (Saturated 6g); Cholesterol 64mg; Sodium 449mg; Carbohydrate 45g (Dietary Fiber 2g); Protein 31g.

Tip: If you want to make your own pesto, just toss some fresh basil leaves, pine nuts, olive oil, garlic, and Parmesan in a blender or food processor. Pesto is super versatile; you can use it on any pasta or on a sandwich or pizza.

Vary It! Leave out the chicken for a nice vegetarian version.

Grilling with Gusto

Grilling is an easy way to create a healthy meal with very little effort. Believe it or not, you don't even need a traditional grill. A simple grill pan on a stove burner or an electric grill/panini maker works just as well as a massive outdoor gas-powered version. Or stick with the old charcoal and lighter fluid style portable grill. The choice is yours.

In this section, you can find some delicious ideas for grilling. Of course, feel free to use any type of meat you have on hand and any vegetables you enjoy. Don't be tied to the recipes for specific ingredients; use them as a guide to build your own creations that suit your taste.

If you want to get extra flavor by marinating your meat prior to cooking, it's best to start marinating the meat the night or the morning before you want to grill. However, I find that adding a sauce and spices to food as you're cooking it does a great job of adding flavor, too, and it requires less planning.

 Many store-bought marinades and premarinated meats contain gluten. Read the labels before you buy and make sure there are no unidentified "natural spices" or specific gluten-containing ingredients. Fortunately, marinades and sauces marked gluten-free are pretty easy to find, and marinating your food in a gluten-free Italian salad dressing is a tasty alternative to using an official marinade.

While you're grilling the meat for your meal, throw some veggies on, too. You can put them on a skewer to avoid losing them through the grate, or you can put a piece of foil sprayed with nonstick cooking spray between the heat and your produce. The vegetables cook right through the foil, and there's no mess to clean afterward.

Chicken Sausage and Peppers

Prep time: 5 min • **Cook time:** 15 min • **Yield:** 2 servings

Ingredients	*Directions*
1 medium green bell pepper, cut into 1-inch chunks 1 cup pineapple chunks	*1* Heat your grill to medium heat. While the grill is heating, put the bell pepper and pineapple on a skewer or sheet of foil.
2 links (8 ounces) gluten-free chicken sausage ½ cup gluten-free teriyaki sauce	*2* Put the sausages, fruit, and vegetables on the grate of the hot grill. Turn the sausages frequently. If you bought precooked sausage, just cook long enough to brown your sausages and soften the vegetables, about 7 to 10 minutes. If you bought raw sausage, cook it until it's no longer pink, about 15 minutes.
	3 When the meat is thoroughly cooked, lower the heat, brush the sauce onto the meat and veggies, and cook for another couple of minutes.

Per serving: Calories 248 (From Fat 40); Fat 4g (Saturated 1g); Cholesterol 93mg; Sodium 3,442mg; Carbohydrate 25g (Dietary Fiber 2g); Protein 26g.

Tip: My favorite sausage for this is Aidells Artichoke & Garlic Smoked Chicken Sausage — marked gluten-free. I get it at a regular grocery store chain.

Vary It! If you don't have teriyaki sauce, use ½ cup gluten-free soy sauce plus 2 tablespoons honey.

Vary It! For teriyaki chicken kabobs, replace the chicken sausage with a 6-ounce chicken breast, cut into cubes. Turn the skewers every couple of minutes, until the chicken is browned on the outside and no longer pink on the inside and the bell peppers are tender.

Tip: This dish is great served with rice.

Sizzling Steak Kabobs

Prep time: 5 min • **Cook time:** 15 min • **Yield:** 2 servings

Ingredients	*Directions*
8 ounces sirloin steak, cut into chunks	*1* Heat your grill to medium heat.
Salt to taste	*2* Season the steak with salt and pepper. If you have skewers, alternate the meat with the bell pepper, onion, tomatoes, and mushrooms. If not, put the veggies on a sheet of foil.
Black pepper to taste	
1 medium green bell pepper, cut into 1½-inch chunks	
1 small onion, cut into 1½-inch chunks	*3* Place the steak and veggies on the hot grill. Turn frequently, cooking about 10 to 15 minutes, depending on the heat of the grill and how well-done you like your food.
6 cherry tomatoes	
6 button mushrooms	

Per serving: Calories 166 (From Fat 49); Fat 6g (Saturated 2g); Cholesterol 64mg; Sodium 199mg; Carbohydrate 5g (Dietary Fiber 1g); Protein 23g.

Note: If you aren't in a rush, you can increase the flavor by marinating the raw meat in a gluten-free Italian dressing or meat marinade (see Figure 12-2). Put the sauce, meat, and veggies in a plastic bag, and let everything marinate for 30 minutes to 12 hours in the refrigerator. Turn the bag a couple of times during marinating to evenly coat the meat and vegetables. When you grill, lower the heat slightly to avoid burning the sauce.

Using a Plastic Bag to Marinate Food

Place food in a plastic bag. → Pour marinade into the bag. → Press all of the air out of the bag. → Seal shut, making sure the food is surrounded by the marinade, folding over if necessary.

Figure 12-2: Marinating is easy with sealable bags.

Sweet and Spicy Grilled Chicken

Prep time: 5 min • **Cook time:** 20 min • **Yield:** 2 servings

Ingredients	Directions
6-ounce boneless, skinless chicken breast, cut in half	**1** Heat your grill to medium-low heat.
1 tablespoon brown sugar **½ teaspoon chili powder**	**2** Rinse the chicken in cool water and pat it dry with a paper towel.
½ teaspoon garlic salt **½ teaspoon paprika**	**3** Combine the brown sugar, chili powder, garlic salt, and paprika in a small bowl. Rub the spice mix onto the chicken breast halves.
	4 Put the chicken on the grill and cook it for 8 to 10 minutes per side, until the chicken is no longer pink in the middle and the outside is brown but not burnt. Cut a little slit to check doneness if needed.

Per serving: Calories 120 (From Fat 19); Fat 2g (Saturated 1g); Cholesterol 47mg; Sodium 290mg; Carbohydrate 7g (Dietary Fiber 0g); Protein 17g.

Tip: Medium to medium-low heat is the key to success here because it doesn't overcook the sugary rub and lets the chicken cook through.

Tip: To cut down on cooking time, use chicken tenders or pound the chicken breast thinner by placing it in a plastic bag and hitting it with a meat mallet or a heavy object, like a small frying pan or a rolling pin (see Figure 12-3). Then add your spice rub and grill in about half the time!

Chicken Cutlets Pounded to an Even Thickness

Figure 12-3: Flattening a chicken breat cuts grilling time and promotes even cooking.

Sizzling Steak Fajitas

Prep time: 5 min • **Cook time:** 10 min • **Yield:** 1 serving

Ingredients	Directions
5-ounce thin-cut skirt steak, cut into ½-inch strips **1 teaspoon butter** **½ of a small onion, sliced**	*1* Heat your grill to medium-low heat. Place the steak on the hot grill and cook about 10 to 15 minutes, depending on the heat of the grill and how well-done you like your food.
¼ cup coarsely chopped green bell pepper **½ teaspoon garlic salt** **2 large gluten-free tortillas**	*2* In a small skillet, heat the butter over medium-high heat until it's melted. Add the onion, bell pepper, and garlic salt. Cook, stirring occasionally, until the veggies are tender.
2 tablespoons sour cream **2 tablespoons shredded cheddar cheese**	*3* Heat the tortillas in the microwave on high for 10 seconds, or until they're warm.
	4 Divide the steak and onion-pepper mixture between the two tortillas. Top with sour cream and cheddar cheese.

Per serving: Calories 770 (From Fat 324); Fat 36g (Saturated 15g); Cholesterol 105mg; Sodium 1,312mg; Carbohydrate 67g (Dietary Fiber 7g); Protein 40g.

Tip: Use leftover steak or pick up pregrilled steak in the freezer or meat section of your grocery store to cut the cooking time. If you go this route, skip Step 1. Cook the veggies for a couple of minutes in Step 2 before adding the steak to the pan.

Note: Use oil instead of butter for a dairy-free option.

Note: Add lettuce, chopped tomato, and salsa to your fajita toppings if you want. Serve with beans, rice, and guacamole. Find a guacamole recipe in Chapter 14.

Vary It! If you find the gas tank empty on your grill, you can cook your steak in a skillet. Just toss the raw steak into the skillet in Step 2 with the onion, bell pepper, and garlic salt and cook until the steak is no longer pink, a few minutes on each side.

Making Casseroles and Marvelous Main Dishes

Feeling homesick? Is your friend feeling down in the dumps? Is it your night to cook for the roommates? Invited to a potluck? A casserole may be the answer. One-dish meals are an awesome way to feed a crowd easily. You can assemble the ingredients, store the dish in the refrigerator or freezer, and pop the meal in the oven when you're ready to cook with no additional prep needed.

Don't have a crowd to feed? Enjoy leftovers another day — you can even freeze the leftovers in individual serving sizes to make your own frozen lunches and dinners. In this section, I walk you through making simple one-dish meals and main dishes that take about 30 minutes to prepare.

Cream of Anything soup mix

Many casserole recipes call for cream soups. Store-bought versions usually contain gluten, but here's a great base to keep on hand and add to recipes when you need cream-of-whatever. You'll have enough mix to make the equivalent of ten cans of soup. You can store the mix in your pantry for up to a year. Just be sure to label the container and include directions for completing the recipe.

To make the soup mix, simply combine the following ingredients in a large plastic bag:

- 2 cups nonfat dry milk

- ¾ cup cornstarch

- ¾ cup reduced-sodium chicken or vegetable bouillon powder (**Note:** Herb Ox makes a gluten-free, MSG-free bouillon powder that's sold at most grocery stores)

- 2 tablespoons dried onion flakes

- ½ teaspoon black pepper

To prepare the soup, add ⅓ cup mix and 1¼ cups cold water in a small pot. Whisk to combine. (**Tip:** Adding warm water to powdered ingredients creates lumps, so always add a cold liquid to powdered ingredients.) Add ½ cup chopped celery, cooked chicken, or chopped mushrooms, depending on which type of cream soup your recipe calls for, to equal one can of cream soup. Cook over medium heat, stirring or whisking continuously, until the soup is thick.

30-Minute Paella

Prep time: 5 min • **Cook time:** 25 min • **Yield:** 4 servings

Ingredients	*Directions*
6-ounce boneless, skinless chicken breast, roughly diced 8 ounces chorizo sausage links, thickly sliced ½ of a green bell pepper, diced ½ of a red bell pepper, diced 1 medium onion, diced 2 cups uncooked rice 2 cups water 15-ounce can crushed tomatoes 1 gluten-free chicken bouillon cube 1 teaspoon garlic salt ½ teaspoon dried oregano 12 small (about 4 ounces) frozen precooked shrimp 1 cup frozen peas	*1* Heat a large skillet (one that has a lid) over medium-high heat. Cook the chicken and sausage uncovered, stirring now and then, until the meat is browned, about 5 minutes. Remove the chicken and sausage from the skillet and set the meat aside. *2* Wipe almost all the grease out of the skillet, leaving about a teaspoon's worth in the pan. Return the skillet to the burner. *3* Add the green bell pepper, red bell pepper, and onion to the skillet. Cook them for about 2 to 3 minutes, until they're brown. *4* Stir in the rice, water, tomatoes, chicken bouillon, garlic salt, and oregano, and add the chicken and sausage back to the skillet. Cover the skillet with the lid and reduce the heat to low. Simmer for 10 minutes. *5* Add the shrimp and peas to the skillet. Simmer, uncovered, for 10 minutes or until the liquid is evaporated.

Per serving: Calories 775 (From Fat 216); Fat 24g (Saturated 9g); Cholesterol 97mg; Sodium 1,613mg; Carbohydrate 98g (Dietary Fiber 6g); Protein 37g.

Note: Bags of shrimp usually list the shrimp size based on the number of shrimp per pound, so lower numbers mean larger shrimp. Small shrimp are usually labeled 51/60, meaning there are 51 to 60 shrimp per pound; in this case, each shrimp weighs about 0.3 ounces or a little less.

Easy Lasagna Pie

Prep time: 5 min • **Cook time:** 25 min • **Yield:** 4 servings

Ingredients	*Directions*
1 pound lean ground beef	*1* Preheat the oven to 375 degrees.
½ cup tomato sauce, plus more for serving	*2* Heat a large skillet over medium-high heat. Brown the ground beef, breaking up the beef with a spatula as you cook it. Drain the grease. Stir the tomato sauce into the beef.
⅓ cup ricotta cheese	
3 tablespoons grated Parmesan cheese	*3* Mix the ricotta cheese, Parmesan cheese, and salt in a small bowl.
½ teaspoon salt	
1 cup mozzarella cheese	*4* Spray a 9-inch pie plate with nonstick cooking spray and spread half the beef mixture in the pie plate. Drop the cheese mixture by spoonfuls onto the beef mixture. Sprinkle on ½ cup of the mozzarella. Top with the remaining beef mixture.
½ cup gluten-free biscuit or roll mix	
1 cup milk	
2 eggs	
	5 In a medium bowl, whisk together the biscuit mix, milk, and eggs. Pour it over the meat and cheese layers.
	6 Bake the pie for 20 minutes, or until a knife inserted in the center comes out clean. Sprinkle the pie with the remaining ½ cup mozzarella and bake 2 to 3 minutes longer.
	7 Let the pie cool for 5 minutes. Serve with additional heated tomato sauce.

Per serving: Calories 471 (From Fat 232); Fat 26g (Saturated 13g); Cholesterol 181mg; Sodium 953mg; Carbohydrate 19g (Dietary Fiber 1g); Protein 19g.

Tip: Simple and frugal, here's a twist on lasagna that everyone will love! Double the recipe and make it in a 9-x-13-inch pan if you want to feed a crowd.

Vary It! You can substitute soft tofu for the ricotta cheese to cut fat and boost the protein in this lasagna. Or you can use cottage cheese instead of ricotta, depending on your taste or the ingredients you have on hand.

Vary It! If you want to leave out the milk in Step 4, use water instead.

Oven-Fried Chicken Tenders

Prep time: 5 min • **Cook time:** 20 min • **Yield:** 4 servings

Ingredients	*Directions*
1 pound boneless, skinless chicken tenders **1 cup gluten-free Rice or Corn Chex cereal, crushed into crumbs** **½ cup gluten-free biscuit mix** **½ teaspoon black pepper** **1 teaspoon garlic salt** **½ teaspoon paprika** **½ to 1 cup lowfat milk**	*1* Preheat the oven to 400 degrees. Line a 9-x-13-inch pan or a cookie sheet with foil and spray it with nonstick cooking spray. *2* Pour the cereal crumbs, biscuit mix, pepper, garlic salt, and paprika into a large plastic bag. *3* Dip the chicken in a bowl of milk. Put the chicken into the bag a few pieces at a time, and shake the bag to coat the chicken with the crumbs. *4* Place the chicken onto the prepared pan or cookie sheet and bake for about 15 minutes. Turn each piece over and cook another 5 minutes, or until the chicken is thoroughly cooked, crispy, and no longer pink inside.

Per serving: Calories 278 (From Fat 42); Fat 5g (Saturated 1g); Cholesterol 98mg; Sodium 527mg; Carbohydrate 19g (Dietary Fiber 1g); Protein 19g.

Note: Throw out any extra coating mix. It touched raw chicken, so you can't save and reuse the coating.

Creating a comfortable crunch

To get a crispy coating or crunchy topping, try using these gluten-free ingredients:

- ✔ Crushed tortilla chips or Funyuns
- ✔ Toasted gluten-free bread, crumbled in a blender
- ✔ Crushed gluten-free rice or corn cereal or crackers
- ✔ Toasted sesame seeds, nuts, or shredded coconut (broiled on a baking sheet until lightly browned)
- ✔ Instant mashed potato buds

Coconut-Crusted Mahi-Mahi

Prep time: 5 min • **Cook time:** 15 min • **Yield:** 4 servings

Ingredients	*Directions*
½ cup gluten-free panko breadcrumbs	**1** Preheat the oven to 400 degrees. Line a baking sheet with parchment paper or foil sprayed with nonstick cooking spray.
¼ cup gluten-free sweetened, flaked coconut	
1 tablespoon gluten-free all-purpose flour	**2** In a shallow dish, mix the breadcrumbs, coconut, flour, cayenne, salt, and pepper.
¼ teaspoon cayenne pepper	
Salt to taste	**3** One at a time, dip the mahi-mahi fillets in water and roll them in the breadcrumb mix. Pat down the breadcrumb mixture on top of the fish to ensure liberal coverage.
Black pepper to taste	
Four 6-ounce mahi-mahi fillets	
2 tablespoons melted butter or olive oil	**4** Place the mahi-mahi fillets on the baking sheet and drizzle them with melted butter or olive oil.
	5 Bake the mahi-mahi for about 15 minutes, until the crust is golden and the fish flakes with a fork.

Per serving: Calories 247 (From Fat 82); Fat 9g (Saturated 5g); Cholesterol 149mg; Sodium 318mg; Carbohydrate 6g (Dietary Fiber 1g); Protein 34g.

Tip: If your mahi-mahi is frozen, be sure to thaw it before cooking. It's tough to get coating to stick to frozen fish, and frozen fish takes longer to cook and gets watery in the oven.

Tip: If you can't find gluten-free panko, you can use cracker crumbs or other gluten-free breadcrumbs. Check out Chapter 16 for directions on making your own breadcrumbs.

Tip: Serve your mahi-mahi with a serving of vegetables and hot rice.

Savory Sausage-Stuffed Portobello Mushrooms

Prep time: 5 min • **Cook time:** 25 min • **Yield:** 2 servings

Ingredients	*Directions*
8 ounces Italian sausage	*1* Preheat the oven to 375 degrees.
2 large portobello mushrooms	
½ cup gluten-free breadcrumbs	*2* Heat a large skillet over medium heat. Crumble and cook the Italian sausage until it's brown. Drain the sausage on paper towels.
¼ cup shredded Parmesan cheese	
1 teaspoon garlic salt	*3* While the sausage is cooking, gently wash the portobello mushrooms and scoop out the insides with a spoon.
1 teaspoon Italian seasoning	
Pinch of shredded mozzarella cheese	
½ cup marinara (tomato) sauce for serving	*4* In a medium bowl, stir together the cooked sausage, Parmesan, breadcrumbs, garlic salt, and Italian seasoning.
	5 Place both mushroom caps in an 8-x-8-inch baking dish. Fill each cap with half the sausage mixture and top with a pinch of mozzarella cheese.
	6 Bake for 20 minutes.
	7 Serve with marinara sauce on the side.

Per serving: Calories 335 (From Fat 192); Fat 21g (Saturated 8g); Cholesterol 56mg; Sodium 1,477mg; Carbohydrate 15g (Dietary Fiber 3g); Protein 20g.

Note: This recipe is so easy and delicious! Serve it as a main dish for two people or enjoy it as four separate side portions. You can use this sausage stuffing for regular-sized mushroom caps as well. No matter how much I make, people ask for more.

Note: Check the recipe for Spaghetti and Marinara Sauce earlier in this chapter to make your own marinara sauce.

Tip: Make your own breadcrumbs from stale gluten-free bread. Find out how in Chapter 16.

Simple Shepherd's Pie

Prep time: 5 min • **Cook time:** 25 min • **Yield:** 6 servings

Ingredients	*Directions*
8 ounces extra lean ground beef	*1* Preheat the oven to 400 degrees.
¼ cup chopped onion	*2* Heat a medium-sized skillet over medium-high heat. Add the ground beef, onion, Worcestershire sauce, salt, and Italian seasoning. Cook until the ground beef is brown, stirring occasionally and breaking up the meat with a spatula. Drain the grease from the pan.
1 tablespoon gluten-free Worcestershire sauce	
1 teaspoon salt	
½ teaspoon Italian seasoning	
2 cups frozen or canned mixed vegetables	*3* Stir the mixed vegetables into the cooked beef mixture. Pour that mixture into an 8-x-8-inch oven-safe dish.
2 cups mashed potatoes	
	4 Top the meat and veggie mixture with the mashed potatoes.
	5 Bake uncovered at 400 degrees for 20 minutes.

Per serving: Calories 155 (From Fat 48); Fat 5g (Saturated 3g); Cholesterol 17mg; Sodium 751mg; Carbohydrate 18g (Dietary Fiber 4g); Protein 9g.

Note: To feed 10 to 12 people, double the recipe and bake it in a 9-x-13-inch dish.

Tip: Make your mashed potatoes using real instant mashed potato flakes, or follow the directions in the nearby sidebar to make easy mashed potatoes from scratch.

Note: Lea & Perrins Worcestershire sauce is gluten-free.

Mashing potatoes

Preparing mashed potatoes from scratch isn't difficult, but it does take an extra 15 to 20 minutes. Any kind of potatoes will work, but I enjoy Yukon Gold. They turn out very creamy and have a mildly sweet flavor. Try a few different types to see what you like.

Here are the basic steps:

1. **Peel the potatoes (if desired) and cut the potatoes into 2- to 3-inch chunks.** Experiment with leaving the skins on for extra nutrition and texture. Small red potatoes are great with the skins.

2. **Put the potatoes in a large pot of salted, boiling water.** Boil the potatoes until they're tender, about 15 to 20 minutes. The timing depends on the size of your potato pieces. Poke them with a fork to check tenderness.

3. **Drain the water and add a few tablespoons of milk and butter to the pan of potatoes.** Any type of milk, from fat-free to heavy cream, will work. You can even use a dairy-free milk option.

4. **Mash the hot potatoes with a potato masher (find one in the kitchen gadget aisle of most grocery stores) or an electric mixer.**

5. **Add more milk and butter as needed until you get the texture and taste you want. Salt and pepper to taste.** Other possible add-ins include sour cream, bacon, cheese, garlic, and fresh herbs.

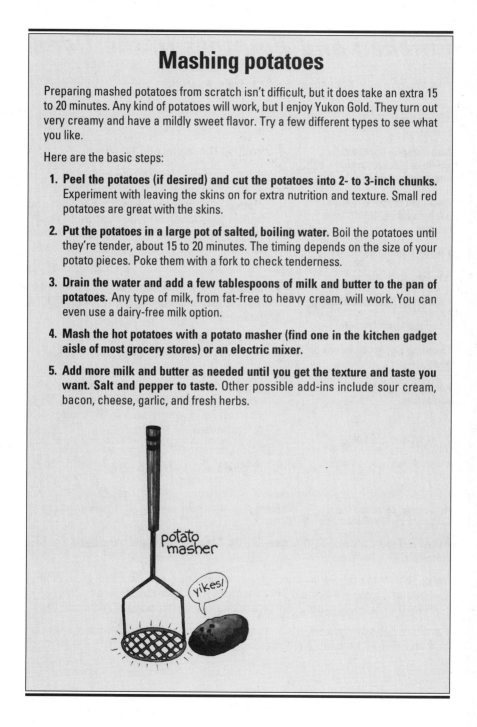

Chicken and Potatoes in the Oven

Prep time: 5 min • **Cook time:** 25 min • **Yield:** 6 servings

Ingredients	*Directions*
Two 4-ounce boneless, skinless chicken breasts, cut into 2-inch chunks	*1* Preheat the oven to 425 degrees.
2 medium russet potatoes, peeled and cut into 2-inch chunks	*2* In an 8-x-8-inch baking dish, add the chicken, potatoes, olive oil, garlic salt, and Italian seasoning. Stir the mixture to coat the chicken and potatoes with the oil and spices.
1 tablespoon olive oil	
½ teaspoon garlic salt	
1 teaspoon Italian seasoning	*3* Lightly cover the baking dish with a piece of aluminum foil (but don't seal it closed). Bake for 20 minutes.
1 cup marinara (tomato) sauce	
15-ounce can green beans or peas	*4* Pull the baking dish out of the oven and remove the foil. Add the pasta sauce and green beans or peas. Stir and cook uncovered for another 5 to 10 minutes, until the chicken is no longer pink in the center and the potatoes are tender.
Parmesan cheese for sprinkling	
	5 Sprinkle with Parmesan cheese.

Per serving: Calories 137 (From Fat 39); Fat 4g (Saturated 1g); Cholesterol 22mg; Sodium 413mg; Carbohydrate 15g (Dietary Fiber 3g); Protein 10g.

Note: To feed a crowd (10 to 12 people), double the recipe and bake it in a 9-x-13-inch dish.

Note: This recipe is from my great-grandmother, Lucy, who was from Italy. When asked what it was called, she'd say in her best New York Italian accent, "It's chicken. It's potatoes. In the oven." It's a long-time family favorite and super easy.

Tip: Store this dish covered in the refrigerator for up to a week. Reheat a plate full for about 45 to 60 seconds in the microwave.

Polenta-Stuffed Peppers

Prep time: 5 min • **Cook time:** 10 min • **Yield:** 4 servings

Ingredients	Directions
2 large green bell peppers	*1* Cut the bell peppers in half lengthwise. Remove the stems, seeds, and ribs from the peppers. Lay the peppers open side up in a microwave-safe dish.
½ cup instant polenta	
2 cups water	
2 tablespoons butter	*2* In a medium pot, bring the polenta, water, butter, and garlic salt to a boil over high heat. Immediately lower the heat to medium. Whisk the polenta continuously, cooking until the water is absorbed and the polenta has expanded. Whisk in the corn and cheese until the cheese is melted.
½ teaspoon garlic salt	
½ cup corn kernels	
1 cup shredded pepper Jack cheese	
	3 Pour the cooked polenta evenly into the peppers. Microwave on high for 3 to 4 minutes, or until the peppers are tender.

Per serving: Calories 278 (From Fat 131); Fat 15g (Saturated 9g); Cholesterol 41mg; Sodium 345mg; Carbohydrate 29g (Dietary Fiber 4g); Protein 10g.

Vary It! Bake the polenta in the oven at 425 degrees for 20 to 25 minutes if you prefer a firmer, crunchier dish.

Tip: Store the polenta-stuffed peppers covered in the refrigerator for up to a week. Reheat in the microwave for about 30 to 45 seconds.

Personal Chicken Pot Pies

Prep time: 5 min • **Cook time:** 20 min • **Yield:** 8 mini pies

Ingredients	*Directions*
8 ounces boneless, skinless chicken breast, diced	*1* Preheat the oven to 400 degrees. Spray 8 small ramekins with nonstick cooking spray.
2 cups gluten-free biscuit mix (plus ingredients the mix requires for biscuits)	*2* Spray a small skillet with nonstick cooking spray and sauté the diced chicken over medium-high heat until it's no longer pink.
12-ounce box gluten-free cream of chicken soup	
1½ cups frozen or canned mixed vegetables	*3* While the chicken is cooking, make the biscuit dough. Prepare the mix according to the package directions for biscuits and stir in ½ cup of the cheese.
1 cup shredded Monterey Jack cheese	
1 teaspoon onion powder	*4* Stir together the cooked chicken, soup, mixed vegetables, the remaining ½ cup cheese, onion powder, and garlic salt in a medium bowl.
1 teaspoon garlic salt	
	5 Spoon about 1 cup of the chicken mixture into each ramekin and top each with about ¼ cup biscuit dough.
	6 Bake for 13 to 15 minutes, or until the biscuits are lightly browned.

Per serving: Calories 364 (From Fat 153); Fat 17g (Saturated 9g); Cholesterol 130mg; Sodium 796mg; Carbohydrate 33g (Dietary Fiber 2g); Protein 18g.

Vary It! If you don't have ramekins, pour the chicken mixture into an oven-safe 8-x-8-inch baking dish sprayed with nonstick cooking spray. Top it with the biscuit mixture and bake in a 400-degree oven for 13 to 15 minutes, or until the biscuits are lightly browned.

Tip: To save time, use 2 cups rotisserie chicken instead of raw chicken.

Tip: Store the pot pies covered in the fridge for a few days. Reheat one for 45 to 60 seconds in the microwave.

Sloppy Joe Cornbread Casserole

Prep time: 5 min • **Cook time:** 30 min • **Yield:** 6 servings

Ingredients	*Directions*
1¼ pounds (20 ounces) lean ground beef	*1* Preheat the oven to 350 degrees.
¼ cup finely chopped onion	*2* Heat a large skillet over medium-high heat. Add the beef, onion, and Worcestershire sauce. Cook, stirring frequently and breaking up the meat with a spatula, until the beef is brown. Drain the grease.
2 teaspoons gluten-free Worcestershire sauce	
12-ounce package gluten-free cornbread mix (plus ingredients the mix requires for cornbread)	*3* While the meat is browning, prepare the cornbread mix according to the package directions (but don't bake it yet!).
15-ounce can corn, drained	
15-ounce can tomato sauce	*4* Mix the corn, tomato sauce, and brown sugar with the meat. Pour the meat mixture into an 8-x-8-inch baking dish.
2 tablespoons brown sugar	
¾ cup shredded cheddar cheese	*5* Sprinkle the meat mixture with ¼ cup of the cheddar cheese. Drop the cornbread mixture by spoonfuls on top. Add the remaining ½ cup cheese.
	6 Bake 20 to 25 minutes, or until the cornbread is cooked through.

Per serving: Calories 600 (From Fat 227); Fat 25g (Saturated 8g); Cholesterol 110mg; Sodium 700mg; Carbohydrate 64g (Dietary Fiber 4g); Protein 30g.

Vary It! To make this a quicker-to-table dish, leave out the onion, Worcestershire sauce, tomato sauce, and brown sugar and use store-bought canned sloppy joe sauce instead. Double-check the sauce for gluten-free status.

Bueno Beef Burrito Bake

Prep time: 5 min • **Cook time:** 25 min • **Yield:** 6 servings

Ingredients	Directions
1 cup gluten-free biscuit mix 16-ounce can refried beans ¼ cup water	**1** Preheat the oven to 400 degrees. Spray an 8-x-8-inch baking dish with nonstick cooking spray.
1 pound lean ground beef, cooked and drained 1 cup salsa	**2** In small bowl, stir together the biscuit mix, beans, and water. Spread the mixture into the baking dish.
1 cup shredded cheese, any type ¼ cup black olives	**3** Top the dough with the ground beef, then salsa, and then cheese.
¼ cup chopped fresh tomatoes	**4** Bake for 20 minutes.
¼ cup fat-free sour cream ¼ cup chopped green onions	**5** Top with the olives, tomatoes, sour cream, and green onions.

Per serving: Calories 355 (From Fat 118); Fat 13g (Saturated 6g); Cholesterol 48mg; Sodium 859mg; Carbohydrate 35g (Dietary Fiber 5g); Protein 35g.

Tip: Make this with ground turkey or use lowfat cheese for a lower-fat version.

Tip: To feed a crowd, double this recipe and prepare it in a 9-x-13-inch pan.

Dreamy Creamy Chicken Enchiladas

Prep time: 5 min • **Cook time:** 25 min • **Yield:** 6 servings

Ingredients	Directions
Two 10-ounce cans premium white chicken in water, drained	*1* Preheat the oven to 375 degrees.
12-ounce box or can gluten-free cream of chicken soup	*2* In a small bowl, stir together the chicken, soup, sour cream, garlic salt, chilies, and 1 cup of the cheese.
1 cup fat-free sour cream	
1 teaspoon garlic salt	*3* Spoon about 2 tablespoons of the chicken mixture into the center of each tortilla, reserving a bit of the chicken mixture for the top of the enchiladas. Roll up the enchiladas and place them side by side in a 9-x-13-inch baking dish.
3-ounce can green chilies	
1½ cups Monterey Jack or Mexican mix shredded cheese	
12 white corn tortillas	*4* Top the rolled enchiladas with the remaining chicken mixture, olives, and ½ cup cheese.
¼ cup black olives	
	5 Bake for 20 to 25 minutes, until the cheese is bubbly.

Per serving: Calories 392 (From Fat 122); Fat 14g (Saturated 7g); Cholesterol 72mg; Sodium 1,352mg; Carbohydrate 36g (Dietary Fiber 4g); Protein 33g.

Note: Find a recipe for Cream of Anything Soup in the sidebar earlier in this chapter.

Tip: Use 2½ cups leftover cooked chicken in place of the canned chicken.

Quick Chili

Prep time: 5 min • **Cook time:** 25 min • **Yield:** 4 servings

Ingredients	*Directions*
1 pound lean ground beef 28-ounce can crushed tomatoes	*1* Heat a large skillet over medium-high heat. Brown the ground beef, stirring and breaking up the meat with a spatula. Drain the grease from the pan if necessary.
15-ounce can kidney beans, drained 1 tablespoon gluten-free chili powder	*2* Add the tomatoes, beans, chili powder, cumin, and garlic salt to the beef in the skillet. Stir.
1 teaspoon cumin ½ teaspoon garlic salt	*3* Let the mixture come to a boil, and then reduce the heat to a simmer. Cook the chili uncovered for 15 to 20 minutes.
Shredded cheddar cheese for topping Corn chips for topping	*4* Serve the chili in bowls. Top it with a pinch of cheese and a few corn chips.

Per serving: Calories 287 (From Fat 83); Fat 9g (Saturated 3g); Cholesterol 31mg; Sodium 606mg; Carbohydrate 27g (Dietary Fiber 8g); Protein 25g.

Part III

Going Beyond Three Squares

Five Great Ways to Use Stale Gluten-Free Bread

Even if your pricey gluten-free bread has aged beyond sandwich quality, you don't need to toss it in the garbage. Here are five ideas for using your stale bread:

✓ **Croutons:** Make croutons by buttering the bread, cutting it into cubes, and broiling it until it's very crispy. Store croutons in the freezer and use them anytime.

✓ **Breadcrumbs:** Pulverize the bread in a blender or food processor to make breadcrumbs for coatings, meatballs or meatloaf filler, or casserole toppings.

✓ **French toast:** Use the bread for French toast, where stale bread is best.

✓ **Bread pudding:** Use it for making bread pudding.

✓ **Garlic toast:** Make garlic toast by brushing the bread with olive oil, adding Italian seasonings and garlic salt, and broiling until crispy.

web extras

Discover delicious and satisfying pizza toppings for a quick meal or late-night snack in the article "Topping Ideas for Gluten-Free Pizza" at www.dummies.com/extras/studentsglutenfreecookbook.

In this part . . .

- ✔ Go beyond the basic three meals and find terrific gluten-free recipes for salads, soups, sides, and even study snacks.
- ✔ Make delicious desserts for a quick indulgence or special occasion.
- ✔ Find out how to use and revive leftovers to get the most from your grocery budget.

Chapter 13

Sensational Soups, Salads, and Sides

In This Chapter

▶ Making soups

▶ Fixing sassy side salads

▶ Preparing simple but sophisticated side dishes

*M*ost restaurant and store-bought soups are loaded with flour or wheat-based pasta; salads are laden with gluten-filled ingredients and dressings; and sides are often swimming in unsafe sauces for the gluten-intolerant diner. Luckily, that doesn't mean you need to give up these staples of everyday eating! By creating your own creamy soups, sassy salads, and sophisticated and delicious sides with the easy directions in this chapter, you can enjoy a hearty bowl of steamy soup and saucy accompaniments just like you did before you began your gluten-free diet.

Enjoy these satisfying foods as a stand-alone snack, light meal, or quick bite between classes. Or serve them alongside a main dish to add some flair.

Supping on Soups

Sipping soups is great when you need some comforting food, you're nursing a stuffy nose, or you just want to warm your belly. Soups can also be the perfect meal to take with you in a cup when you need to eat away from home.

Many soups — both the brothy, clear variety and the thick and creamy kind — are traditionally made with gluten-containing ingredients. To make your own healthy yet decadent gluten-free soups, use some of these ideas:

✔ For thickness, add cooked, mashed starchy vegetables to soups. Try butternut squash, sweet potatoes, russet potatoes, cauliflower, pumpkin puree, beans, or broccoli to get a bit of flavor and a nutrient boost, too.

✔ For creaminess, add some reduced-fat or fat-free sour cream or plain Greek yogurt to your soup at the end of the preparation process.

✔ Puree soups in a blender with a bit of cooked rice to add thickness without fat.

✔ Throw in some instant real mashed potato flakes to make soups thick and creamy.

✔ Use reduced or nonfat milk thickened with gluten-free flour or cornstarch.

More and more commercially available soups are labeled gluten-free, so if you're interested in the convenience of store-bought soups, check the label. You can also search online for the gluten-free soup offerings of specific companies. See Chapter 19 for recommendations.

Grandma's Chicken Tortilla Soup

Prep time: 5 min • **Cook time:** 25 min • **Yield:** 8 servings

Ingredients	*Directions*
1 tablespoon vegetable oil	*1* Heat the oil in a large pot over medium heat. Sauté the chicken, onion, carrots, bell pepper, and rice for about 5 minutes. The chicken will continue cooking in the soup.
1 pound chicken breasts, cut into ½-inch strips	
½ of a medium onion, diced	
½ cup thinly sliced carrots	*2* Add the chicken broth and let the soup come to a simmer, with small bubbles just beginning to break the surface.
¼ of a green bell pepper, diced	
⅓ cup white rice (not instant)	*3* Add the tomatoes to the pot. Reduce the heat to medium-low and cover the pot. Simmer the soup until the rice is tender, about 20 minutes.
32 ounces nonfat gluten-free chicken broth	
15-ounce can diced tomatoes	
15-ounce can pinto beans, drained and rinsed	*4* Add the beans, corn, and cilantro to the soup. Taste the soup and add salt as needed. When the soup returns to a simmer, it's ready to serve.
15-ounce can corn, drained	
3 to 4 fresh cilantro sprigs, chopped	
Salt to taste	*5* Top each bowlful of soup with crushed tortilla chips.
1 cup crushed corn tortilla chips	

Per serving: Calories 238 (From Fat 61); Fat 7g (Saturated 1g); Cholesterol 34mg; Sodium 844mg; Carbohydrate 28g (Dietary Fiber 5g); Protein 17g.

Note: You can use 2 cups fresh or frozen corn instead of canned without adjusting cooking time. Corn cooks quickly, and the crispness of fresh corn is nice. For softer kernels, add fresh corn to the soup a few minutes earlier than indicated in the recipe.

Tip: Top this soup with your favorite toppings. Try grated cheddar cheese, sliced avocado, sour cream, black olives, chopped tomatoes, and even shredded lettuce.

Note: Cover and refrigerate this soup for up to a few days. Reheat it in the microwave or in a pot on the stove over medium heat until it's steaming.

Beefy Quinoa Soup

Prep time: 5 min • **Cook time:** 25 min • **Yield:** 4 servings

Ingredients	*Directions*
1 tablespoon vegetable oil	*1* Heat the oil in a large pot over medium-high heat.
8 ounces stew beef, cut into cubes	
½ cup finely diced onion	*2* Place the beef, onions, carrots, and celery in the pot. Sauté for about 5 minutes, until the veggies start to soften and the meat is brown.
½ cup finely diced carrots	
½ cup finely diced celery	
4 cups gluten-free beef broth	*3* Add the broth, quinoa, rosemary, thyme, and parsley to the pot. Let the soup come to a simmer, with the bubbles just beginning to break the surface.
¼ cup quinoa, rinsed	
½ tablespoon dried rosemary	
½ tablespoon dried thyme	*4* Reduce the heat to medium-low. Cover and simmer the soup for about 15 minutes.
½ tablespoon dried parsley	
¼ cup green beans	*5* Add the green beans and continue to simmer another 5 minutes, or until the quinoa is tender. Season the soup with salt and pepper to taste.
Salt to taste	
Black pepper to taste	

Per serving: Calories 201 (From Fat 74); Fat 8g (Saturated 2g); Cholesterol 35mg; Sodium 1,119mg; Carbohydrate 14g (Dietary Fiber 3g); Protein 18g.

Note: The smaller you cut your meat and veggies, the less time it takes to cook them in Step 2.

Vary It! Make this into a vegetarian soup by using vegetable broth instead of beef broth and adding 1½ cups additional vegetables instead of beef. Mushrooms and diced tomatoes are good!

Vary It! Use rice if you don't have quinoa.

Tip: I prefer canned Italian cut green beans in this recipe. They're thick and short and work well for soup. Fresh or frozen would work, too. If you choose to use fresh or frozen green beans, wait until the last 5 or 10 minutes of cooking time to add them to the soup to avoid overcooking them.

Loaded Baked Potato Soup

Prep time: 5 min • **Cook time:** 20 min • **Yield:** 4 servings

Ingredients	Directions
2 large russet potatoes	*1* Wash the potatoes and pat them dry. Microwave the potatoes on high for 6 to 8 minutes on a microwave-safe plate, until the potatoes are soft when you pierce them with a fork.
1½ cups gluten-free chicken broth	
2½ cups lowfat milk	
⅓ cup plus 2 tablespoons shredded cheddar cheese	*2* Cut the potatoes in half and let them cool for a few minutes. Scoop out the middle of the potatoes and coarsely mash the insides with a potato masher or a fork. Discard the skin.
1 tablespoon dried onion flakes	
Salt to taste	
Black pepper to taste	*3* In a large pot, combine the potatoes, chicken broth, milk, ⅓ cup of the cheese, onion flakes, and salt and pepper. Cook on medium-low, until the soup is warm and the cheese is melted, stirring often. Don't boil the soup.
2 tablespoons lowfat sour cream	
3 slices bacon, cooked and crumbled	
2 tablespoons chopped fresh chives	*4* Divide the soup into four bowls and top each serving with ½ tablespoon cheese and the sour cream, bacon, and chives.

Per serving: Calories 264 (From Fat 98); Fat 11g (Saturated 5g); Cholesterol 28mg; Sodium 695mg; Carbohydrate 29g (Dietary Fiber 2g); Protein 13g.

Vary It! Use lowfat turkey bacon to cut the fat content in this soup.

Note: Cover and refrigerate this soup for up to 3 days. Reheat it in a bowl for about a minute in the microwave, or heat it in a pot on the stove over medium heat until the soup is steamy.

Creamy Tomato Basil Soup

Prep time: 5 min • **Cook time:** 15 min • **Yield:** 4 servings

Ingredients	*Directions*
28-ounce can crushed tomatoes	*1* In a large uncovered pot, cook the tomatoes, basil, broth, milk, garlic salt, and pepper over medium heat for 10 to 15 minutes.
10 to 15 fresh basil leaves, finely chopped	
2 cups gluten-free chicken or vegetable broth	*2* Top the soup with gluten-free croutons.
1½ cups fat-free milk	
½ teaspoon garlic salt	
Black pepper to taste	
Gluten-free croutons	

Per serving: Calories 142(From Fat 33); Fat 4g (Saturated 1g); Cholesterol 4mg; Sodium 929mg; Carbohydrate 23g (Dietary Fiber 4g); Protein 7g.

Note: To use fresh tomatoes, peel and seed about 4 tomatoes and pulse them in the blender with the fresh basil leaves; then follow the directions as stated in the recipe.

Vary It! Add ¼ cup shredded cheddar or Parmesan cheese while cooking, or sprinkle cheese on top before serving.

Tip: Follow the homemade-crouton directions in the next section for an extra tasty topping.

Note: If you don't have fresh basil, add about 1 tablespoon dried basil.

Note: Cover and store this soup in the fridge for up to a week.

Broccoli Cheese Soup

Prep time: 5 min • **Cook time:** 20 min • **Yield:** 4 servings

Ingredients	Directions
3 cups lowfat or fat-free milk **1 cup gluten-free chicken broth** **12-ounce package frozen broccoli florets** **4 ounces Velveeta** **½ cup shredded Swiss cheese** **¾ teaspoon garlic salt** **¼ teaspoon black pepper**	**1** Place the milk, chicken broth, broccoli, Velveeta, Swiss cheese, garlic salt, and pepper in a large pot over medium heat. Stir until the cheese is melted. Cook uncovered, stirring occasionally, for 15 minutes, or until the broccoli is tender. **2** Mash the soup with a potato masher to break up the broccoli a little more.

Per serving: Calories 264 (From Fat 126); Fat 14g (Saturated 9g); Cholesterol 45mg; Sodium 975mg; Carbohydrate 16g (Dietary Fiber 3g); Protein 19g.

Note: Even if you're not much of a broccoli person, this soup is great! My dad used to jokingly say, "Why eat broccoli? Eat chocolate and take a vitamin!" But even he loves this soup.

Sassy Side Salads

From an exotic quinoa salad to standard American, Greek, or Italian side salad options, this section offers enticing recipes for vegging up your meals. These salads are a great accompaniment to a gluten-free meal, but they also make a good snack or light lunch or dinner on their own, especially if you serve them with one of the delicious soups I include earlier in this chapter. You can also find meal-sized salads in Chapter 10.

Topping your greens

For me, a great salad is judged by what it has in it besides lettuce. The more stuff, the better. Throwing in some extra fixin's can add extra nutrition, too.

Try some of these ingredients:

- ✔ **Beans:** Try garbanzo beans (chickpeas), kidney beans, black beans, or green beans for added fiber.

- ✔ **Seeds:** Try sesame seeds, pine nuts, pumpkin seeds, chia seeds, or flax seeds. Seeds add protein, fiber, and trace vitamins and minerals as well as a nice crunch.

- ✔ **Nuts:** Nuts add crunch along with protein, fiber, and healthy fats.

- ✔ **Tomatoes:** Like some lycopene? Tomatoes are high in this antioxidant.

- ✔ **Fruit:** Throw in some apple chunks, raisins, or dried cranberries. They're a lowfat way to add vitamins and sweetness.

- ✔ **Cheese:** Add some flavor and protein with cheese or a dairy-free cheese substitute.

- ✔ **Chicken, ham, or turkey:** Mix in some lowfat meats to make your salad more filling and protein-filled.

- ✔ **Bacon:** Crumbled bacon adds a little protein and a lot of flavor. Use lowfat turkey bacon for a slightly healthier version.

Making croutons

Try making homemade croutons! They're easy to prepare, and this is a great way to use up your stale bread. Follow these easy steps to make your own gluten-free croutons:

1. **Butter both sides of gluten-free bread (or drizzle the bread with olive oil) and sprinkle on your favorite spices.**

   I use garlic salt and Italian seasoning. You can also try dill, Parmesan, chili powder, or whatever you like.

2. **Cut the bread into crouton-sized cubes and place them on a baking sheet.**

3. **Put the croutons in the oven on broil (no need to preheat the oven).**

   The closer the pan is to the heating element at the top of the oven, the quicker the croutons will cook. Watch for the bread to turn brown and crispy all over the top, not just on the edges. If the croutons aren't super crispy, they'll get soggy in your salad.

4. **Remove the croutons from the oven, stir them with a spatula or large spoon, and broil the croutons again until you see the top of the bread getting crisp.**

   Repeat several times until the bread is crisp all the way around.

5. **After cooling the croutons, place them in a large plastic bag and freeze them.**

   You can use the croutons straight from the freezer. Just throw them on a salad or in a bowl of soup, or use them as a casserole topping.

Picnic Veggie Salad

Prep time: 2 min • **Chill time:** 30 min • **Yield:** 2 servings

Ingredients	*Directions*
15-ounce can mixed vegetables, drained	*1* Combine the mixed vegetables, egg, mayonnaise, cheddar, salt, and pepper in a small bowl. Stir and then chill the salad for at least 30 minutes.
1 hard-boiled egg, chopped	
2 to 3 tablespoons light mayonnaise	
¼ cup cheddar cheese chunks	
Salt to taste	
Black pepper to taste	

Per serving: Calories 211 (From Fat 113); Fat 13g (Saturated 5g); Cholesterol 113mg; Sodium 596mg; Carbohydrate 15g (Dietary Fiber 4g); Protein 10g.

Note: This side salad is not fancy, but it's been a family favorite for two generations, and it just happens to be gluten-free!

Note: Cover leftovers and save them in the fridge for a few days.

Note: Find directions on hard-boiling eggs in Chapter 8.

BLTA Salad

Prep time: 5 min • **Yield:** 2 servings

Ingredients	*Directions*
2 cups chopped iceberg lettuce	*1* Divide the lettuce into a couple of bowls.
1 tomato, chopped	*2* Add the tomato and avocado to the lettuce. Top the salads with crumbled bacon and ranch dressing.
1 avocado, chopped	
3 slices bacon, cooked and crumbled	
4 tablespoons gluten-free ranch dressing	

Per serving: *Calories 285 (From Fat 221); Fat 25g (Saturated 5g); Cholesterol 13mg; Sodium 343mg; Carbohydrate 14g (Dietary Fiber 9g); Protein 8g.*

Note: Check the ranch dressing for gluten-free status.

Tip: My new favorite dressing line is Bolthouse Farms. Find this yogurt-based, lowfat, preservative-free, gluten-free dressing in the refrigerator of your produce section.

Breezy Caprese Salad

Prep time: 5 min • **Yield:** 2 servings

Ingredients	*Directions*
1 large tomato	*1* Slice the tomato and the mozzarella into ¼-inch thick slices.
4 ounces fresh mozzarella cheese	
5 to 7 baby spinach leaves	*2* Alternate the tomato, cheese, and spinach leaves on a plate, stacking them and overlapping them slightly.
1 tablespoon olive oil	
4 teaspoons balsamic vinegar	*3* Drizzle the arranged cheese and veggies with oil, balsamic vinegar, salt, and pepper.
Salt to taste	
Black pepper to taste	

Per serving: Calories 249 (From Fat 191); Fat 21g (Saturated 9g); Cholesterol 41mg; Sodium 191mg; Carbohydrate 6g (Dietary Fiber 1g); Protein 11g.

Tip: Get the freshest ingredients possible for the best flavor in this dish. It's a great salad to enjoy after a trip to a farmers' market.

Vary It! Use fresh basil leaves instead of spinach if you prefer a more powerful flavor.

Momma Mia Italian Potato Salad

Prep time: 5 min • **Cook time:** 20 min • **Yield:** 4 servings

Ingredients	Directions
½ **tablespoon salt**	*1* Boil a large pot of water with ½ tablespoon salt over high heat.
2 large russet potatoes	
2 tablespoons olive oil	*2* Cut each of the potatoes into four large chunks and place them in the boiling water. When water returns to boil, turn the heat down to medium and continue boiling until the potatoes are tender when you poke them with a fork, about 10 to 15 minutes.
2 teaspoons Italian seasoning	
2 tablespoons chopped flat-leaf parsley	
1 teaspoon garlic salt	
1 stalk celery, chopped	
	3 Drain and cool the potatoes. Peel and cut them into smaller chunks.
	4 Stir together the oil, Italian seasoning, parsley, and garlic salt in a small bowl. Add the oil mixture and celery to the potatoes and stir to coat the potatoes. Add more oil or garlic salt to taste.

Per serving: Calories 149 (From Fat 62); Fat 7g (Saturated 1g); Cholesterol 0mg; Sodium 694mg; Carbohydrate 21g (Dietary Fiber 2g); Protein 2g.

Tip: Don't peel and dice the potatoes before cooking them. They can fall apart and get mushy if you boil them when they're small. Peeling and cutting the larger cooked potato chunks is a breeze.

Note: This potato salad is a great alternative to the traditional mayonnaise-laden potato salad, and it's especially good for an outdoor event. If you have any leftovers, fry them for breakfast with some eggs.

Note: Cover and store this potato salad in the refrigerator for up to a week.

Corny Bean Salad

Prep time: 5 min • **Yield:** 4 servings

Ingredients	Directions
15-ounce can corn, drained	*1* Combine the corn, black beans, onion, parsley, olive oil, and balsamic vinegar in a serving bowl. Toss the ingredients. Add salt and pepper to taste.
15-ounce can black beans, rinsed and drained	
½ cup finely chopped red onion	
¼ cup chopped flat-leaf parsley	*2* Serve this salad cold or at room temperature. No cooking!
2 tablespoons olive oil	
1 tablespoon balsamic vinegar	
Salt to taste	
Black pepper to taste	

Per serving: Calories 189 (From Fat 73); Fat 8g (Saturated 1g); Cholesterol 0mg; Sodium 446mg; Carbohydrate 25g (Dietary Fiber 6g); Protein 6g.

Note: This veggie side salad is light and delicious. It looks and tastes like much more work than it really is.

Note: You can replace the canned corn with 2 ears fresh corn, cooked and cut off the cob, or about 2 cups thawed frozen corn. Check out the section "Picking and preparing corn on the cob" later in this chapter for tips on finding and preparing the tastiest corn.

Greek Veggie Salad

Prep time: 5 min • **Chill time:** 30 min • **Yield:** 2 servings

Ingredients	Directions
1 large tomato, diced	**1** Mix the tomato, cucumber, onion, olives, cheese, oil, lemon juice, oregano, salt, and pepper in a serving bowl.
1 large cucumber, diced	
¼ of a red onion, diced	
8 Kalamata olives, sliced in half and pitted	**2** Refrigerate for at least 30 minutes and serve the salad chilled.
¼ cup crumbled feta cheese	
2 tablespoons olive oil	
1 teaspoon lemon juice	
½ teaspoon oregano	
Salt to taste	
Black pepper to taste	

Per serving: Calories 254 (From Fat 198); Fat 22g (Saturated 5g); Cholesterol 17mg; Sodium 611mg; Carbohydrate 12g (Dietary Fiber 3g); Protein 5g.

Tip: Enjoy this Greek treat as a side salad or top it with some chopped grilled chicken to make it a complete meal!

Simply Sophisticated Sides

When starting to cook gluten-free, simpler is often better — after all, just deciphering ingredients takes some work. You may stick with one-ingredient main dishes such as grilled meats and fish and very simple sides until you get used to the do's and don'ts. But when you're ready to experiment, try some of the quick, easy, and satisfying recipes that follow.

Pairing sides with main dishes

To figure out which side dishes to pair with which main dishes, follow this simple rule: If your main dish has multiple ingredients, stick with a simple side salad or sautéed veggies. If your main dish is simple, jazz up your meal with a more complex side.

Contrasting colors, flavors, and textures is also a good idea. So if your main dish is creamy, your sides shouldn't be. If you have a spicy main dish, keep your side mild. And don't fill a plate with everything beige. That can be a cute décor scheme for a living room, but try to liven things up with your meals. Variety tends to make meals more interesting and healthier, too.

Cooking fresh veggies

There are as many different ways to prepare vegetables as there are vegetables, but here are some basic techniques:

- ✔ **Steaming:** Use a steamer basket to hold the veggies above a small amount of boiling water in a saucepan, or put the vegetables in a small amount of boiling water. Cover the saucepan to hold the steam in.

  To steam in the microwave, add a few tablespoons of water to the veggies in a microwave-safe bowl and cover it with plastic wrap. Microwave for 3 to 4 minutes, depending on type and amount of veggies. Try this with carrots, asparagus, broccoli, and others.

- ✔ **Boiling:** Cut vegetables into chunks before boiling to reduce the cooking time. Cover the vegetables with water, bring it to a boil, and let the veggies cook until they're tender. This method is best for making mashed potatoes.

- ✔ **Sautéing:** Cook vegetables in a skillet over medium-high heat with a small amount of butter or oil, stirring occasionally, until the veggies are tender. For even cooking, use a large enough pan so the veggies can spread out in one layer.

✔ **Frying:** Cut vegetables into small pieces and cook them in about a tablespoon of hot oil in a skillet on the stove over medium heat until they're tender. Lower the temperature if oil splatters out of the pan. To deep fry, use a few inches of oil. Pour the used oil in a jar, put the lid on, and dump it in the trash after the oil hardens.

✔ **Stewing and braising:** Simmer or boil the vegetables over low heat in very little liquid. This causes veggies like tomatoes to make their own sauce, for a stew-like result.

✔ **Baking or microwaving:** Vegetables such as potatoes and squash can be cooked in their skins. Any vegetables can be stuffed or mixed with other ingredients or sauces and then baked or microwaved.

✔ **Broiling:** Broiling cooks vegetables rapidly. Adjust the oven rack so the vegetables are 6 to 10 inches from the top heating element to create a crisp top crust on any veggies that are already softened. Watch carefully to be sure the vegetables don't burn. This is a great way to give new life to a dish full of leftover veggies or those that are in their last days.

✔ **Grilling:** You can cook large vegetables directly on the grill. Grill small ones on a sheet of foil or wrap them in foil for steaming, or put them on a skewer and turn them every few minutes on the grill. Zucchini, mushrooms, peppers, onions, and potatoes all work great on the grill.

Picking and preparing corn on the cob

One of my favorite side dishes is fresh corn, so it's a good thing that picking the tastiest fresh corn is a breeze. First, look for the freshest ears of corn you can find. Choose corn husks that are green in color with light brown silk attached. Pull a piece of the husk a little away from the top so you can see the kernels inside. They should be plump, juicy, and firm. If the kernels are dry, the corn is old, so pick a different ear.

To store fresh corn, leave it in the husks and put it in your refrigerator. But don't store it too long; corn becomes less sweet as time passes!

When you're ready to *shuck*, or clean, the corn, peel off the husk from the top — just pull it down. Do this with each piece of the husk until it's all pulled down to the stem. Then grab the husk and pull it off, breaking the stem with it. To remove the strands of silk, wipe your dry hand over the corn from the top to the bottom several times. Wipe a clean, damp paper towel over the corn to clean off the remainder of the silk. Finally, rinse the ear of corn well under cool tap water. Now the corn is ready to cook and eat.

There are many quick and easy ways to cook corn on the cob. Here are a few of them:

- ✔ Microwave it in the husk for about 6 minutes. Then shuck the corn and add butter and spices. The husk creates a packet of steam that makes a perfect ear of corn.

- ✔ Shuck the corn, add butter and spices, and place the corn in a microwave-safe dish. Cover the corn and microwave it for 5 to 8 minutes.

- ✔ Shuck the corn and place the ears in a large pot of salted boiling water for about 5 minutes. Immediately remove the corn from the water and add butter and spices.

- ✔ Shuck the corn and add butter and spices. Place the corn on the grill and turn it occasionally. Delicious corn will be ready in 5 to 10 minutes.

- ✔ Place the ears of corn in the husks directly on the grill when you put the meat on. They'll turn black outside, but the corn inside will be steamy and ready when the meat is ready. Shuck the corn and add butter and spices.

Spices can include salt, pepper, chili powder, garlic salt, dill, onion powder, or any other spice you like. But fresh corn can also be great without adding a thing. Give it a try!

Sinfully Cinnamon Baked Apples

Prep time: 2 min • **Cook time:** 5 min • **Yield:** 4 servings

Ingredients	Directions
4 tart apples	**1** Peel and core the apples. Cut them into small chunks.
2 tablespoons butter	
½ tablespoon cinnamon	**2** Place the apples in a microwave-safe dish and top them with butter, cinnamon, and sugar. Cover the dish with plastic wrap and microwave the apples for about 4 minutes, or until apples are soft.
¼ cup brown sugar	
¼ cup chopped pecans	
	3 Stir the apple mixture and then drain out most of the liquid, leaving only a small amount in the dish. Sprinkle the apples with nuts and microwave for another 30 seconds.

Per serving: *Calories 237 (From Fat 104); Fat 12g (Saturated 4g); Cholesterol 15mg; Sodium 6mg; Carbohydrate 36g (Dietary Fiber 5g); Protein 1g.*

Tip: These apples are great for a dessert or side dish!

Note: Try Granny Smith apples. Their tartness balances the sweetness of the brown sugar.

Polenta Parmesan

Prep time: 2 min • **Cook time:** 2 min • **Yield:** 4 servings

Ingredients	*Directions*
18-ounce roll polenta	*1* Slice the polenta into about eight ½-inch slices.
1 cup tomato sauce	
1 cup shredded mozzarella cheese	*2* Place the polenta on a microwave-safe plate. Cover each slice of polenta with tomato sauce, cheese, and Italian seasoning.
1 tablespoon Italian seasoning	
	3 Microwave the polenta for 60 to 90 seconds.

Per serving: Calories 198 (From Fat 64); Fat 7g (Saturated 4g); Cholesterol 25mg; Sodium 883mg; Carbohydrate 24g (Dietary Fiber 2g); Protein 10g.

Vary It! For a crispier dish, bake the polenta in a 375-degree oven for 15 minutes.

Vary It! Use ½ tablespoon fresh chopped basil and ½ tablespoon fresh chopped oregano in place of the Italian seasoning.

Dilly Mashed Cauliflower

Prep time: 5 min • **Cook time:** 15 min • **Yield:** 4 servings

Ingredients	*Directions*
1 large head cauliflower	*1* Wash the cauliflower under running water, break it apart, and remove the large stems.
1 teaspoon salt	
2 tablespoons butter	*2* Place the cauliflower in a pot and cover the cauliflower with about 3 inches of water. Add about a teaspoon of salt.
¼ cup lowfat milk	
1 teaspoon garlic salt	
1 teaspoon dried dill	*3* Bring the water to a boil over high heat. Then lower the heat to medium and cook for 7 to 10 minutes, or until the cauliflower stems are tender when you poke them with a fork.
	4 Drain the water from the pot. Add the butter, milk, garlic salt, and dill to the cauliflower.
	5 Beat the cauliflower with an electric mixer on medium speed until the cauliflower is smooth. Add more milk if needed to create a smoother texture.

Per serving: Calories 110 (From Fat 57); Fat 6g (Saturated 4g); Cholesterol 16mg; Sodium 369mg; Carbohydrate 12g (Dietary Fiber 5g); Protein 5g.

Vary It! Leave out the dill if you're not a fan. Add curry, chili powder, Italian seasoning, or Cajun seasoning, or just enjoy the buttery taste with no extra spices.

Note: Cauliflower is a delicious low-carb, high-nutrient substitute for potatoes.

Certifiably Cheesy Polenta

Prep time: 5 min • **Cook time:** 30 min • **Yield:** 6 servings

Ingredients	*Directions*
½ cup polenta	*1* Preheat the oven to 400 degrees. Spray an 8-x-8-inch baking dish with nonstick cooking spray.
¼ cup (4 tablespoons) butter	
2 cups water	*2* Add the polenta, butter, and water to a small pot. Bring the mixture to a boil over high heat and then lower the heat. Cook and stir until the polenta is thickened.
¼ cup milk	
1 cup shredded cheddar cheese	
1 teaspoon garlic salt	*3* Pour the polenta mixture in the prepared baking dish. Add the milk, cheese, garlic salt, and beaten egg to the polenta. Stir to combine the ingredients.
1 egg, beaten	
	4 Bake the polenta for 25 minutes, or until the mixture is firm.

Per serving: Calories 215 (From Fat 135); Fat 15g (Saturated 9g); Cholesterol 73mg; Sodium 370mg; Carbohydrate 13g (Dietary Fiber 1g); Protein 8g.

Note: This is my favorite side dish, and I make it often. It's wonderful served with beef, chicken, pork, or barbecue sausage. You can even eat it on its own for breakfast the next day!

Parmesan Baked Tomatoes

Prep time: 5 min • **Cook time:** Less than 10 min • **Yield:** 4 servings

Ingredients	Directions
2 large tomatoes **1 tablespoon olive oil**	*1* Cut the tomatoes in half and place them in an oven-safe dish, cut side up.
1 teaspoon Italian seasoning **Salt to taste** **Black pepper to taste**	*2* Drizzle the tomatoes with olive oil. Sprinkle the tomatoes with Italian seasoning, salt, and pepper, and then top them with cheese.
½ cup shredded mozzarella cheese	*3* Broil the tomatoes in the oven for 5 to 10 minutes, until cheese is bubbly.

Per serving: Calories 95 (From Fat 65); Fat 7g (Saturated 3g); Cholesterol 13mg; Sodium 140mg; Carbohydrate 5g (Dietary Fiber 1g); Protein 4g.

Vary It! You can replace the Italian seasoning with ½ teaspoon chopped fresh basil and ½ teaspoon chopped fresh oregano.

Marvelous Mac and Cheese

Prep time: 5 min • **Cook time:** 30 min • **Yield:** 6 servings

Ingredients	*Directions*
2 cups (about 8 ounces) rice elbow macaroni	*1* Preheat the oven to 375 degrees.
1½ cups fat-free milk	*2* Cook the elbow macaroni until it's slightly tender, using the minimum time listed on the package.
1 tablespoon cornstarch	
Salt to taste	
Black pepper to taste	*3* In a saucepan, stir together the milk, cornstarch, salt, pepper, and cayenne. Bring the milk to a simmer, with the bubbles just starting to break the surface. Add the Velveeta and Swiss cheese. Simmer and stir until the cheese melts.
Dash of cayenne pepper	
6 ounces Velveeta, cubed	
1 cup shredded Swiss cheese, plus a pinch for the top	
¼ cup gluten-free panko breadcrumbs	*4* Place the cooked macaroni in an 8-inch square baking dish sprayed with nonstick cooking spray. Toss the macaroni with the cheese sauce. Sprinkle the top of the mac and cheese with panko and a pinch of Swiss cheese.
	5 Bake the mac and cheese for 15 minutes. Remove it from the oven and let it sit for about 5 minutes before serving.

Per serving: Calories 353 (From Fat 122); Fat 14g (Saturated 9g); Cholesterol 41mg; Sodium 541mg; Carbohydrate 40g (Dietary Fiber 2g); Protein 17g.

Note: You can still enjoy macaroni and cheese on a gluten-free diet! I prefer Tinkyada rice pasta. Kinnikinnick Foods makes gluten-free panko breadcrumbs.

Note: Instead of using panko, you can top the mac and cheese with gluten-free croutons — I tell you how to make croutons earlier in "Making croutons." Or put gluten-free bread in a blender or food processor and make your own breadcrumbs.

Note: Gluten-free pasta doesn't make great leftovers! Lower the amount of ingredients if you don't think you'll eat all this in one meal.

Swingin' Sweet Potato Fries

Prep time: 10 min • **Cook time:** 25 min • **Yield:** 4 servings

Ingredients	*Directions*
1 or 2 large (about 1½ pounds) sweet potatoes	*1* Preheat the oven to 425 degrees. Spray a baking sheet with nonstick cooking spray.
1½ tablespoons olive oil	
Salt to taste	*2* Peel the sweet potatoes. Cut them into small, evenly sized strips or wedges, about ½-inch wide.
Black pepper to taste	
Dash of cayenne pepper	
	3 On the baking sheet, drizzle olive oil over the sweet potatoes and sprinkle them with salt, pepper, and cayenne. Stir to coat the potatoes. Spread the fries on the baking sheet in a single layer.
	4 Bake the fries for 10 minutes. Then turn the fries and cook for another 10 minutes. Turn the fries again and cook for another 5 minutes, or until the potatoes are thoroughly cooked. Fries should be lightly brown on the outside and tender when poked with a fork.

Per serving: Calories 91 (From Fat 46); Fat 5g (Saturated 1g); Cholesterol 0mg; Sodium 77mg; Carbohydrate 11g (Dietary Fiber 1g); Protein 1g.

Vary It! Sprinkle the fries with cinnamon for a sweet twist.

Vary It! Leave the potato skins on for texture and extra nutrients.

Vary It! Use russet potatoes for great traditional baked fries.

Smashed Potatoes

Prep time: 5 min • **Cook time:** 20 min • **Yield:** 4 servings

Ingredients	Directions
1½ pounds (about 8) small white potatoes	**1** Preheat the oven to 425 degrees. Spray a baking sheet with nonstick cooking spray.
2 tablespoons olive oil	**2** Microwave the potatoes on a microwave-safe dish on high for 3 to 4 minutes, or until they're soft.
Salt to taste	
Black pepper to taste	
1 teaspoon Italian seasoning	**3** Put the potatoes on the baking sheet and use the back of a large spoon to flatten each potato until it's about ½ inch thick.
	4 Drizzle olive oil over the potatoes and sprinkle them with salt, pepper, and Italian seasoning. Stir to coat.
	5 Bake the potatoes for 10 minutes. Turn the potatoes and bake them for another 5 minutes, until they're browned.

Per serving: Calories 189 (From Fat 63); Fat 7g (Saturated 1g); Cholesterol 0mg; Sodium 87mg; Carbohydrate 29g (Dietary Fiber 3g); Protein 4g.

Chili-Topped Potato

Prep time: 2 min • **Cook time:** 6 min • **Yield:** 1 serving

Ingredients	Directions
1 medium russet potato	*1* Wash and dry the potato and place it on a microwave-safe plate.
7 ounces (½ can) lowfat chili, with or without beans	
¼ cup reduced-fat cheddar cheese	*2* Microwave on high until the potato is soft all the way through, about 5 minutes. Pierce it with a fork to see if it's done.
¼ cup fat-free sour cream	
1 teaspoon chopped fresh cilantro	*3* Cut the potato in half, fluff it, and top it with chili and cheese. Microwave the potato for 1 more minute.
	4 Top the potato with sour cream and chopped cilantro (see Figure 13-1).

Per serving: Calories 455 (From Fat 78); Fat 9g (Saturated 5g); Cholesterol 50mg; Sodium 1,129mg; Carbohydrate 66g (Dietary Fiber 9g); Protein 29g.

Note: Check the chili for gluten-free status.

Note: This makes a great quick lunch or dinner all by itself!

Chopping Fresh Herbs

1. Rinse and dry well

2. chop roughly
*NOTE: For herbs like rosemary and thyme, remove and chop leaves. Discard thick stem.

3.  gather and chop some more
Use rocking motion
move knife around

Figure 13-1: How to chop fresh herbs.

Southwest Corn Dog Muffins

Prep time: 5 min • **Cook time:** Less than 20 min • **Yield:** 4 servings

Ingredients	Directions
1 package gluten-free cornbread mix (plus ingredients the mix requires for muffins)	**1** In a medium bowl, prepare the cornbread batter according to the package directions for muffins. Preheat the oven as directed.
4-ounce can green chilies (not drained)	**2** Stir the green chilies and cheese into the cornbread batter.
1½ cups shredded pepper Jack or cheddar cheese	**3** Spray a 12-cup muffin pan or line it with paper muffin cups. Divide the batter evenly among the muffin cups.
4 lowfat hot dogs, cut into thirds	**4** Push one hot dog piece down into the middle of each muffin.
Yellow mustard for dipping	**5** Follow the baking directions on the cornbread package for muffins, baking about 15 to 17 minutes.
	6 Serve with yellow mustard.

Per serving: Calories 447 (From Fat 160); Fat 18g (Saturated 11g); Cholesterol 109mg; Sodium 1,096mg; Carbohydrate 53g (Dietary Fiber 4g); Protein 22g.

Note: Check the hot dogs for gluten-free status.

Note: Serve this satisfying side with an entree salad or take it to the next tailgate!

Tip: Gluten-free muffins, breads, and cupcakes are always easier to handle when they're prepared in paper muffin cups because of their crumbly texture.

Tip: Freeze your leftover muffins and reheat later — about 1 to 1½ minutes on high in the microwave.

Parmesan Asparagus with Breadcrumbs

Prep time: 5 min • **Cook time:** Less than 10 min • **Yield:** 4 servings

Ingredients	Directions
1 pound fresh asparagus spears 1 tablespoon water Olive oil for drizzling Salt to taste Black pepper to taste ¼ to ½ cup shredded Parmesan cheese 2 tablespoons gluten-free breadcrumbs	*1* Put the asparagus on a microwave-safe plate. Add about a tablespoon of water and cover the dish with plastic wrap. Microwave the asparagus on high for about 3 to 4 minutes. *2* In a baking dish, add the asparagus and drizzle it with olive oil, salt, and pepper. Top the asparagus with the Parmesan and breadcrumbs. *3* Broil the asparagus until the topping is golden brown on top.

Per serving: Calories 77 (From Fat 46); Fat 5g (Saturated 1g); Cholesterol 4mg; Sodium 185mg; Carbohydrate 5g (Dietary Fiber 1g); Protein 4g.

Tip: Check out broiling tips in Chapter 10.

Vary It! You can use about 16 ounces of canned asparagus spears instead of fresh. Heat the spears about 2 minutes in the microwave and then follow directions as given.

Tip: To make you own gluten-free breadcrumbs, put stale bread slices into a blender or food processor. Throw in some garlic salt and Italian seasoning to make them Italian style, or add paprika, onion powder, garlic powder, and red pepper to make 'em Cajun. Label your bags and keep them indefinitely in the freezer to use when a recipe — like this one! — calls for breadcrumbs.

Quick Parmesan Drop Biscuits

Prep time: 5 min • **Cook time:** 20 min • **Yield:** 4 servings

Ingredients	Directions
3 cups gluten-free bread and roll mix	**1** Preheat the oven to 375 degrees. Spray a baking sheet with nonstick cooking spray.
2 cups milk or water	
1 teaspoon garlic salt	**2** Combine the bread mix, milk, and garlic salt in a medium bowl. Stir the dough with a large fork until the lumps are gone.
1½ cups shredded Parmesan cheese	
	3 Scoop spoonfuls out of dough about 2 inches in diameter and roll them into the Parmesan cheese until they're coated. Place the biscuits about 2 inches apart on the baking sheet.
	4 Bake the biscuits about 20 minutes, until they're golden brown.

Per serving: Calories 530 (From Fat 128); Fat 14g (Saturated 8g); Cholesterol 40mg; Sodium 1,631mg; Carbohydrate 77g (Dietary Fiber 2g); Protein 17g.

Note: These biscuits are quick and delicious. No one will guess they're gluten-free. They're golden brown and crispy and cheesy on the outside and soft and chewy on the inside. I use Kinnikinnick Kinni-Kwik Bread and Bun Mix for this recipe and prepare it with milk. You can also use Bisquick Gluten Free mix.

Chapter 14

Smart Study Snacks

Studying usually requires bursts of energy and ongoing sustenance to keep a growling stomach from becoming a distraction. Especially late at night, finding quick and satisfying snacks can require creativity. Fortunately, you can keep many foods on hand that don't require any prep work and that you may not even realize are gluten-free.

This chapter offers snack ideas for when you need something simple and satisfying — whether during your solo study sessions or when you're working with a group — for an extra boost of energy.

Enjoying Simple Snacks

For easy food preparation, it's best to have ready-to-enjoy foods and staple ingredients in the kitchen. So if your friend with a car offers to take you on a grocery run, use the opportunity to stock up on some of the following staples that you can eat as they are or use in the recipes in this chapter:

✔ Fresh fruit, applesauce, raisins or other dried fruit, fruit leather

✔ Cut-up veggies, avocado, edamame (green soybeans)

 ✔ String cheese, yogurt (regular dairy or nondairy or Greek)

 ✔ Hard-boiled eggs

 ✔ Nuts, pumpkin or sunflower seeds, peanut or cashew butter

 ✔ Salsa, hummus, beans

 ✔ Corn tortillas and tortilla chips (see Figure 14-1 to find out how to make your own tortilla chips)

 ✔ Gluten-free granola, granola bars, Chex cereal (only certain flavors are gluten-free), rice cakes, and protein bars

 ✔ Popcorn, gluten-free pretzels, trail mixes, cookies, pudding

 ✔ Pickles, olives

When shopping for foods, always check labels for gluten-free status.

When you want a fancier snack than, say, peanut butter straight from the jar or a hard-boiled egg or avocado scooped out with a spoon, try out the recipes in this chapter. You'll spice up your study time in about 5 minutes so you can get energized and hit the books again.

Shaking up plain popcorn

Popcorn is an awesome gluten-free and fiber-rich snack. After you pop a bag of plain microwave popcorn, shake some add-ins into the bag to power it up! Here are some of my favorite ways to enjoy popcorn:

 ✔ **Snickerdoodle Popcorn:** Add sugar and cinnamon to taste.

 ✔ **Cheesy Southwest Popcorn:** Throw in some Parmesan cheese and a dash of cayenne pepper.

 ✔ **Campfire Popcorn:** Mini marshmallows and chocolate chips hit the spot.

 ✔ **Pizza Popcorn:** Add garlic powder, oregano, Parmesan cheese, and chopped pepperoni for an Italian treat.

Ladybugs on a Log

Prep time: 5 min • **Yield:** 1 serving

Ingredients	Directions
2 stalks celery 2 to 3 tablespoons almond butter 2 teaspoons dried cranberries	**1** Wash and dry the celery stalks and cut them into 3-inch pieces. Discard the leaves.
	2 Spread almond butter in the curved area of each piece of celery.
	3 Top the almond butter with a few dried cranberries.

Per serving: Calories 239 (From Fat 170); Fat 19g (Saturated 2g); Cholesterol 0mg; Sodium 104mg; Carbohydrate 16g (Dietary Fiber 3g); Protein 6g.

Vary It! For a savory twist on this sweet treat, use cream cheese instead of almond butter and top the snack with black olives instead of dried cranberries.

Apple Nachos

Prep time: 5 min • **Yield:** 2 servings

Ingredients	Directions
2 tart apples	**1** Cut each apple in half, remove the core, and slice the apple into thin wedges.
1 teaspoon lemon juice	
2 tablespoons creamy peanut butter	**2** To prevent the apples from browning, put the apples in a plastic bag with the lemon juice. Shake the bag to coat them.
2 tablespoons chopped pecans	
2 tablespoons sweetened coconut flakes	**3** Place the apples on a plate, spreading them out evenly.
¼ cup chocolate chips	
Drizzle of chocolate sauce	**4** Warm the peanut butter in the microwave for about 10 to 15 seconds, until it's runny. Drizzle the peanut butter on the apples.
Drizzle of caramel sauce	
	5 Top the apples with pecans, coconut, chocolate chips, chocolate sauce, and caramel sauce.

Per serving: Calories 404 (From Fat 196); Fat 22g (Saturated 7g); Cholesterol 0mg; Sodium 130mg; Carbohydrate 54g (Dietary Fiber 7g); Protein 6g.

Tip: Double this recipe for your whole study group to share.

Note: The tartness of Granny Smith apples makes this snack especially refreshing.

Sweet, Creamy Fruit Dip and Apples

Prep time: 5 min • **Yield:** 4 servings

Ingredients	Directions
8-ounce block cream cheese, room temperature ¾ **cup brown sugar** **3 small tart apples, cold**	**1** Combine the cream cheese and brown sugar in a medium bowl. Using a fork or electric hand mixer, mix the dip until it's smooth. Refrigerate the dip until you're ready to serve it.
	2 Halve, core, and then slice the apples into wedges just before serving them.
	3 Dip each apple slice in the cream cheese–brown sugar mixture and enjoy!

Per serving: Calories 414 (From Fat 181); Fat 20g (Saturated 13g); Cholesterol 62mg; Sodium 184mg; Carbohydrate 57g (Dietary Fiber 3g); Protein 5g.

Note: I prefer Granny Smith apples for this recipe. The tartness of the apples is a nice contrast to the sweetness of the dip.

Tip: For the best texture and flavor, use regular cream cheese, not lowfat. If you're concerned about fat and calories, just eat a smaller portion! Savor it and share with your friends.

Tip: If you're not sharing this, cut one apple at a time until you've used all the dip. Or to prevent browning, put the apple slices in a baggie with a couple of tablespoons of lemon juice. Shake to ensure the apples are covered with juice. The apple slices will keep in the fridge for a day or so, but I'm betting your dip will be gone by then, anyway.

Cocoa Crunchies

Prep time: 10 min • **Yield:** 10 servings (1 cup each)

Ingredients	*Directions*
13-ounce box (about 9 cups) of Rice Chex Cereal	*1* Pour the cereal into a large bowl.
½ cup (8 tablespoons) butter 1 cup chocolate hazelnut spread ¾ cup semisweet chocolate chips	*2* In a large saucepan, heat the butter, chocolate hazelnut spread, semisweet chocolate chips, and white chocolate chips over medium-low heat until they're just melted.
¾ cup white chocolate chips 2½ cups powdered sugar (or less)	*3* Remove the pan from the burner and immediately pour the chocolate mixture over the cereal. Gently stir until the cereal is coated, trying not to crush the cereal.
	4 Add half the powdered sugar to the mixture and toss to coat. Add more sugar as needed.

Per serving: Calories 578 (From Fat 215); Fat 24g (Saturated 12g); Cholesterol 27mg; Sodium 370mg; Carbohydrate 91g (Dietary Fiber 2g); Protein 5g.

Vary It! You can make this sweet treat in the microwave. Just put the Rice Chex in a large bowl. In a separate microwave-safe bowl, heat the butter, chocolate hazelnut spread, and chocolate chips in the microwave at 50 percent in 30-second increments. Stir after every 30 seconds, heating the chocolate until it's melted and smooth. Pour the sauce over the Rice Chex, gently stir, and coat with powdered sugar.

Note: You can store this in an airtight container for quite a while, until it begins to taste stale. It will likely be gone way before that happens.

Pronto Guacamole

Prep time: 5 min • **Yield:** 2 servings

Ingredients	Directions
1 large ripe avocado	**1** Cut the avocado in half, remove the pit, and scoop out the flesh with a spoon.
½ teaspoon lemon juice	
1 teaspoon garlic salt	**2** Mash the avocado with a fork until it's smoothish.
2 tablespoons jarred salsa	
	3 Stir the lemon juice, garlic salt, and salsa into the mashed avocado.

Per serving: Calories 158 (From Fat 135); Fat 15g (Saturated 2g); Cholesterol 0mg; Sodium 600mg; Carbohydrate 8g (Dietary Fiber 4g); Protein 2g.

Tip: Serve the guacamole with chips or cut vegetables. Figure 14-1 shows how to make your own gluten-free tortilla chips.

Tip: Double or triple this dip for friends. One avocado serves about two snackers.

Tip: If you're not eating this right away, lay plastic wrap over the surface and then around the edges of the bowl so there's no space between the dip and the plastic wrap. Air makes guacamole turn brown, though it doesn't affect the flavor.

How to Fry Corn Tortillas for Chips

Cut the tortillas into eight pieces.

Let the pieces dry out on the counter.

Heat the oil in a heavy pan and deep fry a few at a time.

Stir constantly so they don't stick together. They should be slightly browned and crispy. 45 seconds to 1 minute.

Remove chips from oil. Drain off excess oil on paper towels.

Sprinkle with salt if desired.

Figure 14-1: Homemade tortilla chips.

Cracker Egg Bites

Prep time: 5 min • **Cook time:** Less than 1 min • **Yield:** 1 serving

Ingredients	Directions
1 hard-boiled egg	*1* Slice the egg into five slices.
5 gluten-free crackers	
1½ slices cheese (or ¼ cup shredded)	*2* Top each cracker with one egg slice. Top the egg with cheese.
	3 Microwave the egg on high until the cheese is bubbly, about 40 seconds.

Per serving: Calories 232 (From Fat 139); Fat 15g (Saturated 8g); Cholesterol 242mg; Sodium 273mg; Carbohydrate 8g (Dietary Fiber 0g); Protein 14g.

Note: You can also broil these egg bites in the oven instead of microwaving them. Turn to Chapter 7 for more on boiling eggs and Chapter 9 for tips for using a broiler.

Vary It! This quick and easy protein-filled snack can double as a light meal if you're in a hurry. You just need an egg slicer or a sharp knife.

Speedy Nachos

Prep time: 5 min • **Cook time:** Less than 1 min • **Yield:** 4 servings

Ingredients	Directions
15-ounce can refried beans	**1** Spread the beans on a microwave-safe dinner plate.
4 ounces tortilla chips (about 20 chips)	
½ cup shredded cheese	**2** Stick the chips in the beans, covering the plate in a circular pattern from the middle all the way to the outer rim.
2 tablespoons olives	
2 tablespoons sliced jalapeños	**3** Sprinkle the chips with cheese, olives, jalapeños, and tomatoes.
2 tablespoons chopped tomatoes	
2 tablespoons sour cream	**4** Microwave the nachos on high until the cheese is bubbly, about 30 seconds.
2 tablespoons salsa	
2 tablespoons guacamole	**5** Add the sour cream, guacamole, and salsa just before eating, or serve these toppings on the side.

Per serving: Calories 338 (From Fat 151; Fat 17g (Saturated 6g); Cholesterol 27mg; Sodium 713mg; Carbohydrate 37g (Dietary Fiber 8g); Protein 12g.

Note: Find a recipe for Pronto Guacamole earlier in this chapter.

Tuna Salad

Prep time: 5 min • **Yield:** 2 servings

Ingredients	*Directions*
5-ounce can tuna in water, drained	*1* Combine the tuna, yogurt, garlic salt, and lemon juice in a small bowl. Stir to mix.
¼ cup plain Greek yogurt	
½ teaspoon garlic salt	
Dash of lemon juice	

Per serving: Calories 108 (From Fat 22); Fat 3g (Saturated 1g); Cholesterol 2mg; Sodium 425mg; Carbohydrate 1g (Dietary Fiber 0g); Protein 19g.

Vary It! Use mayonnaise instead of the Greek yogurt if that's what you have in the fridge.

Note: Use this tuna salad as a topping for gluten-free crackers, gluten-free pretzel twists, rice cakes, or cucumber slices.

Tip: If you like some crunch in your tuna salad, toss in some chopped celery or even a few chopped walnuts.

Petite Pesto Pizza Bites

Prep time: 5 min • **Cook time:** 1 min • **Yield:** 5 mini pizzas

Ingredients	*Directions*
5 gluten-free crackers	**1** Top each cracker with pesto, cheese, and a slice of mushroom.
5 teaspoons pesto	
5 teaspoons mozzarella cheese	**2** Microwave the pizza bites on high until the cheese is melted, about 30 to 60 seconds.
5 mushroom slices	

Per serving: Calories 42 (From Fat 28); Fat 3 (Saturated 1g); Cholesterol 4mg; Sodium 57mg; Carbohydrate 2g (Dietary Fiber 0g); Protein 2g.

Amazing Energy Bites

In this section, I provide a few recipes for portable, pick-me-up snacks that feature nuts, dried fruit, and gluten-free oats. Most of them are no-bake.

Why are some of the ingredients in these high-calorie snacks considered healthy? Here are the health benefits of some of my favorites:

- ✔ **Nuts:** Nuts are loaded with protein, which keeps you going for the long haul. Nuts also contain antioxidants, which protect cells from damage, and omega-3 fatty acids, which provide energy for the body and help lower bad cholesterol.

- ✔ **Pumpkin seeds:** Pumpkin seeds are high in essential amino acids and zinc. They contain iron and a large variety of other minerals as well as protein and fiber. Pumpkin seeds also help prevent kidney stones and, according to some people, combat depression.

- ✔ **Peanut butter:** Peanut butter is high in protein and rich in heart-healthy fats. It offers more than 30 essential nutrients and phytonutrients. Plus, its combination of fiber and protein satisfies hunger for hours.

- ✔ **Cranberries:** Cranberries are packed with antioxidants, and this power berry prevents harmful bacteria from sticking to the walls of the urinary tract, thus cutting down on the likelihood of infections. Cranberries are also high in other phytonutrients that seem to be important for protecting the body against heart disease, cancer, and conditions such as memory loss.

- ✔ **Raisins:** Raisins are high-energy, lowfat snacks that are packed with antioxidant and anti-inflammatory benefits, along with boron, which protects against osteoporosis and converts estrogen and vitamin D to their most active forms. Raisins contain compounds including oleanolic acid, which inhibits some bacteria responsible for tooth decay and plaque formation. They're heart friendly because they may help reduce levels of bad cholesterol. Being fiber dense, they also aid in digestion.

Although oats are naturally gluten-free, they're often grown and processed in a way that contaminates them with gluten-containing grains. When buying oats, look for brands that are labeled "certified gluten-free" on the package. This indicates that the oats were grown, harvested, and packaged separately from wheat and barley.

Snacking without pigging out

Keeping portion sizes reasonable is important when you're eating high-energy snacks. Here are some suggestions for snacking without overeating:

✔ Question your motives before looking for food. If you just want an excuse to stop working, try other methods of productive procrastination — go for a walk, return books to the library, start some laundry . . .

✔ Close your books, step away from the computer, and concentrate on the delicious food you're eating. You'll be less likely to overeat, you'll taste things, and you'll get to relax for a few minutes.

✔ Take the food out of the storage container so you can see what and how much you're eating. Use small plates or bowls to make the food look bigger.

✔ Scale down recipes or buy food in smaller packages if you can't trust yourself not to eat the whole thing in one sitting.

✔ Don't deprive yourself. Eat reasonable amounts of the gluten-free stuff you love!

Nutty Granola Pie

Prep time: 5 min • **Cook time:** Less than 1 min • **Yield:** 8 servings

Ingredients	Directions
1 cup gluten-free oats	*1* Spray a 9-inch pie plate with cooking spray.
1 cup gluten-free crisp rice cereal	*2* Mix the oats, rice cereal, pecans, and raisins in the prepared pie plate. Pour honey over the mixture and stir until it's well coated. Press the mixture firmly into the pie plate.
½ cup pecans	
¼ cup raisins	
½ cup honey	*3* Heat the nut butter in the microwave on high until it's runny, about 30 seconds. Drizzle the heated nut butter over the mixture.
¼ cup nut butter	
	4 Refrigerate the pie until it's cool. Then cut it into 8 wedges.
	5 Store leftovers (as if!) covered in the refrigerator.

Per serving: Calories 241 (From Fat 87); Fat 10g (Saturated 1g); Cholesterol 0mg; Sodium 72mg; Carbohydrate 38g (Dietary Fiber 3g); Protein 5g.

Tip: To press a sticky mixture easily into a pan, place your hand in a small plastic bag (glove-like) and spray the bag with cooking spray. You can now press mess-free. Or if you don't have a bag, just coat your fingers with cooking spray so the mixture doesn't stick to you while pressing.

Note: Check the rice cereal for gluten-free status.

Leah's Cookie Dough Clusters

Prep time: 5 min • **Yield:** 4 servings

Ingredients	Directions
¾ **cup gluten-free oats** ⅓ **to ½ cup peanut butter**	**1** Combine the oats, peanut butter, cocoa, and honey in a bowl and stir to mix.
½ **tablespoon unsweetened cocoa**	**2** Form mixture into eight 1-inch balls.
1 tablespoon honey	**3** Refrigerate and enjoy the cold clusters as you like.

Per serving: Calories 224 (From Fat 119); Fat 13g (Saturated 3g); Cholesterol 0mg; Sodium 102mg; Carbohydrate 24g (Dietary Fiber 6g); Protein 10g.

Vary It! Switch out the peanut butter for any type of nut butter or sunflower-seed butter. You can also substitute agave syrup for the honey.

Tip: Toast the oats before mixing to lose the raw-oat taste. Spread them on a baking sheet and bake them in a 350-degree oven for 5 to 10 minutes.

Note: These cookies contain no egg, so you can safely munch these no-bake goodies without worrying about food poisoning. My daughter, Leah, is gluten-free and sugar-free. While making cookies one night, she got sidetracked by the yummy dough and finished it before adding all the ingredients. Now this is her go-to no-bake treat.

Note: Check the oats for gluten-free status.

Chex Munch Mix

Prep time: 5 min • **Yield:** 4 servings

Ingredients	Directions
2 cups **Chocolate Chex cereal**	**1** Combine the Chocolate Chex cereal, Honey Nut Chex cereal, cashews, pumpkin seeds, butterscotch chips, and dried cranberries in an airtight container. Shake to mix.
2 cups **Honey Nut Chex cereal**	
1 cup **salted cashew pieces**	
½ cup **pumpkin seeds**	
½ cup **butterscotch chips**	
½ cup **dried cranberries**	

Per serving: Calories 617 (From Fat 288); Fat 32g (Saturated 10g); Cholesterol 0mg; Sodium 530mg; Carbohydrate 76g (Dietary Fiber 3g); Protein 12g.

Vary It! I'm often asked to bring this mix when I'm invited to gatherings; people love this unexpected combination of yummy ingredients. Alter this recipe to use what you have on hand or prefer.

Note: Most brands of butterscotch chips are gluten-free, but some aren't! Read the labels carefully and select chips that are free from gluten and don't contain malt.

Amanda's Sweet and Salty Trail Mix

Prep time: 5 min • **Yield:** 8 servings (½ cup each)

Ingredients	Directions
2 cups roasted, salted whole almonds **1 cup dried apples** **½ cup yogurt-covered raisins** **½ cup golden raisins** **½ cup dried cranberries**	*1* Combine the almonds, apples, yogurt-covered raisins, golden raisins, and cranberries in an airtight container. Shake to mix.

Per serving: Calories 336 (From Fat 177); Fat 20g (Saturated 3g); Cholesterol 0mg; Sodium 134mg; Carbohydrate 36g (Dietary Fiber 6g); Protein 9g.

Note: This mix is the favorite of my future daughter-in-law, Amanda. She loves the healthy flavors and the perfect ratio of sweet and salty.

Note: Store this mix in an airtight container until it's gone.

Cinnamon-Glazed Pecans

Prep time: 5 min • **Cook time:** 1 hour • **Yield:** 8 servings (¼ cup each)

Ingredients	*Directions*
1 egg white, room temperature 8 ounces pecan halves 2 tablespoons cinnamon ½ cup white sugar	*1* Preheat the oven to 200 degrees. Line a baking pan with parchment paper or aluminum foil.
	2 In a deep bowl, beat the egg white with an electric hand mixer on high until the egg white is stiff. The egg should turn foamy and white and hold its shape when you lift out the beater.
	3 Carefully stir the pecans into the egg white. Stir together the cinnamon and sugar and add the mixture to the pecans, stirring until the nuts are evenly coated.
	4 Pour the mixture in the prepared baking pan. Bake the mixture for about 1 hour, stirring every 15 minutes, until the coating is hardened on pecans.
	5 Let the pecans cool. Store them in an airtight container with a lid.

Per serving: Calories 251 (From Fat 184); Fat 21g (Saturated 2g); Cholesterol 0mg; Sodium 7mg; Carbohydrate 18g (Dietary Fiber 4g); Protein 3g.

Tip: To separate egg white from yolk, crack the egg gently and use the two halves of the shell to hold in the yolk while the white runs into a bowl. Discard the yolk or use it in another recipe. Take care to fully separate the white from the yolk — the white won't whip up like it needs to if there's yolk in the mixture. Flip to Chapter 8 for illustrated directions for separating an egg.

Tip: Whipping egg whites is most effective with room-temperature egg whites. Leave your egg out of the fridge for at least 15 minutes for best results.

Tip: If you cover the pan in parchment before pouring on the glazed pecans, the food won't stick during baking and you won't even have to wash the pan afterward!

Chapter 15

Dazzling Desserts

In This Chapter

▶ Whipping up quick desserts
▶ Putting some time into special desserts
▶ Jazzing up gluten-free mixes

*E*xtreme food restrictions can make any diet difficult to follow over the long haul, even if you're fully committed to pursuing a healthier lifestyle. When you're eliminating gluten in particular, you automatically cut out so many go-to foods. If you try to avoid desserts at the same time, you may end up feeling wildly deprived and unsatisfied. So go easy on yourself. Eat desserts in moderation and allow yourself an occasional indulgence while you're working on your core diet.

Besides, desserts aren't all bad. Dark chocolate, for instance, boosts brain function, reduces heart disease risk, and is packed with immunity-boosting antioxidants.

To ensure your desserts come out great, consider these tips:

✔ Choose recipes that have only a little flour to substitute instead of a large amount.

✔ Practice your recipe so you can make necessary adjustments before making the dessert for someone special or a big event.

✔ When using a cake recipe, consider making cupcakes. They usually bake up to be less crumbly and dense than a whole gluten-free cake, and it's easier to get cupcakes to bake all the way through without drying out the rest of the cake.

✔ Buy an all-purpose flour blend, preferably with xanthan gum already included. Those mixes cost a bit more, but you'll need to buy xanthan gum for baking anyway, and that's pricey.

✔ Consider using cake, cookie, and brownie mixes as the base to begin your dessert instead of a gluten-free flour blend on occasion. I've made literally hundreds of cookies and many desserts that have been a total flop over the years, so going with a mix that's tried and true *can* mean money savings for you in the long run.

✔ Many cookies, cupcakes, cakes, and cheesecakes store very nicely in the freezer. Freeze some of them while they're still fresh.

Assembling a Sweet Treat in a Snap

Putting together a sweet treat doesn't need to require a day of baking or mean opening a nutrient-void bag of candy. Find out how to prepare quick and not-so-bad-for-you desserts in this section.

To prevent your gluten-free goodies from sticking to the pan and to make cleanup quick, line your baking sheet with parchment paper.

If you choose to use nonstick cooking spray instead of parchment paper, don't use nonstick *baking* spray; it usually contains flour. Regular nonstick cooking spray is gluten-free.

Peanut Butter Cup Soft Serve

Prep time: 5 min • **Yield:** 4 servings

Ingredients	*Directions*
4 ripe bananas, cut into chunks and frozen **3 tablespoons peanut butter** **4 peanut butter cups, crushed** **1 teaspoon pure vanilla extract**	*1* Place the frozen banana, peanut butter, peanut butter cups, and vanilla in a blender. Puree just until creamy — only a few seconds. *2* Serve immediately or, to firm up this treat a little more, freeze for 5 to 10 minutes.

Per serving: Calories 271 (From Fat 102); Fat 11g (Saturated 3g); Cholesterol 1mg; Sodium 110mg; Carbohydrate 41g (Dietary Fiber 5g); Protein 6g.

Vary It! Try making this soft serve with chocolate hazelnut spread instead of peanut butter for a more chocolaty version. Throw in some chocolate chips, M&Ms, cocoa powder, fresh or frozen fruit, mini marshmallows, fresh vanilla beans, or nuts if you're feeling extra indulgent.

Tip: Keep plastic bags of peeled and sliced frozen bananas so they're ready for a quick treat anytime! Choose ripe bananas for freezing, avoiding the ones with green on the peel. Some brown spots are okay.

Tip: To make a single scoop, use 1 frozen banana, 1 peanut butter cup, ¼ teaspoon vanilla, and 1 tablespoon peanut butter.

Note: Store leftovers covered in the freezer for up to 2 weeks.

Note: Check the gluten-free status of the peanut butter cups.

White Chocolate Macadamia Nut Cookies

Prep time: 10 min • **Cook time:** 12 min • **Yield:** 6 servings (5 cookies each)

Ingredients	Directions
1¼ cups light brown sugar	**1** Preheat the oven to 350 degrees. Line a baking sheet with parchment paper or aluminum foil sprayed with nonstick cooking spray.
¾ cup shortening	
1 egg	
1 teaspoon pure vanilla extract	**2** Using an electric mixer, blend the brown sugar, shortening, egg, and vanilla on high until the mixture is fluffy.
1 teaspoon baking powder	
¼ teaspoon salt	
1¾ cups all-purpose gluten-free flour	**3** Add the baking powder, salt, and flour to the sugar mixture. Continue mixing on low until the dough is well-blended.
1 cup white chocolate chips	
1 cup macadamia nuts, chopped	**4** Using a spoon, stir in the white chocolate chips and nuts.
	5 Drop teaspoons of dough onto the baking sheet about 2 inches apart.
	6 Bake the cookies for 12 minutes, or until they're set in the middle.

Per serving: Calories 836 (From Fat 469); Fat 52g (Saturated 14g); Cholesterol 37mg; Sodium 215mg; Carbohydrate 90g (Dietary Fiber 5g); Protein 8g.

Tip: I use Jules Gluten Free flour blend, which contains xanthan gum, when baking these cookies. If you use a brand with no xanthan gum, add 1½ teaspoons xanthan gum to this recipe.

Vary It! Use the same amount of unsalted butter (1½ sticks, or 12 tablespoons) instead of shortening if you prefer a crisp texture and buttery taste. Just keep in mind that your cookies will be flatter if you choose to forgo the shortening. For best results, soften the butter by leaving it on the counter for an hour or two before making your cookies, or microwave for 10 to 15 seconds before mixing in.

No-Bake Peanut Butter Bars

Prep time: 10 min • **Chill time:** 30 min • **Yield:** 8 servings (2 squares each)

Ingredients	*Directions*
1 cup gluten-free graham cracker crumbs **1 cup peanut butter**	*1* In a medium bowl, mix the graham cracker crumbs, peanut butter, and butter. Stir in the powdered sugar.
½ cup (8 tablespoons) unsalted butter, melted	*2* Press the mixture into an 8-x-8-inch pan.
1¼ cups powdered sugar **8 ounces (½ can) chocolate fudge frosting**	*3* Microwave the frosting for 15 seconds. Stir the frosting and spread it on the peanut butter crust.
	4 Chill the dessert for at least 30 minutes. Then cut it into 2-inch squares.

Per serving: Calories 506 (From Fat 302); Fat 34g (Saturated 12g); Cholesterol 31mg; Sodium 240mg; Carbohydrate 46g (Dietary Fiber 2g); Protein 8g.

Vary It! Try almond butter, cashew butter, or sunflower seed butter instead of peanut butter to change the taste of this delicious dessert. If you choose to stick with peanut butter, use crunchy or smooth, full fat or reduced fat, depending on your preferences.

Note: Several companies sell gluten-free graham crackers and graham cracker crumbs. If you can't find this product at your regular grocery store, check a natural foods store. Just make sure that the label says gluten-free!

Tip: Store any leftovers covered in the refrigerator or cut your extra peanut butter squares into chunks and freeze them. Use the chunks with Peanut Butter Cup Soft Serve (earlier in this chapter), in cake batter or cookie dough, or in milkshakes!

Salted Mocha Fudge

Prep time: 5 min, plus 1 hour to chill • **Cook time:** 5 min • **Yield:** 16 servings (4 pieces each)

Ingredients	*Directions*
3 cups semisweet chocolate chips	*1* In a large microwave-safe bowl, combine the chocolate chips, condensed milk, butter, vanilla, and espresso powder.
14-ounce can sweetened condensed milk	
6 tablespoons salted butter	*2* Microwave the mixture uncovered on high for 30 seconds. Stir and continue microwaving in 30-second increments, stirring after each time, until the chocolate chips are melted.
1 teaspoon pure vanilla extract	
1 tablespoon espresso powder	
½ teaspoon coarse sea salt or kosher salt	*3* Line an 8-x-8-inch dish with parchment paper or aluminum foil sprayed with non-stick cooking spray.
	4 Pour the chocolate mixture into the prepared pan and sprinkle it with coarse salt. Refrigerate the fudge until it's set, about an hour.
	5 Cut the fudge into 1-inch squares.

Per serving: Calories 269 (From Fat 143); Fat 16g (Saturated 10g); Cholesterol 20mg; Sodium 138mg; Carbohydrate 34g (Dietary Fiber 2g); Protein 3g.

Vary It! Add white chocolate chips, mini marshmallows, nuts, or peanut butter chips to this fudge!

Vary It! If you don't have espresso powder and still want a coffee flavor, use two packets of Starbucks' VIA instant coffee.

Note: Store leftover fudge in the refrigerator.

No-Fuss Nut Butter Cookies

Prep time: 5 min • **Cook time:** 6-8 min • **Yield:** 4 servings (3 cookies each)

Ingredients	*Directions*
1 cup nut butter **1 cup sugar** **1 egg, beaten**	*1* Preheat the oven to 350 degrees. Line a baking sheet with parchment paper or aluminum foil sprayed with nonstick cooking spray.
	2 Stir together the nut butter, sugar, and egg until the ingredients are well-combined.
	3 Drop teaspoons of cookie dough onto the cookie sheet about 2 inches apart. Flatten them slightly with a fork.
	4 Bake the cookies for 6 to 8 minutes, or until they begin to get crisp around the edges.

Per serving: Calories 592 (From Fat 305); Fat 34g (Saturated 7g); Cholesterol 47mg; Sodium 315mg; Carbohydrate 62g (Dietary Fiber 4g); Protein 18g.

Note: These are the easiest cookies you can make from scratch! Whip them up anytime you want a dozen warm cookies.

Vary It! Use peanut butter, sunflower seed butter, cashew butter, or almond butter for these treats. Add mini chocolate chips or a tablespoon of cocoa powder if you want a touch of chocolate.

Mini Cookies-and-Cream Cheesecakes

Prep time: 10 min • **Cook time:** 15 min • **Yield:** 6 servings (2 cakes each)

Ingredients	Directions
20 gluten-free chocolate sandwich cookies	**1** Preheat the oven to 350 degrees.
Two 8-ounce packages regular cream cheese, softened	**2** Line a 12-cup muffin pan with paper liners and place a whole cookie at the bottom of each one.
3 tablespoons sugar	
2 eggs	**3** Crush 6 of the cookies.
1 teaspoon pure vanilla extract	**4** In a medium bowl, combine the cream cheese, sugar, eggs, vanilla, and crushed cookies with an electric hand mixer.
	5 Pour the cheesecake mixture into the muffin cups. Bake for 15 minutes, until middle is set.

Per serving: Calories 444 (From Fat 288); Fat 32g (Saturated 18g); Cholesterol 145mg; Sodium 350mg; Carbohydrate 32g (Dietary Fiber 1g); Protein 9g.

Vary It! You can make this standard cheesecake with any type of gluten-free cookies. Try it with gingersnaps, chocolate chip cookies, or snickerdoodles!

Tip: Soften the cream cheese by leaving it on the counter for half an hour or so. Or unwrap the two packages and microwave the cream cheese for 15 to 20 seconds.

Note: These are best served chilled for about 30 minutes or more, until no longer warm.

No-Bake Berry Cheesecake

Prep time: 15 min • **Chill time:** 25 min • **Yield:** 8 servings

Ingredients	Directions
1½ cups gluten-free graham cracker crumbs	*1* Put the graham cracker crumbs in a medium bowl. Add the butter and sugar and mix well.
6 tablespoons unsalted butter, melted	
¼ cup sugar	*2* Press the crumb mixture into 9-inch pie plate. Refrigerate for 10 to 15 minutes.
Two 8-ounce packages cream cheese, softened	
14-ounce can sweetened condensed milk	*3* While the crust is chilling, mix the cream cheese, condensed milk, lemon juice, and vanilla with an electric mixer on high until the filling is smooth.
¼ cup lemon juice	
1 teaspoon pure vanilla extract	*4* Pour the cream cheese mixture into the prepared crust. Chill the cheesecake for at least 15 minutes.
2 cups berries	
	5 Serve the cheesecake with berries on top or on the side.

Per serving: Calories 342 (From Fat 264); Fat 29g (Saturated 18g); Cholesterol 85mg; Sodium 196mg; Carbohydrate 16g (Dietary Fiber 2g); Protein 5g.

Note: My mom's been making this cheesecake, which is a bit more like a pie, since I was a kid. When my family went gluten-free, it was an easy fix to switch out the crust to get rid of the gluten.

Vary It! You can serve this cheesecake with any type of fruit. Fresh berries are firmer than frozen berries, which turn to a delicious berry sauce when defrosted. To make this dessert extra sweet, drizzle chocolate syrup on top.

Tip: If using frozen berries, empty the berries into a bowl and thaw them at room temperature, in the refrigerator, or in the microwave for 30 to 45 seconds before serving the cheesecake.

Tip: Soften the cream cheese by leaving it on the counter for half an hour or so. Or unwrap the two packages and microwave the cream cheese for 15 to 20 seconds.

Tip: To make graham cracker crumbs from whole graham crackers, place about 15 to 20 crackers in a plastic bag and crush them into fine crumbs with a rolling pin to equal 1½ cups.

Devoting Time to Special Desserts

Finish your meal on a sweet note with traditional desserts, including old-fashioned Texas cobbler, rich chocoholic-worthy pie and cake, fluffy mixtures, and a pumpkin dessert that's perfect for fall and winter.

This section includes a few of my family's favorite holiday dessert recipes. They're not difficult to make, but they may take a bit longer to prepare than other recipes in this book. You can save a bit of prep time by laying out all your ingredients before you even begin to work your dessert magic.

If you're wondering how to convert some of your family favorite dessert recipes to gluten-free versions, check out the tips in Chapter 18.

 Make just about any dessert into individual serving sizes by evenly dividing the mixture into small custard cups, ramekins, or a muffin pan. No matter how long a recipe says to bake the dish, begin checking for doneness after 15 or 20 minutes by inserting a toothpick in the center. The toothpick should come out clean or have just a crumb or two stuck to it, not wet batter. Or cut a recipe in half and use an 8-inch square dish instead of the 9-x-13-inch dish.

Preparing a pie crust

Make a simple pie crust by pressing one of these combinations into a baking dish or pie plate that you've sprayed with nonstick cooking spray:

- ✔ 2 cups finely crushed gluten-free cookies and 4 tablespoons melted butter

- ✔ 2 cups crushed gluten-free graham cracker crumbs mixed with 4 tablespoons melted butter and ¼ cup sugar

- ✔ 1 cup finely crushed nuts, 2 tablespoons melted butter, and ¼ cup sugar (Crush the nuts in a plastic bag with a rolling pin or something similar.)

Three-Layer Chocolate Cloud

Prep time: 20 min • **Cook time:** 15 min • **Yield:** 16 servings

Ingredients	Directions
⅓ cup (5⅓ tablespoons) unsalted butter, melted	*1* Preheat the oven to 350 degrees.
¼ cup sugar	*2* Pour the butter on the bottom of a 9-x-13-inch pan.
1 cup gluten-free all-purpose flour	
1 cup chopped pecans	*3* Mix the sugar, flour, and pecans in a small bowl.
8-ounce package cream cheese, softened	*4* Pat down the pecan mixture in the pan, and bake the crust for 15 minutes. Let the crust cool to room temperature, about 15 minutes.
1 cup powdered sugar	
Two 8-ounce containers whipped topping, thawed	
6-ounce box instant chocolate pudding	*5* With an electric hand mixer, mix the cream cheese and powdered sugar on low speed. Fold in one 8-ounce container of whipped topping. Spread the mixture onto the crust.
4-ounce box instant vanilla pudding	
3 cups milk	*6* Whisk together the chocolate pudding mix, vanilla pudding mix, and milk in a separate medium bowl. Spread the pudding mixture over the cream cheese layer.
	7 Top the pudding layer with the remaining 8-ounce container of whipped topping and serve.

Per serving: Calories 371 (From Fat 187); Fat 21g (Saturated 12g); Cholesterol 32mg; Sodium 316mg; Carbohydrate 42g (Dietary Fiber 2g); Protein 4g.

Tip! This dessert is great for a crowd or a holiday.

Note: Store this dessert covered in the refrigerator for up to a few days.

Tip! Use fat-free whipped topping and milk if you want to save a few calories here. Believe me, you won't miss 'em.

Tip: Soften the cream cheese by leaving it on the counter for half an hour or so. Or unwrap the cream cheese and microwave it for 15 seconds.

Grandma's German Chocolate Pie

Prep time: 5 min • **Cook time:** 35 min • **Yield:** 8 servings

Ingredients	Directions
2 ounces Baker's German's sweet baking chocolate	*1* Preheat the oven to 375 degrees.
¼ cup (4 tablespoons) salted butter	*2* In a medium saucepan over low heat, whisk together the chocolate, butter, sugar, and corn syrup until everything is melted together. Let the chocolate mixture cool.
¾ cup sugar	
½ cup light corn syrup	
3 eggs	*3* Whisk together the eggs, milk, and cornstarch in a medium bowl. Add the egg mixture to the chocolate mixture in the saucepan. Stir in the pecans and vanilla.
¼ cup milk	
1½ tablespoons cornstarch	
1 cup chopped pecans	*4* Pour the mixture into the pie crust.
1 teaspoon pure vanilla extract	
9-inch unbaked gluten-free pie crust	*5* Bake the pie for 35 to 45 minutes, or until the filling is set.

Per serving: Calories 551 (From Fat 184); Fat 20g (Saturated 6g); Cholesterol 86mg; Sodium 335mg; Carbohydrate 86g (Dietary Fiber 1g); Protein 8g.

Vary It! This pie is delicious crustless, too. If you want to try this without the crust, just spray a pie pan with nonstick cooking spray and pour in the filling before baking.

Note: This pie is one of my mother-in-law's specialties. The first time my gluten-free son ate it, he kept asking if we were sure he could have it. It's just almost too good to be true.

Vary It! For a more chocolaty pie, use semisweet baking chocolate (54% cacao) in place of German's (46% cacao).

Tip: Pour this pie filling into small custard cups or a muffin pan to make individual pies or crustless chocolate custards. If you're using custard cups, place them on a baking sheet with a lip and slide it in the oven. Bake for about 20 minutes, or until the filling is set.

Texas Blackberry Cobbler

Prep time: 5 min • **Cook time:** 30 minutes • **Yield:** 16 servings

Ingredients	Directions
½ cup (8 tablespoons) salted butter, melted	*1* Preheat the oven to 350 degrees.
1½ cups sugar (divided in half)	*2* Pour the butter in a 9-x-13-inch baking dish.
1 cup gluten-free all-purpose flour	
2 teaspoons baking powder	*3* In a medium bowl, mix ¾ cup sugar with the flour (plus 1¼ teaspoons xanthan gum if your flour mix doesn't include it), baking powder, and milk.
¾ cup fat-free or lowfat milk	
15-ounce can blackberries, drained	
	4 Pour the batter over the melted butter in the baking dish.
	5 Stir together the fruit and the remaining ¾ cup sugar. Pour the fruit over the batter.
	6 Bake for 30 to 35 minutes, or until the crust has risen and browned and is no longer doughy.

Per serving: Calories 220 (From Fat 106); Fat 12g (Saturated 7g); Cholesterol 31mg; Sodium 171mg; Carbohydrate 29g (Dietary Fiber 1g); Protein 2g.

Note: This favorite family recipe is adapted from my husband's Southern grandmother. I make it with Jules Gluten Free all-purpose flour (which includes xanthan gum), and I cut the amount of sugar from the original. Serve it warm with a scoop of vanilla ice cream for the full Southern experience!

Vary It! Make this cobbler with 2 cups of any fresh, frozen, or canned fruit.

Pumpkin Crumble

Prep time: 10 min • **Cook time:** 30–45 min • **Yield:** 16 servings

Ingredients	Directions
30-ounce can pumpkin puree	**1** Preheat the oven to 350 degrees. Spray a 9-x-13-inch baking dish with nonstick cooking spray.
3 eggs	
1½ cups sugar	
12-ounce can evaporated milk	**2** In a large bowl, mix together the pumpkin puree, eggs, sugar, evaporated milk, pudding mix, cinnamon, and cloves.
Two 3.5-ounce packages butterscotch pudding mix (instant or cook-and-serve)	
2 teaspoons ground cinnamon	**3** Pour the pumpkin mixture into the prepared baking dish.
½ teaspoon ground cloves	
1 package gluten-free cake mix (spice cake or yellow cake)	**4** Pour the dry cake mix on top of the pumpkin mixture. Top with nuts and then pour the melted butter over the cake mix.
1 cup chopped pecans	**5** Bake 30 to 45 minutes, until the pumpkin crumble is firm in the middle.
¾ cup melted butter	

Per serving: Calories 397 (From Fat 148); Fat 16g (Saturated 7g); Cholesterol 65mg; Sodium 372mg; Carbohydrate 61g (Dietary Fiber 3g); Protein 5g.

Note: After you gather the ingredients, this recipe is a breeze to prepare but looks like you slaved over it. It makes an impressive holiday or party dessert for a crowd. It's similar to a pumpkin pie but with a crispy, nutty topping!

Vary It! Use vanilla pudding instead of butterscotch for a toned-down flavor.

Note: Store this dessert covered in the refrigerator and eat it cold when the urge for a sweet treat strikes.

Fancy Flourless Chocolate Cake

Prep time: 20 min • **Cook time:** 35 min • **Yield:** 8 servings

Ingredients	Directions
½ cup semisweet chocolate chips ½ cup (8 tablespoons) salted butter 4 eggs ¾ cup sugar ½ cup unsweetened cocoa 1 teaspoon pure vanilla extract Powdered sugar for dusting	**1** Preheat the oven to 300 degrees. Spray an 8-inch round cake pan or 9-inch pie plate with nonstick cooking spray.
	2 In a medium bowl, melt the chocolate chips and butter in the microwave on high in 30-second increments. Stir the chocolate after each 30-second interval.
	3 Add the eggs, sugar, cocoa, and vanilla to the melted chocolate. Make sure the chocolate isn't too hot when you add the eggs to avoid cooking them. Mix well. Pour the batter into the prepared pan.
	4 Bake for 35 to 40 minutes, or until a toothpick inserted in the middle of the cake comes out clean.
	5 Let the cake cool and then dust it with powdered sugar.

Per serving: Calories 278 (From Fat 160); Fat 18g (Saturated 10g); Cholesterol 124mg; Sodium 150mg; Carbohydrate 30g (Dietary Fiber 2g); Protein 5g.

Note: This easy but fancy cake will have your guests fooled into thinking you slaved away in the kitchen all day. Serve it with ice cream for a special presentation.

Vary It! Make this cake into 12 cupcakes instead of a single cake. Bake for about 20 minutes, or until a toothpick inserted in the middle of a cupcake comes out clean.

Jazzing Up Gluten-Free Mixes

In the olden days of gluten-free baking, which were as recent as 5 to 7 years ago, most gluten-free baking mixes tasted horrible and were difficult to find. Today, many delicious mixes are available, and they're easy to find in most cities and abundant online.

Chances are good that any mix you try now will be great. And if you don't love one brand, try another. They're simple to prepare and often end up saving you money in the long run, because they allow you to avoid buying individual ingredients.

Of course, making the same thing time after time can get boring, so the recipes in this section offer ideas for altering standard mixes. And here are some simple add-in suggestions for jazzing up your mix:

- Almond or mint extract
- Cocoa, espresso powder, or cinnamon
- Instant pudding
- Mini marshmallows
- Semisweet chocolate chips, white chocolate chips, or peanut butter chips
- Crushed gluten-free cookies
- Chopped nuts
- Drizzle of honey topping
- Dried cranberries or raisins

If you're over 21, check your alcohol collection for flavorings. Liqueurs aren't as strongly flavored as extracts, so you may need to add a little extra, but you can bake with crème de menthe or peppermint Schnapps for mint flavor, amaretto for almond, triple sec for orange, Frangelico for hazelnut, and Kahlúa for coffee flavor.

Cinnamon Crumb Cake

Prep time: 5 min • **Cook time:** About 30 min • **Yield:** 16 servings

Ingredients	Directions
15- to 21-ounce box gluten-free yellow cake mix 3 eggs	**1** Preheat the oven to 350 degrees. Spray a 9-x-13-inch glass baking dish with nonstick cooking spray.
½ cup (8 tablespoons) unsalted butter, softened ⅔ cup milk 1 teaspoon pure vanilla extract	**2** In a medium bowl, combine the cake mix, eggs, butter, milk, and vanilla. Mix with an electric mixer for 1 to 2 minutes on high speed. Pour the mixture into the prepared baking dish.
1½ tablespoons ground cinnamon ½ cup brown sugar 2 tablespoons honey	**3** Sprinkle cinnamon over the entire cake and then sprinkle on the brown sugar. Drizzle honey on top.
1 cup chopped pecans	**4** Using a butter knife, cut through the topping and swirl it down into the cake. Cover the cake with pecans.
	5 Bake the cake for the amount of time listed on your cake mix box (usually 25 to 35 minutes), or until a toothpick inserted in the center of the cake comes out clean.

Per serving: *Calories 251 (From Fat 111); Fat 12g (Saturated 5g); Cholesterol 52mg; Sodium 163mg; Carbohydrate 34g (Dietary Fiber 1g); Protein 3g.*

Vary It! You can make Cinnamon Crumb Cupcakes as well. For cupcakes, bake them according to the directions listed on the cake box, usually around 20 minutes.

Rockin' Rocky Road Brownies

Prep time: 5 min • **Cook time:** About 25 min • **Yield:** 16 servings

Ingredients	Directions
15-ounce box gluten-free brownie mix (plus the ingredients to prepare it) 1¼ cups chocolate chips 1¼ cups mini marshmallows ¾ cup chopped pecans	**1** Preheat the oven to the temperature indicated on your brownie mix. Spray an 8-inch square baking dish with nonstick cooking spray.
	2 In a medium bowl, combine the brownie mix and the ingredients called for on the package. Stir in ¼ cup chocolate chips.
	3 Pour the batter into the prepared baking dish. Top with marshmallows, nuts, and the remaining 1 cup chocolate chips.
	4 Bake as directed on the brownie package, until a toothpick inserted in the center of the brownies comes out mostly clean.
	5 Cool the brownies for about 10 minutes before cutting them.

Per serving: Calories 294 (From Fat 160); Fat 18g (Saturated 4g); Cholesterol 35mg; Sodium 72mg; Carbohydrate 35g (Dietary Fiber 2g); Protein 3g.

Vary It! There are so many ways to dress up plain old brownie mix! A few ideas for add-ins are mint chips, peanut butter chips, and s'more ingredients.

Vary It! Swap out pecans for any other nut you have in your fridge or pantry. (No, your roommate doesn't count.)

All-Nighter Red Bull Cupcakes

Prep time: 5 min • **Cook time:** 15 min • **Yield:** 12 servings

Ingredients	*Directions*
15- to 20-ounce box gluten-free yellow cake mix	*1* Preheat the oven to 350 degrees. Line a muffin pan with 12 paper liners.
12 ounces sugar-free Red Bull	
Frosting of your choice	*2* In a large bowl, mix the cake mix and Red Bull with an electric hand mixer on medium speed until the ingredients are combined.
	3 Pour the batter into the muffin pan. Bake according to directions on the box, about 15 minutes.
	4 Let the cupcakes cool. Frost them with a frosting of choice.

Per serving: Calories 236 (From Fat 45); Fat 5g (Saturated 2g); Cholesterol 0mg; Sodium 242mg; Carbohydrate 48g (Dietary Fiber 0g); Protein 1g.

Note: Yes, this sounds like a crazy recipe, but it tastes great and skips all the fat of added butter or oil and calories of added eggs!

Note: I've tried this trick with several different cake mixes. Gluten-free mixes vary greatly in the amount of mix, the taste, and the texture. I think this recipe works best with Betty Crocker gluten-free cake mixes.

Vary It! Try this recipe with Coke Zero and chocolate cake mix. It also works with vanilla cake mix and Sprite Zero, ½ cup cranberries, and ¼ cup sliced almonds. Stir in any mix-ins you like just before pouring the batter into the muffin cups. Then bake.

Chapter 16

Resurrecting Leftovers and Prepping Ahead

A few years ago, my husband and I visited a spa resort in the Caribbean. It was the type of place that, after arriving, you stay put. No exploring the town for a cute bistro or trying out local cuisine. The resort was in the middle of a rainforest, so we were captive to the one restaurant on site. For dinner, we enjoyed a large buffet of fresh fruit, vegetables, breads, and different types of meats and seafood. If corn and lobster were on the buffet one evening, then the next lunch would be lobster and corn chowder. If an abundance of cucumber, tomatoes, and whitefish remained after a meal, then the next meal would feature a cucumber-tomato-fish quiche. Instead of *leftovers,* we came to call this *Caribbean-style dining,* but it's really just a smart and creative use of leftovers!

The lesson: You can make a really good second meal from foods you previously served — that's every bit as tasty as the first — if you apply a little creative thinking.

This chapter is all about how you can save time in the kitchen and reduce your food costs by creating delicious and satisfying meals with leftovers. I also tell you how to store leftovers and point out how to make cooking quicker and easier by prepping ingredients ahead of time and using orphan groceries.

Storing Leftovers

There's a bit of an art to saving leftovers. Store things you want to use again, but don't store them so long that they take on some extra life of their own. In this section, I cover how to reach this delicate balance by storing your leftovers properly and knowing how long to keep them.

Packing up leftovers

Pack up leftovers as soon as you finish your meal so they don't sit out at room temperature for very long. And if you don't plan to use the remainder of the dish within a day or two, transfer the leftovers to a plastic container or glass jar and label it. Especially if you can't tell what the food is just by looking at it and you don't trust yourself to remember when the food was new, stick a piece of tape on top and write the name of the dish and its preparation date.

Don't put highly acidic food, such as tomato-based soups or sauces, into reusable plastic containers. These foods eat through plastic and stain it, possibly contaminating your food with chemicals from the plastics as well. The acid in tomato sauce and barbeque sauce also eats through aluminum foil. Store acidic sauces in the containers they come in or glass jars, cover them well with plastic wrap or foil, and use them within a day or two.

Many leftover ingredients keep very well in a plastic bag, and there's usually a spot to label the date and contents right on the front. One advantage of using this method for storing food is that you can load single servings right into the freezer if you know you won't be getting to it any time soon. Packaging home-cooked leftovers in single serving sizes makes nice, easy meals to be reheated and enjoyed on demand!

If you plan to microwave your leftovers in the plastic container you stored them in, make sure you're buying BPA-free plastic. Otherwise, cancer-causing chemicals can leech into your food as plastics break down when heated. Your best bet is to transfer food to microwave-safe glass, ceramic, porcelain, or paper plates and bowls before heating it. Companies are getting used to health-savvy consumers and some now mark their plastic containers as "BPA free."

Knowing how long to save food

How many times have you rummaged through the fridge for something to eat, only to find some blue and hairy dish that looked more like a science experiment than food? Worse yet, how often do you look through containers and find things that look okay, but you have no idea how long they've been there? If you're like me, you look and sniff and debate whether it's worth taking a risk on whatever your leftovers used to be.

The United States Department of Agriculture (USDA) says leftovers are safe indefinitely in the freezer, but the food may become unappealing due to freezer burn. Things that don't freeze well include casseroles, soups, and other dishes that contain mayonnaise, yogurt, or sour cream.

The USDA also says that egg, chicken, ham, tuna, and macaroni salads last in the fridge (set to 40 degrees or below) for about a week. Soups, cooked meat or poultry, chicken nuggets or patties, and pizza last for 3 to 4 days.

Planning New Meals with Leftovers

Intentionally creating leftovers to use in other dishes can save time in the kitchen, reduce wasted food, and keep the menu interesting. For instance, if you're cooking chicken for dinner one day, make some extra and use the leftover chicken for a salad or chicken tacos the next day. You can serve mashed potatoes as a side dish for a meal and make extra to use on a shepherd's pie (Chapter 12). Or you can cook extra rice when preparing a stir-fry with plans to make fried rice the next day. Here, leftovers aren't simply uneaten, day-old food; they're an ingredient in another recipe!

Here are a few recipes from this book that go together. If you think ahead on day one, you can get a good jump on your meal for day two:

- ✔ **Hard-Boiled Egg Melt (Chapter 7):** Make extra eggs to use in Classic Egg Salad Sandwich (Chapter 10).

- ✔ **Rice for a stir-fry side dish:** Make extra rice to use in Quick Leftover Fried Rice, California Roll Bowl, or Rice, Bean, and Veggie Salad (Chapter 9).

✔ **Easy Italian Sausage and Lentils (Chapter 9) or Italian Sausage Stir-Fry (Chapter 11):** Make extra sausage to use in Baked Ziti with Italian Sausage (Chapter 12).

✔ **Sizzling Steak Kabobs (Chapter 12):** Make extra steak to use in Steak and Baked Potato Salad (Chapter 10).

✔ **Momma Mia Italian Potato Salad (Chapter 13):** Make extra potatoes to use in Steak and Baked Potato Salad (Chapter 10).

✔ **Tempting Teriyaki Chicken Skewers (Chapter 12):** Make extra chicken to use in Warm Chicken Teriyaki Quinoa Salad (Chapter 10).

If you happen to have any of the following ingredients left from last night's dinner, think wrap, sandwich, salad, soup, quesadilla, taco, or omelet for breakfast or lunch:

✔ Hamburger

✔ Roasted or grilled chicken

✔ Ribs or pork chops

✔ Lunchmeat

✔ Grilled fish

✔ Sautéed vegetables

✔ Slices of fruit

✔ Baked or fried potatoes

✔ Partial can of vegetables or sauces

After you begin to prepare a budget-savvy meal of leftovers, you may discover that you're missing some key ingredients. Don't pack it all up and run for fast food. Instead, figure out what you can use to replace the missing ingredients to rescue the meal.

Substitutions are easy if you aren't too tied to your recipes. Think of recipes as guidelines — not a set of rules. For instance, if your recipe calls for green beans and you don't have any, see what you do have. You can switch out the green beans for peas, broccoli, carrots, mushrooms, or just about any other vegetable or bean you do have. On the other hand, if you're trying to make a quiche and you don't have eggs, then you may need to redirect your meal plan!

Here are some common substitutions:

- ✔ Pasta for rice
- ✔ Quinoa for pasta or rice
- ✔ Mashed potatoes for polenta
- ✔ Any type of beans (black, navy, kidney, garbanzo) for another
- ✔ Green beans for peas
- ✔ Zucchini for eggplant
- ✔ Cauliflower for potatoes

You can also plan for leftovers by preparing an entire entree with the intention of storing it as individual servings and warming it up as needed for a quick bite.

Of course, if you loved a dish the first time, don't feel pressured to reinvent it; just reheat and love it again — maybe with a new side dish you prepare with groceries you need to use before they spoil. The next section includes ideas for those kinds of leftovers.

Using Leftover Groceries

According to the U.S. Environmental Protection Agency, Americans throw away nearly 31.6 million tons of food every year. Of course, only a very small portion of that would be food that *you* throw away, but keeping waste to a minimum can save you hundreds of dollars a year.

Perhaps you recently enjoyed a nice dinner out with your parents or you've done a little cooking and now have doggie bags of leftovers sitting around with half-used cans of things and wilting veggies. With a bit of creativity, you can use all that good gluten-free food to whip up a delicious and free new meal for yourself! This section gives you some ideas for using leftover groceries.

If an original meal or partially used food is more than a few days old, throw it out. It's not worth risking your health if leftovers have been around long enough to look or smell iffy.

Getting more mileage from partially used canned goods and sauces

Most of the time when you're cooking for one or two, you don't use all the sauce in a bottle or the contents of a can. Cover them well, refrigerate, and don't hide them on the back of the shelf and forget about them until they're green and fuzzy. Instead, take a look at these ideas for how to transform half a can or jar into some other meal.

Artichoke hearts

A jar of artichoke hearts is very versatile, but you rarely need a whole jar in any recipe unless you're cooking for at least four. Try these ideas:

- ✔ Chop them up and add them to a pizza.

- ✔ Add artichokes to a green salad or a Greek salad that contains feta cheese, olives, chopped tomatoes and cucumbers, and olive oil and vinegar.

- ✔ Throw them into a bowl of pasta; they're especially great with a white sauce like Alfredo.

- ✔ Add artichokes to a quiche or an omelet.

- ✔ Make a warm artichoke dip with chopped artichoke hearts, Parmesan cheese, and mayo. Warm the dip in the microwave and serve it with chips or gluten-free crackers.

Beans

Leftover beans will likely sit in the fridge until they're unrecognizable — unless you have a plan! Here are some ways to use those beans:

- ✔ Add them to soup or salad.

- ✔ Throw them in a stir-fry.

- ✔ Mix them with some rice or quinoa for a hearty protein-filled side dish.

- ✔ Add them to tacos, wraps, or quesadillas.

- ✔ Put beans in the blender with a dash of salt, lemon juice, and olive oil to make a great dip for chips or gluten-free crackers.

Chili

Chili is a great, quick meal all by itself. But what can you do with it the second time around to change it up a bit? Try some of these ideas:

- Stir chili in with spaghetti squash.
- Top a gluten-free hot dog and bun with chili.
- Mix it with corn chips and cheese.
- Spoon it over a baked potato.
- Make a chili burger.
- Use chili to help fill a burrito or quesadilla, along with cheese, sour cream, and lettuce.
- Add chili to a taco salad.
- Mix it with rice or gluten-free pasta and cheese.

Olives

It seems like I always have a plastic bag in the fridge with some olives in it! I never use them all at once. I'm happy to have a few so I can do the following:

- Add olives to a homemade pizza.
- Throw them in a salad.
- Add them to pasta.
- Mix them in with tuna salad or chicken salad.
- Crush them up, add a dash of olive oil, and serve them with gluten-free crackers.

Pesto

With pesto, a little goes a long way. It's expensive, so you definitely want to think of ways to use leftover pesto. Try these tips:

- Spread pesto on a gluten-free pizza crust instead of tomato sauce. The pesto goes well with toppings like chicken and cheese.
- Spread it on a sandwich or wrap.
- Use it in a cold pasta salad. Add your leftover olives, too!

✔ Marinate fish or chicken in pesto, or spread it on steak before serving.

✔ Add it to a BLT.

✔ Mix pesto into your mashed potatoes or cauliflower.

✔ Stir pesto into rice and top with Parmesan cheese.

✔ Spread pesto on a slice of gluten-free bread, cover it with a few spinach leaves and tomato slices, add a little provolone or mozzarella cheese, and broil it.

Salsa

Salsa lasts a long time if you don't eat it with chips every day. It does have many great uses, though:

✔ Use salsa as a salad dressing.

✔ Stir it into rice for an easy Spanish rice.

✔ Add salsa to soups and stews for an extra kick.

✔ Top a baked potato with salsa, sour cream, and cheese.

✔ Add salsa to omelets and quiches.

✔ Add salsa to tacos, quesadillas, and burritos.

✔ Stir salsa into your mac and cheese for a spicy Southwest version.

Sun-dried tomatoes

A jar of sun-dried tomatoes is very concentrated, so you'll definitely have them around long after you use them in your original recipe. Here are a few creative ways to use sun-dried tomatoes:

✔ Spread them on sandwiches (if you have the paste).

✔ Mix sun-dried tomatoes with rice, quinoa, or risotto.

✔ Stir them into mashed potatoes.

✔ Chop them and add them to salads and pizza.

✔ Mix sun-dried tomatoes with broccoli and pine nuts with a drizzle of olive oil.

✔ Mix them in pasta salads.

Tomato-based pasta sauce

Half a jar of pasta sauce is probably in your refrigerator right now. There's always some in mine! Why not try some of these ideas?

- Warm it up as a dip for chicken or gluten-free bread.

- Top slices of polenta with a spoonful of sauce and some Parmesan cheese.

- Make a quick gluten-free English muffin or bagel pizza.

- Add pasta sauce to soup, stew, or homemade chili.

- Mix it in with rice or quinoa.

- Top a burger, hot dog, or grilled chicken sandwich with some pasta sauce and mozzarella cheese.

- Make an Italian stuffed baked potato with pasta sauce, cheese, and olives or sausage.

Refreshing stale bread and crackers

Gluten-free bread and crackers don't usually last as long as their wheat-filled counterparts. Sometimes they even taste dry from day one, but don't get rid of them just yet!

If you see mold on the bread, throw it away. If you keep your gluten-free bread in the freezer until you're ready to use it, it won't get stale or moldy.

Bread

If you don't want the bread for a sandwich, it's still good for some other things. How about some of these ideas?

- Make croutons by buttering the bread, cutting it into cubes, and broiling it until it's very crispy. Store the croutons in the freezer and throw them in a salad anytime. See Chapter 13 for the full directions for making croutons.

- Pulverize the bread in a blender or food processor to make breadcrumbs for coatings, for acting as filler in meatballs or meatloaf, or for topping for a casserole. Add extra seasoning for Italian or Cajun versions.

- Use the bread in Classic French Toast or in Apple French Toast Pie, where stale bread is best. Flip to Chapter 8 for recipes.

✔ Use it in bread pudding.

✔ Make garlic toast by brushing the bread with olive oil, adding Italian seasonings and garlic salt, and broiling until crispy.

Crackers

You'll probably try lots of gluten-free crackers — some you'll love, and some you won't. The ones you love will likely be eaten before they're stale, but the ones you don't care for don't have to be thrown away. Follow these tips to get the most for your money:

✔ Crush up crackers for toppings on casseroles and vegetables.

✔ Use them as a binding for meatloaf, salmon cakes, or crab cakes (use real crab, because imitation crab usually contains wheat).

✔ Use cracker crumbs as a coating for baked or fried chicken or pork chops.

✔ Break crackers into pieces and use them as croutons in soups, chili, and salads.

Check out Chapter 19 for recommendations on great gluten-free crackers.

Reviving aging vegetables

A refrigerator full of less-than-appetizing vegetables is pretty common, especially in the college fridge. Don't despair and don't throw them out before trying to revive or recycle them into a meal that works.

When your veggies are approaching their final days, you can still use them. Try some of these tips:

✔ Bring droopy celery and carrots back to crispness with a little water and vinegar. Cut about an inch off the bottom of the stalks and put them in a mixture of a cup of cold water and a tablespoon of white vinegar for 15 to 30 minutes.

✔ Use the veggies in a stir-fry. After they're chopped up and cooked, the vegetables are great. Find stir-fry recipes in Chapter 11.

✔ Eat raw veggies with hummus or ranch dressing.

✔ Shred carrots, cucumbers, and zucchini and use them in soups, in salads, and on sandwiches.

✔ Sauté your wilted greens with some garlic and olive oil, and they become a gourmet side like you'd find in the finest restaurants.

✔ Add your limp spinach to an omelet or quiche.

✔ Throw your droopy veggies into a soup or stew.

✔ Boil and mash potatoes and sweet potatoes.

✔ Toss your shriveling tomatoes into a sauce.

Saving shriveling fruit

Try some of these tips to use your aging fruit:

✔ Bake soft apples in the microwave with cinnamon and butter. See Chapter 13 for a baked apple recipe.

✔ Make applesauce: In a saucepan, combine 4 apples, ¾ cup water, ¼ cup sugar, and ¼ teaspoon cinnamon. Cover and cook over medium heat for 15 to 20 minutes, or until the apples are soft. Then mash with a fork or potato masher.

✔ Make smoothies!

✔ Freeze berries for use later in a smoothie, in muffins, or as an ice cream topping.

✔ Make popsicles by putting all your aging fruit in the blender and then freezing the puree in small paper or plastic cups with sticks.

✔ Peel and then freeze banana chunks for making soft serve. Check out the Peanut Butter Cup Soft Serve recipe in Chapter 15.

✔ Mash bananas for use in banana bread, or add mashed banana to any pancake or muffin batter to moisten it.

✔ Create a sweet sauce. Just cut the bad parts off the fruit, mix the good parts with a spoonful of sugar, and heat the mixture in a small pot for a few minutes, until the fruit becomes syrupy. Save it in the refrigerator for about a week for use on waffles, pancakes, yogurt, or ice cream.

✔ Cut all your fruit into bite-sized pieces and make a fruit salad.

Redirecting desserts

It may be unnecessary to add a section on what to do with leftover desserts, but here it is just in case. Actually, on a gluten-free diet, your main issue may be that you *don't like* the desserts you try until you master a few recipes or find your favorite brands. Find recipes for great-tasting gluten-free desserts in Chapter 15. But don't throw away those less-than-fabulous desserts and gritty cookies.

Here are a few tricks for repurposing the sweet flops:

- ✔ Take those dry or stale cookies and brownies and crush them up and freeze them. They make great pie crust (see Chapter 15) or ice cream topping. Remember to label the plastic bag "GF Cookie Crumbs" so you know what it is when you need it.

- ✔ Cut up stale cake into cubes, microwave for a few seconds to warm it, and top it with ice cream and chocolate sauce or berries and whipped cream.

- ✔ Throw cookie, cake, or brownie chunks into a milkshake.

- ✔ Make homemade ice cream sandwiches with leftover cookies. They taste great frozen, even if they're stale.

- ✔ Cut your cake into large chunks and put it in muffin cups with a different topping than it had to begin with. It doesn't look left over, so you can serve it to friends!

- ✔ Make a trifle with fruit and whipped cream with your cake pieces. In a large bowl (preferably with straight sides), layer cake pieces with fruit and whipped cream. Repeat the layers until you reach the top of the bowl.

- ✔ Put cake scraps into a well-greased waffle iron and toast them until they're golden. Line a bowl with the toasted cake and fill it with ice cream, toppings, and whipped cream. Then eat the edible cake bowl.

- ✔ Add leftover candy bars to cookie dough or cake or brownie batter.

Prepping Ingredients Ahead of Time

To allow yourself the joy of home-cooked meals without the time commitment that such meals often require, try preparing a few ingredients ahead of time. Carve out some time over the weekend or take advantage of a free evening for prep work. That way, you can keep key ingredients ready to go in the fridge or freezer for a fast lunch or dinner.

Here are some foods to make ahead of time:

- ✔ **Cooked ground beef:** Cook a pound of ground beef and freeze it in a plastic freezer bag. If you plan to use it within a day or two, store it in a sealed container in the refrigerator.

- ✔ **Cooked chicken:** Here are some good techniques for cooking chicken to use in multiple recipes. After the chicken cooks, freeze it in a freezer-safe bag or container, unless you're planning to use it in the next day or two. You can save chicken in the freezer for up to a year without compromising quality.

  - • **Sauté:** Rinse boneless, skinless chicken breasts in cool water and pat them dry with a paper towel. Cut the chicken into smaller pieces or strips for faster cooking. Cook the chicken in a skillet or grill pan in just a little oil, turning the chicken to cook each side. Sauté the chicken over medium-high heat until it's no longer pink, about 5 minutes.

  - • **Poach:** Place boneless, skinless chicken breasts in a pot that's large enough to fit the chicken in one layer. Add liquid (water or broth) so that it completely covers the chicken by ½ to 1 inch. After bringing the liquid to a boil over high heat, reduce the heat to low, keeping the liquid at a bare simmer for about 10 minutes. Then turn off the heat and cover the pot, leaving the chicken to finish cooking in the hot water for 10 to 15 more minutes. Shred or chop the chicken before freezing it.

  - • **Roast:** Roasting chicken with the skin on and bone in is simple. Rinse the chicken and pat it dry. Add salt and pepper and pop the chicken in a preheated oven for 45 to 55 minutes, until cooked. Remove the skin and bones before freezing.

- ✔ **Hard-boiled eggs:** Flip to Chapter 7 for tips on boiling eggs. Store your extra hard-boiled eggs covered in the fridge. Make note of the sell-by date on the box, and use them within a couple of weeks of that date.

- ✔ **Cooked rice:** Make extra rice and freeze individual 1-cup servings. Just toss the cooled, cooked rice into plastic freezer bags. When you're ready to use it, place the rice in a microwave-safe dish and warm it up in the microwave on high for a minute or so.

✔ **Sliced or chopped veggies:** Use frozen vegetables instead of keeping fresh ones on hand and cutting them up for each recipe. Or chop fresh produce and store it in the freezer until you're ready to use it. If you plan to use your chopped fresh veggies within a day or two, you can keep them in the fridge.

You can also save on prep time by buying ready-to-go ingredients at the store:

✔ Buy precut food, such as shredded cheese or minced garlic in a jar.

✔ Buy precooked rice in a pouch, which you may find on the shelf or in the freezer. Try Uncle Ben's 90-second plain brown rice in the microwave pouch for a super quick meal solution. Just keep in mind that not all Uncle Ben's products are gluten-free.

✔ Check your grocery store for precooked meats and fish, such as roasted turkey breast, grilled chicken breasts or steak strips, cooked bacon, frozen grilled fish, and sliced deli meats. Consider picking up a rotisserie chicken when you venture out to the grocery store. You can eat it as it comes or use it in a stir-fry, throw it on a salad, stack it on a sandwich, soup up your soup, top a pizza, fill tacos, and more!

Watch out for gluten that may be hiding in marinades, seasonings, and sauces. Check labels carefully.

Part IV

Enjoy an additional student's gluten-free cookbook Part of Tens chapter online at www.dummies.com/extras/studentsgluten freecookbook.

In this part . . .

✔ Choose a college that accommodates gluten-free student living.

✔ Find out how to navigate a less-than-ideal environment when you're on a gluten-free diet.

✔ Discover how to make any recipe gluten-free by using smart substitutions and other adjustments.

✔ Benefit from my countless taste tests with lists of my favorite gluten-free products.

Chapter 17

Ten Tips for Going to College Gluten-Free

*M*any colleges and universities provide great gluten-free choices for students. You should find some level of accommodation made for students on special diets, including the gluten-free diet. You may even find a dedicated dietitian and area of the cafeteria that serves gluten-free pizzas, pastas, sandwiches, cereals, buns, and more.

Some gluten-free choices, even in the least-aware cafeteria, include bunless burgers, roasted and grilled chicken, omelets, baked potatoes, plain rice, fresh fruits and vegetables, yogurt, gelatin, pudding, and ice cream (flavors without cookies, brownies, or dough).

That said, in my experience, most universities have a long way to go before they reach the point of fully accommodating students on a special diet. Some school dietitians just don't seem to understand that the same lunch and dinner offering of a green salad, bunless hamburger, and ice cream every day of the year does not qualify as a complete and satisfying gluten-free menu.

It's hard enough to be gluten-free at home, but trying to maintain the proper diet when you have little or no control over what a cafeteria staff prepares for you (and how they prepare the food) is even tougher! But that doesn't mean it's impossible.

This chapter includes strategic tips for making it easier to stay gluten-free in college. The first few suggestions address how to work with the school, and this is a solid first course of action; but the reality is that most schools aren't yet equipped to provide a totally safe food experience for students on a gluten-free diet. That's why this chapter covers steps you can take yourself.

Tour Colleges

You probably don't want to choose your college based on the school's gluten-free policies because that's ever-changing — fortunately, for the better in most cases. But I do suggest that you show up to your chosen institutions with a plan in hand.

Before you visit, envision your ideal situation and know what you're not willing to live with. The school will likely fall somewhere in the middle of that spectrum, but go prepared to lay out your ideal and see how close the institution is willing and able to come. Are administrators willing to flex a little, or do they show an unwillingness to work with you?

Tour the colleges you most want to attend for their academics and majors and whatever other criteria matter to you. Even if they don't accommodate gluten-free students very well, most colleges require you to live and eat on campus for your first one or two years. After a few school visits, speaking to administrators and cafeteria workers, you should be able to determine how much you want your dietary needs to affect your school choice, if at all.

Peruse Policies

Search online for gluten-free friendly schools and explore the quality of life for gluten-free students living on campus. Here are some helpful websites:

- ✔ Check out the university website to find school policies related to living and eating on campus. I ran across one site that said in bold letters, "Allergies and dietary needs do not grant approval to move off campus before your residency requirement is fulfilled." Okay, you know at that particular school you'll be in the dorm and on the meal plan for three full years! So you need to decide if that can work for you.

- ✔ Best Colleges Online names several colleges that cater to gluten-free students in its article "14 Colleges That Cater to Gluten-Free Students." Visit www.bestcollegesonline. com/blog/2012/01/10/14-colleges-that-cater- to-gluten-free-students/

✔ Go to GlutenFreeTravelSite to read reviews by students rating their universities for gluten-free policies. Visit `http://glutenfreetravelsite.com/glutenfreecollege reviews.php`.

✔ Check out the school's student Facebook page and ask students with food restrictions for their advice and experiences. You can get the real story from the students, usually before you even show up on campus. Plus, you might make a few gluten-free friends who can show you the ropes when you get to campus.

To really understand school policies and offerings, ask about them during your campus tour. Here's a list of questions to ask:

✔ Does the school have a dietitian who works with students on special diets?

✔ Does the school require the purchase of a meal plan? Are exemptions available?

✔ Is there a gluten-free menu online with specific gluten-free meals?

✔ Is an allowance offered for extra gluten-free food I may need to buy?

✔ Is gluten-free food sold in the campus stores or other eating establishments on campus? Can those purchases be used toward the meal plan?

✔ Which small appliances does the school allow in the dorms?

✔ How long does the school require students to live on campus? Are exceptions made for people who don't want to live in dorms for dietary reasons?

Canvass the Cafeteria

During your visit to various colleges, be sure to drop by the dining halls. And as you stroll through the cafeterias, here are some things to look for:

✔ Do signs list the ingredients in each dish and salad dressing that the cafeteria serves?

✔ Are allergens, including gluten, listed on each dish?

✔ Do cafeteria staff members know what gluten is? Can they explain how food is prepared? Ideally, anyone who is cooking or serving food will have basic knowledge of gluten-free options.

✔ Is there a gluten-free section with things such as gluten-free bread and a gluten-free toaster and waffle iron?

✔ Are specific gluten-free choices such as pizza, hamburger buns, cookies, and cereal available?

✔ Does the cafeteria offer stations where you can get custom-made food, such as an omelet or stir-fry?

Watch for gluten-free serving no-no's like this one: My son's university lines the bottom of the bacon pan with bread to soak up extra grease, thereby nullifying the bacon's gluten-free status! Also keep an eye out for things like utensils that go from a dish containing gluten into the gluten-free items. Steer clear if you see these cross-contamination mistakes, and look instead for pre-wrapped options that the servers don't handle.

Address Administrators

Ask the important questions, but don't put too much stock in the guy sitting in the office who doesn't eat in the cafeteria and tells you the school is handling gluten-free issues expertly. At every school we visited, an administrator told us that the dining company has great processes in place to serve gluten-free students. Unfortunately, when we looked closer, we found that it just wasn't true.

Get to know the people on campus who are responsible for core elements of your eating and living experience. Setting up your support team at the beginning of the year is critical to your health, happiness, and well-being during college, so be your own advocate.

Be sure to connect with these four groups either during a campus visit or during your first week of school:

✔ Student Disability Services

✔ Residence Life

✔ Health Services

✔ Dining Services (director)

If you meet with these folks on a campus visit, set up a time for a quick reintroduction during your first week of school so you can remind the chef and Dining Services director of your needs. As you get your food each day, introduce yourself to servers so they get to know you as well. Sometimes the people working in the dining hall can prepare foods especially for you or warn you against items you can't have.

Connect with Other Gluten-Free Students

You'll likely be teaching your school how to best serve gluten-free students like yourself, and that will benefit those who come after you. Consider banding together with other gluten-free students to share information and resources. Find out whether your school has a gluten-free club. If not, consider starting one to gain a stronger voice with the school administrators — or at least to cook a gluten-free meal together now and then.

Gather Groceries

Map out the grocery stores and specialty health stores near the schools you're interested in attending (or have already chosen to attend). When you're in town, visit each store and ask at the customer service desk for a list of gluten-free items that the store sells. Most stores have these lists available. If you don't see your favorites on the list, most store managers are happy to order a few things for you, either upon request or to keep in stock.

If you're not used to buying your own gluten-free groceries, try to get a copy of Cecelia's Marketplace *Gluten-Free Grocery Shopping Guide* (www.ceceliasmarketplace.com). It lists almost 50,000 gluten-free products that you can find at almost any grocery store. Having this information on hand can be a huge time-saver — not to mention a lifesaver. Flip to Chapter 5 for a full rundown on shopping for gluten-free fare.

Research Restaurants

Search online to find restaurants near your school that consider themselves gluten-free friendly. Most places have menus available online, but if not, visit the restaurants that most interest you early on. If nothing else, definitely find out where to get a good gluten-free pizza before the first round of exams begins. Check vegetarian restaurants as well; they often have a nice variety of gluten-free choices.

 If you find a gluten-free bakery/café that delivers in your college town, be sure to tell your mom and dad. Maybe they'll think to order you a dozen cupcakes for dorm delivery on your birthday or send you soup when you're sick!

Order Online

You can order many foods online if you happen to be in the middle of nowhere and can't get find good gluten-free snacks, ingredients, or breads. If you have favorites that are missing from your local area, you can order those as well.

Amazon and many gluten-free shopping sites have hundreds of gluten-free options that come with free shipping if you order enough or have a membership.

Call or Write Home

If you're lucky, you take frequent trips to the campus mailroom to get gluten-free care packages. Call, text, or e-mail the people back home to put in early requests for your favorite cookies, goodies, and ingredients. Even if you have a full kitchen that's well-stocked with your staples for gluten-free cooking, a care package with your favorites from home always feels pretty nice.

Move Out

As soon as possible, move out of the dorm and into a place with your own kitchen. You'll be surprised how drastically your life can improve when you're in control of your own food.

Some schools don't require you to live on campus at all; some allow you to skip or modify the required meal plan; and some allow students to live off campus earlier than the official policy states. It's a nice idea, in theory, to experience dorm living, but if you're on a restricted diet, the more control you have over your food and living situation, the better.

Chapter 18

Ten Simple Ways to Make a Recipe Gluten-Free

In This Chapter

▶ Omitting offending ingredients

▶ Making or buying substitutions

▶ Adding to and adjusting recipes

▶ Experimenting

*T*he easiest way to prepare a gluten-free meal is to follow a gluten-free recipe that's already been tried and published by someone else who sweated out the details to get the ingredients and proportions just right. But that's not always possible. So this chapter provides some suggestions for converting gluten-containing dishes into safe and delicious gluten-free versions.

Although some recipes are easier to adjust than others, almost any recipe can be made gluten-free. The easiest to change are recipes with only small amounts of flour and fare with high fruit and vegetable content. But even if your gluten-heavy Italian recipe calls for wheat pasta, just use a gluten-free pasta instead. And if you're clean out of gluten-free pasta, knowing you can substitute rice, potatoes, risotto, spaghetti squash, or polenta in the recipe can save the day!

Substitutions may be more challenging for baked goods like breads, cakes, and muffins that are traditionally light and fluffy and have high flour content. But you can do it! This chapter offers tips for swapping ingredients to make anything gluten-free.

Omit Ingredients

The first step in making a gluten-containing recipe gluten-free is to know which ingredients to avoid. While you search the ingredient list for items you can leave out, be sure to check the labels on ingredients you plan to use as well.

Here are some not-so-obvious gluten-containing ingredients that you may find in a recipe (more are listed in Chapter 1):

- ✔ Barbeque sauce
- ✔ Barley and barley malt
- ✔ Brewer's yeast
- ✔ Malt vinegar
- ✔ Oats (due to cross-contamination)
- ✔ Soy sauce
- ✔ Teriyaki sauce

Is it possible to leave out ingredients in the recipe that contain gluten and still have a good result? For example, can you omit the soy sauce from a recipe and still end up with a tasty dish?

Replace the Flour

Converting recipes that don't contain a large amount of flour is easiest. If the recipe calls for only a little flour, then just swap out the gluten-containing flour for cornstarch, arrowroot powder, or any gluten-free flour or flour blend.

But if you're preparing a recipe with more than just a few tablespoons of flour, you can't throw in the same volume of gluten-free flour and have a recipe turn out well unless you use a blend. Here are a few tricks to make a recipe work:

- ✔ **Use a blend of gluten-free flours.** You can buy an all-purpose flour blend or make your own. Try 3 parts rice flour, 2 parts potato starch, 1 part tapioca flour, and 1 teaspoon of xanthan gum for every 1½ cups of the flour mixture. So if you use cups for each part, you need about 4 teaspoons of xanthan gum for this batch of gluten-free flour.

Potato starch and potato flour are different, but tapioca starch and tapioca flour are the same thing. Be sure to buy potato starch for your gluten-free flour, or you may end up with a total flop! You can find these in health food stores and in some regular grocery store health food sections.

✔ **Use your flour blend, once mixed, in the same amount as called for in the regular recipe.** For baked goods, make sure your blend includes xanthan gum; if not, you need to add some.

Keep It Together with Xanthan Gum

Xanthan gum is a natural soluble fiber that's produced by fermenting a microorganism with sugar. So why do you need xanthan gum in your gluten-free baked goods? This ingredient helps give dough a sticky consistency, and dough minus gluten really needs some help to stay together! If you're just mixing a little gluten-free flour into gravy or a soup or using it for a coating, then no gum is required.

You need to add xanthan gum only if you're baking with a flour blend that doesn't already contain it, and you need only a little. You'll realize how good this news is when you see the price of a small bag! Depending on what you're baking, 1 teaspoon of xanthan gum for every 1½ cups of flour in the recipe should produce a good result. You may need to experiment to get the exact result you want, but I've never had a problem with using too much — just not enough.

When baking cookies, put in the amount of xanthan gum you think you'll need. Bake just a few cookies. If they look too flat, stir in another ½ teaspoon to the dough and try baking a few more. When you're happy with how the cookies are turning out, fill a cookie sheet or two with dough and bake them all. This is a great way to avoid making a whole sheet of cookies that you end up tossing out. Just remember to write down how much xanthan gum you end up using so you'll know how much to add the next time you use the recipe.

Add Moisture to Baked Goods

Gluten-free flours tend to produce foods that are denser and drier than their gluten-containing cousins. If your gluten-free cake or muffins turn out dry or heavy, here are a few ingredients that you can add the next time to improve the consistency:

- ¼ cup applesauce
- ¼ cup pumpkin puree
- ¼ cup mayonnaise
- ¼ cup sour cream
- 1 or 2 tablespoons vanilla instant pudding mix
- 1 or 2 tablespoons extra milk, butter, or oil

Use Alternative Breading Options

If a recipe calls for a fried or baked crispy coating on meat or veggies, you don't have to do without. Just use ingredients like gluten-free breadcrumbs, gluten-free flours, ground nuts, cornmeal, crushed potato chips or corn chips, instant mashed potato flakes, or crushed gluten-free cereal or crackers. Or you can forgo the coating and grill the food instead.

If you're using an ingredient that's coarser than flour, like crushed corn chips, handle the food carefully and press the crumbs in a bit before baking or frying.

Make Gluten-Free Ingredients

If your recipe calls for croutons, breadcrumbs, or a pie crust, you can leave them out, buy them ready-made, or make your own! Find out how to turn your stale bread into fabulous croutons or bread-crumbs in Chapter 13. I keep a bag of each in the freezer at all times so they're ready whenever I want them.

If pie crust shows up in the recipe, you can make your pie or quiche crustless by adding a few tablespoons of gluten-free flour. The flavor comes through even more without any crust, and you avoid a lot of fat and calories. Or flip to Chapter 15 to find out how to make a simple pie crust from gluten-free graham crackers, cookies, or nuts.

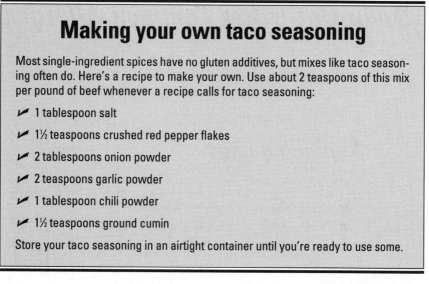

Making your own taco seasoning

Most single-ingredient spices have no gluten additives, but mixes like taco seasoning often do. Here's a recipe to make your own. Use about 2 teaspoons of this mix per pound of beef whenever a recipe calls for taco seasoning:

- 1 tablespoon salt

- 1½ teaspoons crushed red pepper flakes

- 2 tablespoons onion powder

- 2 teaspoons garlic powder

- 1 tablespoon chili powder

- 1½ teaspoons ground cumin

Store your taco seasoning in an airtight container until you're ready to use some.

Get Saucy

Many recipes call for sauces and cream soups, but you may not have a gluten-free version handy. Here's how to whip up these sauces quickly in a pinch:

- Check Chapter 12 for a simple cream soup mix. You can use it in any casserole or side dish recipe that calls for a cream-of-anything soup.

- Make your own teriyaki sauce by combining gluten-free soy sauce (tamari) with honey to taste. Try ½ cup gluten-free soy sauce plus 2 tablespoons honey.

- Make your own barbecue sauce by combining ½ cup ketchup, ⅓ cup brown sugar, 1 tablespoon cider vinegar, 2 teaspoons gluten-free Worcestershire sauce, and 2 teaspoons gluten-free soy sauce (tamari).

- Use cornstarch or gluten-free flour instead of regular wheat flour to thicken any gravy.

Although it's often cheaper to buy a bottle of sauce than it is to buy all the ingredients to make your own, especially for one or two people, making your own sauce is a good idea if you already have all the ingredients on hand.

Swap Out Other Common Allergens

People who have trouble with gluten may also have trouble with dairy, egg, or soy as well. If you're looking for additional substitution solutions for your recipes that go beyond gluten, this section offers tips for replacing these foods to make your favorite dishes safer for yourself and others.

Replacing eggs

You can't really make a great omelet with no eggs, because eggs are the main ingredient. But for a recipe with only a few eggs, try some of these ideas to replace each egg:

- 1 tablespoon flaxseed meal plus 3 tablespoons hot water (let the mixture stand for about 10 minutes before using it)

- 3 tablespoons unsweetened applesauce plus 1 teaspoon baking powder

- Powdered egg replacer such as EnerG or Bob's Red Mill Egg Replacer

Swapping out milk

If cow's milk is your issue, maybe goat's milk is better for you. Try it, or go with one of these vegan solutions in your recipes: Cup for cup, you can replace cow's milk with coconut milk, rice milk, almond milk, or soy milk.

Getting rid of butter

If you're avoiding dairy, then you can't use butter in a recipe. No problem! Just replace 1 stick (8 tablespoons, or ½ cup) of butter with one of these alternatives:

- 8 tablespoons shortening

- 8 tablespoons dairy-free margarine

- 8 tablespoons Earth Balance Buttery Spread or Buttery Stick

- 6 tablespoons unsweetened applesauce plus 2 tablespoons vegetable oil (a lower-fat solution!)

Try Alternative Grains

As part of your gluten-free diet, take the time to experiment with the wide range of gluten-free grains, including these:

✔ **Amaranth:** Add amaranth to soups, to stews, and — in small amounts — to flour mixes to thicken and add nutrition. But don't bake with amaranth; it makes baked goods too dense.

Amaranth contains more protein than any other gluten-free grain. One cup of raw amaranth contains about 28 grams of protein. It's also high in calcium, magnesium, iron, and fiber. In fact, amaranth contains eight or nine times the fiber of white rice!

✔ **Buckwheat:** Don't let the name fool you. Buckwheat is gluten-free and unrelated to wheat. It's not even technically a grain; it's a seed that's a relative of rhubarb. So if you see buckwheat pancakes in a gluten-free cookbook or on a gluten-free menu, go for it. If they're on a regular menu, though, the pancakes may also contain wheat flour. Always check! Buckwheat noodles are popular in Japan, and you may see buckwheat as an ingredient in gluten-free beer.

Buckwheat is high in fiber, manganese, magnesium, and copper, and it's an antioxidant. Buckwheat is being studied for properties that may reduce plasma cholesterol, body fat, and cholesterol gallstones, and it may be useful in the management of type 2 diabetes.

✔ **Millet:** Whole millet adds a crunchy texture to muffin, bread, pancake, and waffle recipes, and you can use millet flours in flour mixes. This ancient grain feeds more than a third of the world's population. Millet is high in fiber, B vitamins, iron, potassium, calcium, zinc, and essential amino acids.

✔ **Sorghum:** America is the largest producer of this ancient grain, but we'd mostly been feeding it to livestock until the past few years. It's become a popular gluten-free staple in flour blends. Alone, it has a gritty taste and texture.

✔ **Teff:** Teff flour works as a small part of a flour mix, or you can use teff whole and uncooked in place of other seeds or nuts. It has a high concentration of a wide variety of nutrients, including calcium, thiamin, and easily absorbable iron. It's very high in fiber and may benefit people with diabetes because it helps control blood sugar levels.

✔ **Quinoa:** Quinoa is usually considered a whole grain, but it's really a seed. Very high in protein, it contains the nine essential amino acids. You can use it in place of rice, or you can sweeten it up a little and add some fruit for breakfast. Quinoa is good cold or hot, as a side dish or salad.

Reference Gluten-Free Recipes

You don't need to give up on favorite family recipes when you give up gluten! You just need to invent gluten-free versions. One way to figure out how to alter your recipe is to hunt for similar gluten-free recipes that have already been tried and published by someone else. If you want to make your grandma's Spritz cookies, for example, there are certainly gluten-free cooks who have figured out similar cookie recipes.

If you can't find a gluten-free recipe for a specific dish, read through several recipes, looking for patterns that can help you alter your recipe. For example

- ✔ Do the similar recipes you find tend to use certain flours? Which ones?

- ✔ Do the recipes call for more or less liquid than the gluten-filled versions?

- ✔ Do they tend to have more eggs or extra vanilla?

- ✔ Do they tend to use the same cooking temperature and time?

With this information, you can get a good idea of how to tweak your own recipes.

Also watch for new cooking tips and techniques that apply especially to gluten-free cooking, like using parchment paper when baking cookies!

Experiment

You may feel a bit like a mad scientist when attempting to turn an old favorite recipe into a gluten-free version, especially if it involves baking. Tap into that! Like a scientist, you should write down what you do and what the results are. Keep track of all the variations you try so you can make adjustments the next time if the food's not just right — or so you can repeat your results!

If at first you don't succeed, try again! Flip to Chapter 16 for ideas on turning failed attempts into edible foods, and don't give up. Preparing gluten-free meals takes practice. With a little guidance and skill-building, you'll get the hang of it.

Chapter 19

Ten Favorite Gluten-Free Product Lists

In This Chapter

▶ Choosing breads, flours, pastas, cereals, and crackers

▶ Selecting soups and other convenience meals

▶ Finding tasty sweets, flours, and baking mixes

*Y*es, this is a cookbook, but you still need to know which pasta to use for a perfect ziti recipe or which flour to use for a cookie recipe so it doesn't flop. You find that information here. You also find some convenience foods you can use when you're on the road or short on time and energy.

Many great new gluten-free products come on the market every month. Unfortunately, many products really aren't so great — they taste gritty or strange or fall apart in a heap of crumbs. Here, I try to save you a lot of time and money by listing my current favorites in ten categories. I haven't tasted everything out there, but I've come pretty close. Of course, new and fantastic gluten-free products will come along after this book is published, but the products in this chapter are the best I've found to date.

You can find these foods online, at many standard grocery stores, and in natural foods stores. If your local store doesn't carry something you like or want to try, check with the customer service desk. They'll often order foods for you.

Breakfast

For mornings when you need all your food prep done for you, consider stocking some of these popular go-to breakfast items in your pantry or freezer:

- **Bagels:** Udi's Gluten Free, Joan's GF Great Bakes

- **Bagel thins:** O'Doughs original, apple cranberry, sprouted whole-grain flax

- **Bars:** Luna protein bars, thinkThin bars, No-Gii bars, That's It. bars, Zing bars, NOW energy bars

- **Breakfast buns:** O'Doughs apple cranberry

- **Cereal:** General Mills Chex cereals (currently six flavors are marked gluten-free), Glutino Apple & Cinnamon, Glutino Berry Sensible Beginnings, Glutino Honey Nut Cereal, Kellogg's Rice Krispies Gluten Free cereal

- **Muffins:** Udi's Gluten Free chocolate, blueberry, lemon streusel

- **Muffin tops:** Udi's blueberry oat, chocolate chia (frozen)

- **Frozen waffles, pancakes, and French toast:** Van's Naturals gluten-free waffles, pancakes, French toast sticks; Trader Joe's gluten-free pancakes

- **Granola:** Bakery on Main (they have some oat-free choices), Udi's Gluten Free

- **Instant oatmeal:** Glutenfreeda, Simpli

Bread

You need good gluten-free bread for the French toast recipes in Chapter 8 and for Chapter 10's sandwich and burger ideas. Ready-to-eat gluten-free bread spans the gamut from gross to amazing. Five years ago, it was pretty much all gross. Now, most of it is somewhere in between. Here are my favorite gluten-free breads:

- **Against the Grain Gourmet:** Baguettes, Vermont country rolls, pumpernickel rolls

- **Canyon Bakehouse:** Hamburger buns, cinnamon raisin bread, rosemary and thyme focaccia, Colorado caraway bread

- **Food for Life:** English muffins

- **Genius by Glutino Gluten-Free:** White sandwich bread, multi-grain sandwich bread

- **Joan's GF Great Bakes:** Bialys, Joan's Italian bread

- **O'Doughs:** Sprouted whole-grain flax bagel thins, apple cranberry bagel thins, plain bagel thins

- **Rudi's Gluten-Free:** Original bread, multigrain bread, raisin bread, tortillas (all flavors), hot dog rolls, hamburger buns

- **Udi's Gluten Free:** White sandwich bread, whole-grain bread, cinnamon raisin bread, millet-chia bread, hot dog rolls, classic hamburger buns, plain bagels

Rudi's and Udi's both make non-gluten-free products as well, so make sure you buy their gluten-free breads.

Tortillas

See Chapter 9 and Chapter 11 for great wrap, taco, and burrito recipes that call for tortillas. Here are the brands I like best:

- **Food for Life:** Brown rice tortillas

- **Mission:** Corn tortillas

- **Rudi's Gluten-Free Tortillas:** Plain, fiesta, spinach

- **Sandwich Petals:** Spinach garlic pesto, Chimayo red chile, agave grain

Crackers

These are my favorite gluten-free crackers for making snack time simple and satisfying:

- **Blue Diamond Nut Thins:** Hint of sea salt, almond, hazelnut, pecan, cheddar cheese, pepper Jack cheese

- **Crunchmaster:** Multi-seed crackers, multigrain crackers (all flavors)

- **Glutino:** Original bagel chips, sea salt snack crackers, original crackers

- **Polka Dot Bake Shop:** Cracked pepper sweet potato crackers

- **Shar:** Table crackers

Pasta

Find fabulous pasta recipes in Chapter 12, and consider using these products for your noodle needs:

- **Amy's:** Rice macaroni and cheese (frozen)
- **Conte's:** Cheese ravioli, spinach/cheese ravioli, stuffed shells (frozen)
- **Glutino:** Macaroni and cheese (frozen)
- **Le Veneziane:** Corn pasta
- **Pasta Fresh:** Five-cheese ravioli, butternut squash ravioli (refrigerated)
- **Tinkyada:** Brown rice pasta

Pizza

Pizza is practically its own food group in college, isn't it? These are my favorite gluten-free frozen pizza choices:

- **Against the Grain Gourmet:** Three-cheese pizza, pesto pizza
- **Conte's:** Margherita pizza with roasted garlic and olive oil
- **Joan's GF Great Bakes:** Joan's NY pizza, Joan's Sicilian pizza
- **Udi's:** Margherita pizza, three-cheese pizza, pepperoni pizza
- **Whole Foods:** Gluten-free pizza

Soups

Chapter 13 has some wonderful, hearty gluten-free soup recipes, but here are a few companies that offer ready-made versions:

- Amy's Organic
- Frontier Soups
- Gluten Free Café
- Imagine Foods
- Kettle Cuisine (frozen)
- Mixes from the Heartland

- ✔ Pacific Natural Foods
- ✔ Thai Kitchen
- ✔ Trader Joe's

Many Progresso and Wolfgang Puck soups are gluten-free, and grocery stores usually offer a few generic gluten-free soup options.

Convenience Meals

Here are great gluten-free foods that you can heat and eat fast:

- ✔ Applegate Naturals grilled chicken nuggets
- ✔ Glutenfreeda shredded beef burrito
- ✔ Happy Pho and Thai Kitchen rice noodle meals
- ✔ Glutino or Amy's rice macaroni and cheese
- ✔ Ian's mini corn dogs and Hebrew National beef franks
- ✔ Starfish gluten-free frozen fish — crispy battered cod, halibut, and haddock
- ✔ Whole Foods gluten-free calzones — Greek and pepperoni

Flours and Mixes

Having the right flour for the job is key to gluten-free baking. Sometimes a flour blend can be a good bet. Here are the best flours and baking mixes I've tried.

Flours

Some gluten-free flour blends come mixed with xanthan gum, which simulates the glue-like property of wheat flour. These mixes cost a bit more, but xanthan gum is quite expensive by itself, so the inclusive flours are usually worth the price.

This list is small, and I've tried many, but here are my all-time favorite gluten-free flours:

- ✔ **Cup-4-Cup (Williams-Sonoma):** Flour (with xanthan gum)
- ✔ **Jules Gluten Free:** All-purpose flour (with xanthan gum)
- ✔ **King Arthur:** Multi-purpose flour

Baking mixes

Find recipes in Chapter 15 to jazz up these great baking mixes:

- **Betty Crocker:** Gluten-free chocolate cake mix, yellow cake mix, cookie mix, Bisquick pancake and baking mix

- **Jules Gluten Free:** Cookie mix, bread mix, cake mix, pancake and waffle mix, graham cracker/gingerbread mix, cornbread mix

- **King Arthur:** Gluten-free muffin mix

- **Kinnikinnick:** Kinni-Kwik bread and bun mix

- **Namaste:** Spice cake mix, waffle and pancake mix

- **Pamela's:** Individual brownie mix

- **Sof'ella:** Gluten-free chocolate cake mix

Sweets

To satisfy that sweet tooth, you can make your own treats with the recipes in Chapter 15 or try these goodies:

- **Dr. Lucy's:** Cookies, all flavors

- **Enjoy Life:** Soft-baked snickerdoodle cookies

- **French Meadow Bakery:** Frozen chocolate chip cookie dough

- **Glow Gluten Free:** Cookies, all flavors

- **Glutino:** Chocolate-covered pretzels, yogurt-covered pretzels

- **Julie's:** Organic ice cream sandwiches

- **Liz Lovely:** Gluten-free and vegan cookies, all flavors

- **Pamela's:** Coffee cake and individual cheesecakes

- **WOW Baking:** Cookies and brownies, all flavors

Appendix A

Resources

Magazines and Books

Referencing a guidebook or gluten-free publication can help you quickly figure out which brands and products are gluten-free and which aren't. Here are my favorites:

- ✔ *Living Without* magazine (www.livingwithout.com)
- ✔ *Delight Gluten-Free Magazine* (www.delightglutenfree.com)
- ✔ *Easy Eats* — digital-only magazine (www.easyeats.com)
- ✔ *Gluten-Free Living* magazine (www.glutenfreeliving.com)
- ✔ *Cecelia's Marketplace Gluten-Free Grocery Shopping Guide* by Matison and Matison (www.ceceliasmarketplace.com)

Apps

A growing number of apps are available for smartphones and tablets to help you find gluten-free food and drinks. Just type "gluten-free" in an online app store to find hundreds of options. For some apps, you just type in or scan a product's barcode to find out whether it's gluten-free. Other apps list products at your store that are gluten-free. Here are a couple of my favorite gluten-free apps:

- ✔ Is That Gluten Free? by Midlife Crisis Apps
- ✔ Find Me Gluten Free by JATX Tech

Blogs, Groups, and Forums

There are lots of great blogs and social media groups you can access to gather information and recipes and connect with others on a gluten-free diet. Here are just a few:

- ✔ **Gluten Freeville:** Find lifestyle info, recipes, reviews, and news. (http://glutenfreeville.com)

- ✔ **Gluten Freeville on Facebook:** Ask and answer all things gluten-free with more than 50,000 (and counting) gluten-free friends. (www.facebook.com/glutenfreeville)

- ✔ **Jules Speaks Gluten Free:** Find great recipes, mixes, and e-books. (http://blog.julesglutenfree.com)

- ✔ **Gluten Free Travel Site:** Read and submit college reviews. (http://glutenfreetravelsite.com/glutenfree collegereviews.php#.UKMA64VcTPE)

- ✔ **University of Arizona Gluten-Free Club on Facebook:** Check your school for a gluten-free club or visit UA's page. (www.facebook.com/UAGlutenFree)

Restaurant Locators

Almost any restaurant you visit will have some things you can order gluten-free. But these sites and apps (or sections of them) focus on gluten-free fare, so you can see reviews, maps, and menus that are specifically gluten-free:

- ✔ **Urbanspoon:** Type in the city. Look to the left under "features" and click on "Gluten-free friendly." (www.urbanspoon.com)

- ✔ **Yelp:** Type "gluten free" in the Search for box and your location in the Near box. (www.yelp.com)

- ✔ **Find Me Gluten-Free:** This app uses your current location to find gluten-free restaurants and stores in your immediate area and links to gluten-free menus. (www.findmegluten free.com)

- ✔ **Gluten Free Registry:** This website and app is a strictly gluten-free review site that includes maps. (www.gluten freeregistry.com)

Deal Sites

Utilize gluten-free deal sites to access coupons and offers from manufacturers, retailers, and restaurants. With these sites, you buy a voucher for a product at a discount and then redeem the voucher at a store or online.

- ✔ **Gluten Free Deals:** http://glutenfreedeals.com

- ✔ **Gluten-Free Saver:** www.glutenfreesaver.com

Appendix B

Metric Conversion Guide

• •

*N**ote:* The recipes in this book weren't developed or tested using metric measurements. There may be some variation in quality when converting to metric units.

Common Abbreviations

Abbreviation(s)	*What It Stands For*
cm	Centimeter
C., c.	Cup
G, g	Gram
kg	Kilogram
L, l	Liter
lb.	Pound
mL, ml	Milliliter
oz.	Ounce
pt.	Pint
t., tsp.	Teaspoon
T., Tb., Tbsp.	Tablespoon

Volume

U.S. Units	Canadian Metric	Australian Metric
¼ teaspoon	1 milliliter	1 milliliter
½ teaspoon	2 milliliters	2 milliliters
1 teaspoon	5 milliliters	5 milliliters
1 tablespoon	15 milliliters	20 milliliters
¼ cup	50 milliliters	60 milliliters
⅓ cup	75 milliliters	80 milliliters
½ cup	125 milliliters	125 milliliters
⅔ cup	150 milliliters	170 milliliters
¾ cup	175 milliliters	190 milliliters
1 cup	250 milliliters	250 milliliters
1 quart	1 liter	1 liter
1½ quarts	1.5 liters	1.5 liters
2 quarts	2 liters	2 liters
2½ quarts	2.5 liters	2.5 liters
3 quarts	3 liters	3 liters
4 quarts (1 gallon)	4 liters	4 liters

Weight

U.S. Units	Canadian Metric	Australian Metric
1 ounce	30 grams	30 grams
2 ounces	55 grams	60 grams
3 ounces	85 grams	90 grams
4 ounces (¼ pound)	115 grams	125 grams
8 ounces (½ pound)	225 grams	225 grams
16 ounces (1 pound)	455 grams	500 grams (½ kilogram)

Length

Inches	Centimeters
0.5	1.5
1	2.5
2	5.0
3	7.5
4	10.0
5	12.5
6	15.0
7	17.5
8	20.5
9	23.0
10	25.5
11	28.0
12	30.5

Temperature (Degrees)

Fahrenheit	Celsius
32	0
212	100
250	120
275	140
300	150
325	160
350	180
375	190

(continued)

Temperature (Degrees) *(continued)*

Fahrenheit	Celsius
400	200
425	220
450	230
475	240
500	260

Index

Notes

Notes

Notes

Notes

Math & Science

Algebra I For
Dummies, 2nd Edition
978-0-470-55964-2

Anatomy and
Physiology
For Dummies,
2nd Edition
978-0-470-92326-9

Astronomy
For Dummies,
3rd Edition
978-1-118-37697-3

Biology For Dummies,
2nd Edition
978-0-470-59875-7

Chemistry
For Dummies,
2nd Edition
978-1-1180-0730-3

Pre-Algebra Essentials
For Dummies
978-0-470-61838-7

Microsoft Office

Excel 2013
For Dummies
978-1-118-51012-4

Office 2013 All-in-One
For Dummies
978-1-118-51636-2

PowerPoint 2013
For Dummies
978-1-118-50253-2

Word 2013 For Dummies
978-1-118-49123-2

Music

Blues Harmonica
For Dummies
978-1-118-25269-7

Guitar For Dummies,
3rd Edition
978-1-118-11554-1

iPod & iTunes
For Dummies,
10th Edition
978-1-118-50864-0

Programming

Android Application
Development
For Dummies,
2nd Edition
978-1-118-38710-8

iOS 6 Application
Development
For Dummies
978-1-118-50880-0

Java For Dummies,
5th Edition
978-0-470-37173-2

Religion & Inspiration

The Bible
For Dummies
978-0-7645-5296-0

Buddhism For
Dummies, 2nd Edition
978-1-118-02379-2

Catholicism For
Dummies, 2nd Edition
978-1-118-07778-8

Self-Help &
Relationships

Bipolar Disorder
For Dummies,
2nd Edition
978-1-118-33882-7

Meditation For
Dummies, 3rd Edition
978-1-118-29144-3

Seniors

Computers For Seniors
For Dummies,
3rd Edition
978-1-118-11553-4

iPad For Seniors
For Dummies,
5th Edition
978-1-118-49708-1

Social Security
For Dummies
978-1-118-20573-0

Smartphones &
Tablets

Android Phones
For Dummies
978-1-118-16952-0

Kindle Fire HD
For Dummies
978-1-118-42223-6

NOOK HD
For Dummies,
Portable Edition
978-1-118-39498-4

Surface For Dummies
978-1-118-49634-3

Test Prep

ACT For Dummies,
5th Edition
978-1-118-01259-8

ASVAB For Dummies,
3rd Edition
978-0-470-63760-9

GRE For Dummies,
7th Edition
978-0-470-88921-3

Officer Candidate
Tests, For Dummies
978-0-470-59876-4

Physician's Assistant
Exam For Dummies
978-1-118-11556-5

Series 7 Exam
For Dummies
978-0-470-09932-2

Windows 8

Windows 8
For Dummies
978-1-118-13461-0

Windows 8
For Dummies,
Book + DVD Bundle
978-1-118-27167-4

Windows 8 All-in-One
For Dummies
978-1-118-11920-4

ⓔ Available in print and e-book formats.

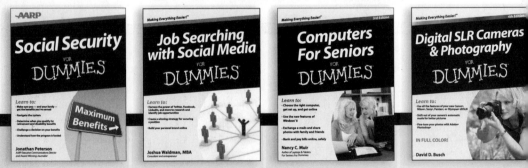

Available wherever books are sold. For more information or to order direct: U.S. customers visit www.Dummies.com or
call 1-877-762-2974.U.K. customers visit www.Wileyeurope.com or call (0) 1243 843291.
Canadian customers visit www.Wiley.ca or call 1-800-567-4797.

Connect with us online at www.facebook.com/fordummies or @fordummies

Take Dummies with you everywhere you go!

Whether you're excited about e-books, want more from the web, must have your mobile apps, or swept up in social media, Dummies makes everything easier .

Visit Us

Like Us

Follow Us

Watch Us

Join Us

Pin Us

Circle Us

Shop Us

Dummies products make life easier!

- DIY
- Consumer Electronics
- Crafts
- Software
- Cookware
- Hobbies
- Videos
- Music
- Games
- and More!

For more information, go to **Dummies.com®** and search the store by category.